CW00970670

THE FREDERICK DOUGLASS PAPERS

Series Two: Autobiographical Writings

VOLUME 1: NARRATIVE

Portrait of a young Fredrick Douglass. (Artist unknown, n.d.)

THE
FREDERICK DOUGLASS
PAPERS

Series Two: Autobiographical Writings
Volume 1: Narrative

John W. Blassingame,

John R. McKivigan,

and Peter P. Hinks, Editors

Gerald Fulkerson, Textual Editor

James H. Cook, Victoria C. Gruber,
and C. Jane Holtan, Editorial Assistants

Yale University Press   New Haven and London

Copyright © 1999 by Yale University. All rights reserved. This book may not be reproduced, in whole or in part, including illustrations, in any form (beyond that copying permitted by Sections 107 and 108 of the U.S. Copyright Law and except by reviewers for the public press), without written permission from the publishers.

Set in Times Roman type by The Composing Room of Michigan, Inc. Printed in the United States of America.

Library of Congress Cataloging-in-Publication Data

Douglass, Frederick, 1818–1895.

    The Frederick Douglass papers. Series two, Autobiographical writings / John W. Blassingame, John R. McKivigan, and Peter P. Hinks, editors ; Gerald Fulkerson, textual editor ; James H. Cook, Victoria C. Gruber, and C. Jane Holtan, editorial assistants.

        p.   cm.

    Includes bibliographical references and index.

    Contents: v. 1. Narrative —

    ISBN 0-300-07196-5 (v. 1 : alk. paper)

    1. Douglass, Frederick, 1818–1895.   2. Abolitionists—United States—Biography. 3. Afro-American abolitionists—Biography.   4. Antislavery movements—United States. 5. Slaves—Maryland—Social conditions.   6. Plantation life—Maryland—History—19th century.   7. Fugitive slaves—Maryland—Biography.   I. Blassingame, John W., 1940– II. McKivigan, John R., 1949– .   III. Hinks, Peter P.   IV. Title.

    E449.D734   1999

    973.8′092—dc21

    [B]   98-26125

A catalogue record for this book is available from the British Library.

The paper in this book meets the guidelines for permanence and durability of the Committee on Production Guidelines for Book Longevity of the Council on Library Resources.

10 9 8 7 6 5 4 3 2 1

COMMITTEE ON
SCHOLARLY EDITIONS

AN APPROVED EDITION

MODERN LANGUAGE
ASSOCIATION OF AMERICA

The emblem of the Committee on Scholarly Editions indicates that this volume is based on an examination of all available relevant textual sources, that it is edited according to principles articulated in the volume, that the source texts and the edited text's deviations from them are fully described, that the editorial principles and the text and the apparatus have undergone a peer review, that a rigorous schedule of verification and proofreading was followed to insure a high degree of accuracy in the presentation of the edition, and that the text is accompanied by appropriate textual and other historical contextual information.

EDITORIAL ADVISORY BOARD

Mary F. Berry
Richard J. M. Blackett
David B. Davis
Carl Degler
John Hope Franklin
Robert Hall
Louis R. Harlan
Darlene C. Hine
Howard Lamar
David Montgomery
George Shepperson
Clare Taylor
Howard Temperley
George B. Tindall
C. Vann Woodward

Contents

Acknowledgments

Publication of the first volume of the Autobiographical Writings Series by the Frederick Douglass Papers marks a landmark in the history of this editorial project. In 1994, the bulk of the project's documents and editorial tools, created during two decades of work at Yale University, was transferred to West Virginia University. At that time, John W. Blassingame, founding editor and guiding spirit of this project since its inception in 1973, turned over the role of principal investigator to John R. McKivigan, who had worked on his staff at Yale from 1979 until joining the faculty at West Virginia University in fall 1989. To ensure continuity in the editorial quality of the Douglass Papers volumes, Blassingame has remained with the project in the new position of General Editor. He consulted closely with McKivigan both in devising the editorial procedures and in examining the final manuscript of this volume before its submission to the press.

Many individuals at three academic institutions need to be thanked for their assistance to the Frederick Douglass Papers in recent years, especially Charles Long and Raymond Novak at Yale University and Rudolph P. Almasy, Barbara J. Howe, Gerald E. Lang, Ronald L. Lewis, Nancy G. McGreevy, M. Duane Nellis, and Christine L. Tarabrella at West Virginia University. Their generous help minimized the disruption inherent in transferring a long-established editorial project to a new home. The Douglass Papers also is greatly indebted to its program officers, Richard Sheldon of the National Historic Publications and Records Commission and Douglas Arnold at the National Endowment for the Humanities, for their advice and support during this process.

Over the years many graduate research assistants and undergraduate honors students contributed to the preparation of this volume, including Cecelia Bucki, Marcus Bruce, and Reeve Houston at Yale University, Brian Berkley and Maureen McCormick at West Virginia University, and Georgia Harmon Butts, Scott Mathis, and Brett Fulkerson at Freed-Hardeman University. The editors benefitted greatly from their scholarship and attention to detail.

Special thanks are owed to a number of other individuals. Richard G. Carlson, a former member of the Douglass Papers staff, contributed to formulating the editorial procedures for this series. Our textual editor,

Gerald Fulkerson, acknowledges the assistance of his Freed-Hardeman University colleague, Don Shull, in sight collating the various editions of the *Narrative*. Noel Polk, professor of English at the University of Southern Mississippi, consulted with the editors and performed the machine collation of the earliest *Narrative* edition for the Douglass Papers. Timothy Dow Adams, professor of English at West Virginia University, provided valuable guidance to the editors on current literary theory concerning the interpretation of autobiographies. The project is also greatly indebted to Lori B. Bessler at the State Historical Society of Wisconsin and Jane Miller at Freed-Hardeman University for locating and supplying many obscure research materials for this volume.

Abbreviations

ACAB	*Appleton's Cyclopaedia of American Biography*
ASB	*Anti-Slavery Bugle*
BDAC	*Biographical Directory of the American Congress*
DAB	*Dictionary of American Biography*
DANB	*Dictionary of American Negro Biography*
DHU	Moorland-Spingarn Library, Howard University
DLC	Library of Congress
DNB	*Dictionary of National Biography*
FDP	*Frederick Douglass' Paper*
JNH	*Journal of Negro History*
Lib.	*Liberator*
MdAA	Hall of Records Commission, Annapolis, Md.
MdHi	Talbot County Courthouse, Easton, Md.
MdHM	*Maryland Historical Magazine*
MdTCH	Talbot County, Maryland, Courthouse
NASS	*National Anti-Slavery Standard*
NCAB	*National Cyclopaedia of American Biography*
NHi	New-York Historical Society
NS	*North Star*
PaF	*Pennsylvania Freeman*

Introduction to Series Two

One of an exceedingly small number of nineteenth-century Americans to publish more than one autobiography in their lifetimes, Frederick Douglass occupies a unique place in the annals of American literature. Publishing three autobiographies between 1845 and 1892, Douglass left an unparalleled record of the events of his life and his shifting perceptions of them over time. Each of these autobiographical works reflects significant differences in age, memory, and objectives at the time of writing. The *Narrative of the Life of Frederick Douglass* was published first in Boston in 1845, *My Bondage and My Freedom* was published in New York in 1855, and *Life and Times of Frederick Douglass* was published in Hartford, Connecticut, in 1881 and extended in 1892. Douglass published all but one of his autobiographical writings in his lifetime. The one exception was the diary that he intermittently kept between 1886 and 1894. Consisting of seventy-one manuscript pages, the diary covers Douglass's trip to England, France, Italy, Greece, and Egypt. Far more than any other Douglass documents, his autobiographical writings are vivid recreations of his private internal life and of the complex worlds of slavery and freedom he inhabited.

Douglass's autobiographies have attracted the attention of numerous scholars. William L. Andrews, Houston Baker, Stephen Butterfield, G. Thomas Couser, Henry Louis Gates, Sidonie Smith, Marion Wilson Starling, Robert Stepto, Albert E. Stone, Eric Sundquist, and many others have examined Douglass's autobiographies as literature.[1] Historians David Blight, Philip Foner, Rayford Logan, William S. McFeely, and Benjamin

---

1. William L. Andrews, *To Tell a Free Story: The First Century of Afro-American Autobiography, 1760–1865* (Urbana, Ill., 1986), 280–91; Houston A. Baker, "The Problem of Being: Some Reflections on Black Autobiography," *Obsidian: Black Literature Review,* 1 : 18–30 (1975); Stephen Butterfield, *Black Autobiography in America* (Amherst, Mass., 1974), 65–89; G. Thomas Couser, *American Autobiography: The Prophetic Mode* (Amherst, Mass., 1979), 51–61; Henry Louis Gates, *Figures in Black: Words, Signs, and the "Racial" Self* (New York, 1987), 98–124; Sidonie Smith, *Where I'm Bound: Patterns of Slavery and Freedom in Black American Autobiography* (Westport, Conn., 1974), 3–27; Marion Wilson Starling, *The Slave Narrative: Its Place in American History* (Boston, 1981), 32–39; Robert Stepto, *From Behind the Veil: A Study of Afro-American Narrative* (Urbana, Ill., 1979), 3–31; Albert E. Stone, "Identity and Art in Frederick Douglass's Narrative," *College Language Association Journal,* 17 : 192–213 (December 1973); Eric J. Sundquist, ed., *Frederick Douglass: New Literary and Historical Essays* (Cambridge, Mass., 1990), 1–22.

Quarles were instrumental in reprinting some of Douglass's autobiographies with introductions describing the publication history and critical reception of the works. These scholars contributed significantly to our understanding of Douglass's autobiographical writings.[2]

At the suggestion of National Endowment for the Humanities site visit teams and reviewers, the Frederick Douglass Papers explored the voluminous writings of modern textual editors in developing an editorial policy for the autobiographical writings. A textual editor has determined the significant variations in different editions, the corruption in the text, printers' errors, and the author's alterations. Such analysis was crucial in order to establish authoritative editions of Douglass's autobiographies consistent with modern editing practices. A description of the textual methodology employed in the editing of Douglass's *Narrative,* the first volume of the Autobiographical Writings Series, immediately follows the text below.

Following the example of many recent scholarly editions, the Douglass Papers place concise annotations identifying individuals, places, events, and literary allusions found in the text of Douglass's autobiographies in an appendix following the text of each autobiography. To enhance the reader's comprehension and appreciation of Douglass's texts, the editors have included additional appendixes to each autobiography. Each of these appendixes contains contemporary documents, maps, or illustrations that illuminate some aspect of the elusive milieu surrounding the text of Douglass's autobiographies. The Editorial Method Statement explains the principles guiding the selection of such materials.

Historians have long recognized the central place of Douglass in his times. There have been more than a dozen biographies of Douglass, and contemporary historians mention him frequently in their writings.[3] A further increase in the recognition by historians and literary scholars of Doug-

2. David W. Blight, ed., *Narrative of the Life of Frederick Douglass, An American Slave, Written by Himself* (Boston, 1993); Frederick Douglass, *My Bondage and My Freedom,* ed. Philip S. Foner (1855; New York, 1969); Rayford Logan, ed., *The Life and Times of Frederick Douglass, Written by Himself: His Early Life as a Slave, His Escape from Bondage, and His Complete History* (New York, 1962); William L. Andrews and William S. McFeely, eds., *Narrative of the Life of Frederick Douglass, An American Slave, Written by Himself* (New York, 1997); Benjamin Quarles, ed., *Narrative of the Life of Frederick Douglass, An American Slave* (Cambridge, Mass., 1960).

3. For example, Kenneth Stampp in his study of slavery, *The Peculiar Institution: Slavery in the Ante-Bellum South* (New York, 1956), refers to Douglass twenty times; James M. McPherson, *The Struggle for Equality: Abolitionists and the Negro in the Civil War and Reconstruction* (Princeton, N.J., 1964), fifty-seven; August Meier, *Negro Thought in America, 1880–1915* (Ann Arbor, Mich., 1963), twenty-one; and practically all general surveys of American history mention him several times.

lass's importance as the central political and intellectual figure of the nine-teenth-century African-American community has occurred in the past two decades. This recognition has led to a flowering of historical scholarship regarding Douglass.[4]

Literary scholars likewise regard Douglass's autobiographies as semi-nal works in African-American literature.[5] The widespread acceptance of Douglass's writings, especially his *Narrative,* into the canon of American literature since the 1960s coincided with a major scholarly reevaluation of the autobiography genre. Literary theorists such as Paul John Eakin, Paul Jay, James Olney, Sidonie Smith, and William Spengemann have ques-tioned the traditional claims for autobiography as factual life history. They instead argue for a view of the autobiography that foregrounds its "novelis-tic" or "fictive" dimensions. Eakin describes how this new attitude toward autobiography differs from its predecessor: "Most readers naturally assume that all autobiographies are based on the verifiable facts of a life history, and it is this referential dimension, imperfectly understood, that has checked the development of a poetics of autobiography. Historians and social scientists attempt to isolate the factual context of autobiography from its narrative matrix, while literary critics, seeking to promote the apprecia-tion of autobiography as an imaginative art, have been willing to treat such texts as though they were indistinguishable from novels."[6] It did not take

4. Among the most noteworthy recent monographs are: Nathan Irvin Huggins, *Slave and Citizen: The Life of Frederick Douglass* (Boston, 1980); Dickson J. Preston, *Young Frederick Douglass: The Maryland Years* (Baltimore, 1980); Waldo E. Martin, Jr., *The Mind of Frederick Douglass* (Chapel Hill, 1984); Douglas T. Miller, *Frederick Douglass and the Fight for Freedom* (New York, 1988); David W. Blight, *Frederick Douglass's Civil War: Keeping Faith in Jubilee* (Baton Rouge, 1989); and William S. McFeely, *Frederick Douglass* (New York, 1991). A computer-assisted search for articles in scholarly journals on the topic of Frederick Douglass turned up nearly one hundred titles published during the 1980s alone.

5. Harold Bloom, ed., *Modern Critical Interpretations: Frederick Douglass's Narrative of the Life of Frederick Douglass* (New York, 1988); Andrews, *To Tell a Free Story,* 214–39; Deborah McDowell, "In the First Place: Making Frederick Douglass and the Afro-American Tradition," in *Critical Essays on Frederick Douglass,* ed. William L. Andrews (Boston, 1991), 192–214; and Henry Louis Gates, "From Wheatley to Douglass: The Politics of Displacement," in Sundquist, *Frederick Douglass,* 47–65.

6. Paul John Eakin, *Fictions in Autobiography: Studies in the Art of Self-Invention* (Princeton, N.J., 1985), 3. Idem, *Touching the World: Reference in Autobiography* (Princeton, N.J., 1992); Sidonie Smith, *A Poetics of Women's Autobiography: Marginality and the Fictions of Self-Representation* (Bloomington, Ind., 1987); Paul Jay, *Being in Text: Self- Representation from Wordsworth to Roland Barthes* (Ithaca, N.Y., 1984); idem, "What's the Use: Critical Theory and the Study of Autobiography," *Biography: An Interdisciplinary Quarterly,* 10 : 39–54 (1987). Still useful are James Olney, *Metaphors of Self: The Meaning of Autobiography* (Princeton, N.J., 1972), 3–50; and William C. Spengemann, *The Forms of Autobiography: Episodes in the History of a Literary Genre* (New Haven, 1980), xi–xvii.

long for adherents of this latter view to proclaim that Douglass's autobiographies were primarily literary creations. After all, as its title suggests, his first autobiography was acknowledged by Douglass himself to be a "narrative" of a life.[7]

The publication of a critical edition of Douglass's autobiographical writings will not resolve the dispute regarding whether these works should be treated as biographical-historical or as fictional material. Historians will appreciate the editors' efforts to verify references to people and events named in these works, yet such verification will not settle literary scholars' questions regarding the "objective reality" of such references. At the same time, as the fictive dimensions of this genre become more highly regarded by literary scholars, the text itself is more, not less, valued. Our preparation of authoritative editions of Douglass's autobiographical writings will assist future research by those who regard those works as rhetorical constructs or inner narratives rather than historical accounts. By addressing the concerns of different disciplines, the editors hope that this critical edition will meet the demand of a wide scholarly community to have all of Douglass's autobiographical writing, at last, compiled and edited in one common series.

Douglass's autobiographies reveal the rich, variegated, and complex workings of one of nineteenth-century America's greatest minds. Though one might be tempted to equate that greatness with Douglass's tireless activities within the political arena, it was clearly his unique gift for self-definition and self-expression that set him apart from his contemporaries. More than any other written record left in his giant wake, Frederick Douglass's autobiographies have quietly led successive generations of Americans toward the true expression of his genius. The new Yale edition of Douglass's autobiographical writings is intended to provide new generations of readers with the definitive tool to appreciate Douglass's intellectual achievement.

7. Eakin, *Touching the World*, 206–07; William L. Andrews, "African-American Autobiography Criticism: Retrospect and Prospect," in *American Autobiography: Retrospect and Prospect*, ed. Paul John Eakin (Madison, Wis., 1991), 195–215.

Introduction to Volume One

John W. Blassingame

Frederick Douglass's antebellum reputation as a writer rests firmly on the autobiography he published when he was twenty-seven years old. At first glance, Douglass's incomparable literary success is inexplicable. During the two decades he spent as a Maryland slave, for example, Douglass displayed few of the talents that would mark his later literary career. Indeed, one observer who knew Douglass during the years he spent in bondage recalled that he was "an unlearned, and rather ordinary negro." However ordinary Douglass appeared as a slave, he had become an extraordinary man by 1845, seven years after his escape from bondage. If not yet learned, Douglass was at least highly literate by 1845.[1]

In typical nineteenth-century fashion, Douglass was fond of referring to his autobiography in self-effacing terms. Speaking of his *Narrative* in 1845, for instance, he asserted that "a person undertaking to write a book without learning will appear rather novel, but such as it was I gave it to the public."[2] Like many authors, Douglass did not often reflect on or clearly elucidate the nature of his "learning" or the various literary influences bearing upon his writing. Nevertheless, it is obvious that when Douglass began writing his autobiography in the winter of 1844–45, he understood the conventions and literary canons that applied to the genre.[3]

The manifold influences bearing upon Douglass's autobiography included antebellum literary criticism, previously published black and white slave narratives, his knowledge of other autobiographical writings, and several events that took place between 1838 and 1845. Many of the conventions followed by Douglass were similar to those of other nineteenth-

---

1. John W. Blassingame et al., eds., *The Frederick Douglass Papers*, Series 1: *Speeches, Debates, and Interviews*, 5 vols. (New Haven, 1979–92), 1 : 201.

2. Ibid.

3. The paucity of studies of nineteenth-century American criticism of autobiographies forces the interested student systematically to examine the magazines of the period and the collected essays on the literary critics active between 1800 and 1860. A brief overview of nineteenth-century English criticism of autobiographies can be found in Keith Rinehart, "The Victorian Approach to Autobiography," *Modern Philology*, 51 : 177–86 (February 1954); and George P. Landow, ed., *Approaches to Victorian Autobiography* (Athens, Ohio, 1979), 3–26, 39–63, 333–54. The most useful bibliography of works revealing the nature of autobiographies appears in James Olney, ed., *Autobiography: Essays Theoretical and Critical* (Princeton, N.J., 1980).

century American and English autobiographers, black and white. The simi-
larities between black and white autobiographers were most evident in the
narratives of those who had been enslaved or captured by Indians in the
Americas or of white Europeans and Americans who were shipwrecked
and enslaved in Africa.[4]

Because antebellum Americans frowned upon the reading of novels,
they avidly read personal accounts of shipwrecks, slavery, and Indian
captivities that had all of the characteristics of romanticized adventures.
Between 1682 and 1860, for instance, some Indian captivity narratives
went through as many as forty-one editions. Among the earliest forms of
American literature, these narratives expressed the religious sentiment of
the age, employed biblical allusions extensively, exemplified the redemp-
tive power of suffering, and illustrated divine providence. Authors stressed
the didactic purposes served by their accounts. Frequently serialized in
nineteenth-century newspapers and magazines, the narratives had become
stylized, sentimental, melodramatic, and sensational tales containing exaggerated accounts of the barbarities, tortures, and manifold horrors suffered
by the captives. Journalists fabricated many nineteenth-century accounts,
and true stories had to compete with fiction parading as truth.[5]

Perhaps the clearest indication of the merging of black and white
autobiographical traditions at an early point in American literary history is
that some of the first black autobiographies were also, in part, Indian
captivity narratives. Among the African-American autobiographers to detail their captivity by and deliverance from Indians were Briton Hammon
and Joseph Marrant in *A Narrative of the Uncommon Sufferings and Surprising Deliverance of Briton Hammon, a Negro Man* (1760) and *A Narrative of the Lord's Wonderful Dealings with John Marrant, a Black, Taken
Down from His Own Relation* (1785).

---

4. C. Marius Barbeau, "Indian Captivities," *Proceedings of the American Philosophical Soci-
ety,* 94 : 522–48 (December 1950); Richard Van Der Beets, "A Surfeit of Style: The Indian Captivity
Narrative as Penny Dreadful," *Research Studies,* 39 : 297–306 (December 1971); Roy Harvey Pearce,
"The Significance of the Captivity Narrative," *American Literature,* 19 : 1–20 (March 1947); Joseph
Bruchac, "Black Autobiography in Africa and America," *Black Academy Review,* 2 : 61–70 (Spring-
Summer, 1971); Mutulu K. Blasing, *The Art of Life: Studies in American Autobiographical Literature*
(Austin, Tex., 1977); James Riley, *An Authentic Narrative of the Loss of the American Brig Commerce*
(Hartford, Conn., 1836), iii–xiv; Eliza Bradley, *An Authentic Narrative of the Shipwreck and Sufferings
of Mrs. Eliza Bradley* (Boston, 1821); John W. Blassingame, *The Slave Community: Plantation Life in
the Antebellum South,* rev. ed. (New York, 1979), 376–77.

5. Richard Van Der Beets, ed., *Held Captive by Indians: Selected Narratives, 1642–1836*
(Knoxville, Tenn., 1973), xi–xxxi.

A group of powerful literary critics in the United States and the United Kingdom shaped the nineteenth-century autobiographical convention followed by Douglass and other authors. One of the most influential of these critics was an Englishman, the Reverend John Foster, a prolific and popular essayist. An ardent republican, Foster wrote widely on theological and biographical subjects and contributed 184 articles to the *Eclectic Review* between 1806 and 1839. Among the most frequently reprinted of Foster's works was the 1805 collection of his early essays. The book, appearing in several American editions between 1807 and 1845, contained Foster's twenty-one-page essay "On a Man's Writing Memoirs of Himself," which played a primary role in establishing the conventions of English and American autobiography.[6]

Concerned in most of his numerous essays with the formation and evidence of character, Foster drew a distinction between the exterior and the interior of a person's life. He admired "simple conviction" and despised "the sly deceit of self-love" and the "self-describers who . . . think the publication of their vices necessary to crown their fame." As much as he disliked the "confessions" of courtesans, debauchees, drunkards, and criminals, Foster delighted in accounts tracing the various stages that marked an individual's moral, spiritual, and intellectual progress. Above all, he viewed the end of autobiography to be self-understanding, a way for a person "to acquire a complete knowledge of himself" and the course of his growth. It was, of course, axiomatic that a person's self-history differed significantly according to the stage at which it was written, since "in the course of a long life a man may be several moral persons." Recognition of moral, religious, and intellectual advancement and retrogression was essential, according to Foster, because of the lessons they provided and because they constituted a record to compare "with the standard of perfection." Conscience required that there be explicit admission of delinquencies to cultivate humility and diminish vanity and "self-love."[7]

Realizing how difficult it was for people to parade their errors, Foster returned again and again in his essay to the distinction between inner and

---

6. Walter Graham, *Tory Criticism in the Quarterly Review, 1809–1853* (New York, 1921); William Charvat, *The Origins of American Critical Thought, 1810–1835* (1936; New York, 1961), 1–26, 164–205. *Dictionary of National Biography,* 21 vols. (London, 1921–22), 7 : 497–99. John Foster, *Essays in a Series of Letters* (New York, 1853), 66–81. The first edition of Foster's book was published in London in 1805. The American editions available to Douglass appeared in Hartford, 1807, 1844, 1845; Boston, 1811, 1833, 1839; Utica, 1815; Andover, 1826; and New York, 1835.

7. Foster, *Essays in a Series of Letters,* 69, 71–72, 73, 78.

outer character. Inner character he considered more important because an attempt to represent it exposed one to the powerful temptation to be dishonest. Without a truthful recounting of this hidden compartment, autobiography would lose much of its power for self-instruction. Foster also felt that dishonesty in this area would make an autobiography less interesting or capable of eliciting sympathy from readers. Truth, history, and divinity met as the autobiographer struggled to reveal his or her inner character:

> Each mind has an interior apartment of its own, into which none but itself and the Divinity can enter. In this secluded place, the passions mingle and fluctuate in unknown agitations. Here all the fantastic and all the tragic shapes of imagination have a haunt, where they can neither be invaded nor descried. . . . Here projects, convictions, vows, are confusedly scattered, and the records of past life are laid. Here in solitary state sits Conscience, surrounded by her own thunders, which sometimes sleep, and sometimes roar, while the world does not know. . . . If, in a man's own account of himself, written on the supposition of being seen by any other person, the substance of the secrets of this apartment be brought forth, he throws open the last asylum of his character. . . . And if it be not brought forth, where is the integrity or value of the history . . . ?[8]

Although actually offering little advice about how to structure autobiography, his few remarks nevertheless resonated through hundreds of prefaces, reviews, and critical essays for the next century. Again and again the critics upheld his singular directive that "the *style* should be as simple as possible."[9]

The critics who followed Foster exhibited far more interest in the readers than the writers of autobiographies. In contrast to Foster, they stressed the autobiography's power to acquaint the reader with human virtues as well as to furnish relaxation and entertainment. Many critics contended that the chief value of the autobiography was that it was a historical document. Through autobiographies—especially those of public figures—readers could see behind the public facades of great figures and learn in detail from the events and influences that shaped their characters.[10]

Writing for an increasingly literate society, American critics valued autobiographies as instructive books for the education of youth. It was

8. Ibid., 76.
9. Ibid., 74.
10. *New York Review,* 1 : 475–76 (October 1837), 9 : 531–33 (October 1841).

infinitely better, they contended, for youths to read autobiographies than novels. Because autobiographers sketched their lives from childhood to their attainment of eminence and stressed "the cultivation of intellectual and moral power," they could provide lessons, examples, and inspirations to the young.[11]

But what was of special concern to antebellum critics was the credibility of any autobiography. Detailing the factors that limited credibility (senility, egotism, and vanity), the critics tried to develop a series of tests to determine where it existed. As critics became more familiar with the genre, they became more confident of their ability to determine the veracity of autobiographies. By concentrating on the patterns of revelation and concealment in a work, the critics believed that they could uncover an author's true self-portrait. A *New York Review* critic, for instance, writing in October 1838, insisted that by a close reading of an autobiography, one could determine whether it was true because "in autobiography we study character in two modes at once. We have, first, what the individual *says* of himself, and secondly, the *unconscious* revelation which he makes of himself as narrator; the picture in the glass, and the real man seen behind it."[12]

A number of critics drew upon their own experience or sought the proof of the credibility of an autobiography in its narrative technique. Frequently they combined the two tests. A *North American Review* critic, for example, argued in 1844 that the most believable autobiographies were those in which minuteness of detail was a salient feature: "Minuteness of narration, whether in fiction or in real life, has a singular charm for all readers. . . . Now, the *only* truth is the *whole* truth. The complete portrait is the only faithful portrait. The only true history or biography is that which tells all." For most readers the credibility of such accounts would be "attested by our experience, which necessarily comprehends the whole of our own thoughts, motives and actions." The "vast edifice" of a life had to be portrayed because the "piecemeal exhibition of another's life finds no counterpart in our own memories, which embrace every incident in our own career."[13]

---

11. *New England Magazine*, 5 : 32–33 (July 1833), 9 : 140–41 (August 1835); *New York Review*, 7 : 535–37 (July 1840); *North American Review*, 10 : 1–14 (January 1820).

12. *New York Review*, 3 : 403 (October 1838). See also: *North American Review*, 9 : 58–59 (June 1819); *New York Review*, 8 : 1–50 (January 1841); Howard Helsinger, "Credence and Credibility: The Concern for Honesty in Victorian Autobiography," in Landow, ed., *Approaches to Victorian Autobiography*, 39–63.

13. *North American Review*, 54 : 452–53 (October 1844).

Much of what critics thought was likely to be incredible about autobiographies was, they contended, inherent in the genre. Since an autobiography involved revelations about the frequently inaccessible interior of
life, it often raised unanswerable questions about credibility. The personal
secrets of the autobiographer represented what most critics believed constituted the most instructive aspect of his or her self-portrait—thoughts, feelings, imaginations, motives. Critics longed to see what they described as
the autobiographer's "thoughts and feelings in their nakedness . . . his
envy, jealousy, malice, and uncharitableness." They wanted to read the
works of autobiographers willing to risk notoriety and "lay open to the
world the deepest and darkest nooks of their own hearts, however ugly and
loathsome may be the things which dwell therein." True histories of the
inner person would always be rare, however, the critics argued, because
most autobiographers lacked the necessary discrimination, analytical
skills, sincerity, and self-knowledge to write them. A *New England Magazine* writer sadly concluded in 1834, we "know our enemies better than
ourselves, because we judge them with more severity; we can write better
lives of them than memoirs of ourselves."[14]

Yet they also imposed limits on such exposure. Self-revelation must not
be a promiscuous exercise intended merely to shock and arouse the audience but must promote a moral life and show an eventual turning away from
things bad even as they are described in detail.

Nevertheless, the author must have a proper and unavoidable dose of
egotism. Many of the critics argued that egotism naturally determined both
the focus and the design of life histories. Reviewing Johann Wolfgang von
Goethe's autobiography in October 1838, a *New York Review* critic professed that in autobiography "if the author is himself the central point
around which all seems to revolve, this is in conformity with the idea of an
autobiography, and is necessary to unity of design . . . egotism is the very
thing to be desired in such a work."[15]

Following Foster's injunctions, critics also expressed a desire for a
"simple" style in autobiographies. Increasingly, critics translated "simple"
into "appropriate," a variable standard dependent on the times, incidents,
and the lives being described. What was, under this standard, misplaced
ornamentation in one author would be appropriate in another. Critics ex-

14. *New England Magazine,* 6 : 497 (June 1834); *New York Review,* 8 : 1–50 (January 1841);
North American Review, 9 : 58–59 (June 1819), 9 : 341–43 (October 1820).
    15. *New York Review,* 3 : 404 (October 1838).

pected an autobiographer to demonstrate lucidity, modesty, honesty, and economy. Repeatedly, critics praised those self-portraits that were "plain, unaffected" narratives marked by unity of design and artful symmetry. Especially ornate language suggested that the author was insincere.[16]

Many American critics identified Benjamin Franklin as the model autobiographer because of the clarity and economy of his writing. A *North American Review* evaluation of Benjamin Franklin's autobiographical writings in 1818 varied little from the positive assessments of numerous other critics. In spite of "some trifling blemishes," Franklin's work was "always admirable for its precision and perspicuity. It is as transparent as the atmosphere; and his thoughts lie before us like objects seen in one of our finest and clearest days, when their very brightness and distinctness alone give us pleasure."[17]

In the 1830s Douglass first encountered Franklin indirectly in Caleb Bingham's *Columbian Orator*. In his primer, Bingham reprinted Abbé Fauchet's 1790 eulogy of Benjamin Franklin. Fauchet praised Franklin for having "presented new and sublime ideas, in a style simple as truth, and as pure as light." Further he contended that Franklin "laid the sacred foundations of social morality. . . . This amiable moralist descended, in his writings, to the most artless details; to the most ingenuous familiarities; to the first ideas of a rural, a commercial, and a civil life; to the dialogues of old men and children; full at once of all the verdure and all the maturity of wisdom." Fauchet stamped the essentials of antebellum American autobiography in his paean to Franklin and assuredly made his impress upon the young Douglass as well.[18]

Although the *Columbian Orator* was Douglass's key textbook during the time of his enslavement in Maryland, his central texts once he escaped from slavery were abolitionist newspapers, magazines, books, and pamphlets and slave narratives. Such works greatly expanded his knowledge of autobiographies. In abolition sources alone, Douglass read dozens of narratives of fugitive slaves before he sat down to write his autobiography in 1844.

Between 1838 and 1844 Douglass avidly read such antislavery publications as the *Liberator, National Anti-Slavery Standard, Liberty Bell, Emancipator, Anti-Slavery Almanac,* and *American and Foreign Anti-Slavery*

16. *New England Magazine,* 5 : 31–33 (July 1833); *New York Review,* 7 : 535–37 (July 1840).
17. *North American Review,* 7 : 321 (September 1818).
18. Caleb Bingham, ed., *The Columbian Orator* (1797; Boston, 1831), 65–68.

Reporter that contained speeches, interviews, and autobiographies of dozens of fugitive slaves including Lunsford Lane, James Curry, Lewis Clarke, and the *Amistad* rebels. Equally significant, the abolition newspapers and magazines published reviews of the autobiographies of blacks and whites and furnished Douglass with further advice on the elements of the proper autobiography. At a very early period, Douglass also came to know the "slave's biographer," Isaac T. Hopper, who published a long-running popular column of slave narratives in the *National Anti-Slavery Standard* under the heading "Tales of Oppression."[19]

Another source of information about the autobiographical canon that Douglass read repeatedly was Theodore Dwight Weld's *American Slavery As It Is*. Douglass quoted frequently from Weld's work in the speeches he gave between 1841 and 1845. Indeed, *American Slavery As It Is* long represented for Douglass the standard by which to measure all statements about the character of America's peculiar institution. The book was, Douglass wrote in 1853, the "repository of human horrors."[20]

Douglass relied so extensively on personal narratives in *American Slavery As It Is* that they undoubtedly formed the structure, focus, and style of his *Narrative*. He learned, for instance, that most of the accounts that Weld published followed letters vouching for the author's integrity and veracity. Weld himself repeatedly stressed the importance of a truthful portrayal of slavery, urged witnesses to " 'speak what they know, and testify what they have seen,' " and commanded them to demonstrate a "fidelity to truth." Conscious of the incredulity of his northern readers, Weld insisted on making a clear distinction between opinion and fact: "Testimony respects matters of *fact,* not matters of opinion: it is the declaration of a witness as to *facts,* not the giving of an opinion as to the nature or qualities of actions, or the *character* of a course of conduct."[21]

American Slavery As It Is may also have played a crucial role in Douglass's original decision to write and publish his *Narrative*. Signi-

19. For examples of these autobiographical accounts, see: John W. Blassingame, ed., *Slave Testimony: Two Centuries of Letters, Speeches, Interviews, and Autobiographies* (Baton Rouge, 1977), 128–64, 198–245, 690–95; Lydia Maria Child, "Charity Bowery," *Liberty Bell* (Boston, 1839), 26–43; Isaac T. Hopper, "Story of a Fugitive," *Liberty Bell* (Boston, 1843), 163–69; "Story of Anthony Gayle," in *The American Anti-Slavery Almanac, for 1838* (Boston, 1838); 44; "The Conscientious Slave," in *The American Anti-Slavery Almanac, for 1843* (New York, 1843), 42–44; Lydia Maria Child, *Isaac T. Hopper: A True Life* (Boston, 1853).

20. *FDP,* 29 April 1853; Blassingame, *Douglass Papers,* 1 : 42, 52, 75.

21. [Theodore Dwight Weld], *American Slavery As It Is: Testimony of a Thousand Witnesses* (New York, 1839), 9–10, 122; Blassingame, *Douglass Papers,* 1 : 41, 51–52, 254, 279–81, 322, 485.

ficantly, in a prefatory "Note" to his book, Weld announced that the American Anti-Slavery Society intended to publish other "TRACTS, containing well authenticated facts, testimony, personal narratives, etc. fully setting forth the *condition* of American slaves." Each prospective author unknown to the Executive Committee of the Society had to furnish references. Weld specified exactly the kinds of narratives in which the society had an interest:

> Facts and testimony respecting the condition of slaves, in *all respects,* are desired; their food, (kinds, quality, quantity), clothing, lodging, dwellings, hours of labor and rest, kinds of labor, with the mode of exaction, supervision, &c.—the number and times of meals each day, treatment when sick, regulations respecting their social intercourse, marriage and domestic ties, the system of torture to which they are subjected, with its various modes; and *in detail,* their *intellectual* and *moral* condition. Great care should be observed in the statement of facts. Well-weighed testimony and well-authenticated facts, with a responsible name, the Committee earnestly desire and call for.[22]

Given this note, it is probably no accident that the publisher Douglass chose for his first autobiography was the American Anti-Slavery Society and that he found two people, William Lloyd Garrison and Wendell Phillips, "personally known" to its executive committee to write prefatory notes to his *Narrative.*

Although the other autobiographical works Douglass read were probably somewhat less influential than *American Slavery As It Is,* they were no less significant. The most salient features of the slave narratives he read in the abolition press were their brevity, directness, simplicity, and lack of specificity. Often editors prefaced the accounts with declarations that publication had been delayed until the fugitive had reached Canada. Editors of the accounts of fugitives who remained in the United States frequently tried to guarantee their anonymity by giving them fictional names, deleting specific references to their masters and places of enslavement, or citing initials for all personal and place names that might possibly serve as keys to the real identity of the narrator. While helping to ensure the safety of the fugitive, such practices, the amanuenses realized, seriously undermined the

---

22. Weld, *American Slavery,* iv.

credibility of the accounts. In many cases, however, the guarantee of anonymity was the sine qua non for obtaining accounts from frightened fugitives.[23]

Significantly, Douglass had some of his first exposures to the narratives of fugitive slaves in oral rather than written form at the home of the
most prolific of the slaves' amanuenses, Isaac T. Hopper. Reflecting in
1853 on his introduction to Hopper, Douglass asserted that he first saw him
in September 1838 when Hopper was a witness in a fugitive slave case. In a
review of Lydia Maria Child's biography of Hopper, Douglass discussed
his "intimate acquaintance with the venerable, Quakerly gentleman" and
his visits to Hopper's home in the early 1840s, where he "listened to some
of the admirable stories and adventures in the matter of rescuing fugitives."[24]

Possessing a nearly photographic memory and being totally fearless,
Hopper aided hundreds of fugitive slaves, first in Philadelphia and later in
New York. Recording the minutest details from the tales of fugitives,
Hopper published about sixty of the stories in his "Tales of Oppression"
column in the *Standard*. Occasionally, when introducing these narratives,
Hopper explained the techniques he employed and taught Douglass much
about the art of autobiography.[25]

What impressed critics were "unvarnished" stories of the slaves' lives
filled with "unstudied pathos" and "touching" incidents that only an actual
observer could describe. Credibility and plainness were everything.[26]

Thus when the scandal over the narratives of Archy Moore and James
Williams broke in the late 1830s, the continuing viability of the slave
autobiographies was threatened. Published anonymously in 1836, the
Memoirs of Archy Moore produced disarray among the abolitionists when
southerners protested that it was fictional. Reviewers—uncertain about the
work's reliability—wavered between describing it as the factual account of
a slave and a fictional work. In 1837, however, a historian and abolitionist,
Richard Hildreth, admitted that he had created the narrative and disguised it
as genuine autobiography. Deeply embarrassed by this affair, the antislav-

23. Blassingame, *Slave Testimony*, 145–50, 151–64, 213–16; Hopper, "Story of a Fugitive,"
163–69.
24. Blassingame, *Slave Testimony*, 151, 158–59; *FDP*, 25 November 1853.
25. *NASS*, 22, 29 October, 5, 12, 26 November, 3, 10, 24, 31 December 1840, 7 January, 4
February 1841.
26. *Lib.*, 9, 30 March 1838.

ery societies had to rescue this critical tool in their crusade from the refuse pile to which the slaveholders wanted permanently to consign it.[27]

There could not have been a worse time, then, for another crisis of credibility to arise as it did in 1838 with the *Narrative of James Williams*, published by the Massachusetts Anti-Slavery Society and edited by John Greenleaf Whittier. Abolitionists spent much of 1838 countering the attacks on Williams's story. The most systematic defense came from the pen of "Memento." Reminding *Liberator* readers of the general skepticism of Whittier, "Memento" noted that former slaveholder James Birney of Alabama confirmed Williams's characterization of slave life in that state, praised the account of valuable "documentary evidence," and concluded that it was "incontrovertibly true; and is additionally valuable, because it so powerfully corroborates other evidence and facts which have been published."

Because it was "incontrovertibly true," the publication of Williams's story should be followed, "Memento" contended, by a flood of similar ones: "a few more such personal narratives as the life and experience of James Williams will render the boasted 'Southern domestic institutions' as loathsome, as they are cruelly malignant and criminal." What was most significant in the defense was a clear elaboration of the general credibility problem facing all abolitionist writers:

> Amid the strange characteristics of mankind, no one of their moral features is more unaccountable than their complex credulity in some cases, and in others, their marvelous unbelief. This general position is illustrated in an astonishing manner, upon the subject of slavery. It seems as if our northern citizens had determined to resist all evidence respecting the practical concerns of slaveholding, until they are ocularly convinced; while they have resolved never to witness *Life in the Negro Quarters*. It is yet more perplexing, that many of our anti-slavery friends are incredulous respecting the facts which are stated by professed eye-witnesses, and the few competent narrators of slavery as it exists in our country. Thus the only citizens, who personally know what slavery is from their own observation, and who are sufficiently independent to disclose the truth, are not only disbelieved, but are also

27. Richard Hildrith, ed., *Archy Moore, the White Slave; Or Memoirs of a Fugitive* (1856; New York, 1969); Marion Wilson Starling, *The Slave Narrative: Its Place in American History* (Boston, 1981), 227–33.

suspected of untruth, or reproached with falsehood, by the silly retort—
"I will not believe it; it cannot be true."[28]

In spite of the complaints and defense of people like "Memento," the
Executive Committee of the Massachusetts Anti-Slavery Society eventually had to consider the possibility that Williams had fabricated his story.
The committee checked many of the personal and place names mentioned
in Williams's account with knowledgeable southerners who almost universally disputed his claims. After its investigation, the committee published a
full retraction in November 1838 in which it came "fully to the conclusion,—that the statements of the narrative . . . are wholly false" and withdrew the book from sale. The Williams debacle forced all abolitionist
amanuenses to be more cautious, to state whether they were using real or
fictitious personal and place names, and to search systematically for cor-
roborating evidence and authenticating testimony for the oral accounts of
fugitive slaves. Williams haunted Theodore Weld; he sought to exorcise
fraudulent statements from the eyewitness accounts he published in *American Slavery As It Is*. The import of this crisis could not have been lost on
Douglass.[29]

Many of Douglass's views of the purpose and structure of autobiographies were those traditionally expressed by black authors since the eighteenth century. Antebellum black authors were well aware of contemporary
autobiographical canons and especially the didactic purposes served by
such works. Like their white contemporaries, black autobiographers often
reflected on the genre and frequently explained their motives for writing in
their preface and introductions. For example, Olaudah Equiano began his
narrative of 1789 by acknowledging that it was "a little hazardous in a
private and obscure individual" to publish his memoirs, establish the credibility of his account, and "to escape the imputation of vanity." Significantly, the "preface" to Equiano's narrative consisted of his open letter to
the British Parliament petitioning for the abolition of the African slave
trade and presenting his narrative as the evidence he hoped would convince
the members to answer his prayer.[30]

---

28. *Lib.*, 9 March 1838. See also: Starling, *Slave Narrative*, 115–17, 228–33; *Lib.*, 23 September
1838. See also *Narrative of James Williams, An America Slave, Who Was for Several Years A Driver on
a Cotton Plantation in Alabama* (New York, 1838).

29. *Lib.*, 2 November 1838; *African Repository*, 15 : 161–63 (June 1839). See also: Moses
Grandy, *Narrative of the Life of Moses Grandy; Late a Slave in the United States of America*, ed. George
Thompson (London, 1843), ii.

30. For a list of black autobiographies published between 1837 and 1845, see: George P. Rawick,

The sentiments expressed in Equiano's open letter would resonate in all of the autobiographies written by antebellum African Americans. Antebellum black autobiographers consistently asserted that the chief reason for portraying their lives was the need to bear witness against slavery, to wake their fellow Americans to its evil, and to cheer on those who labored in the cause of human freedom. Truth, the antebellum black autobiographers contended, would expose the evil of slavery and contribute to its destruction. Interestingly, American whites formerly enslaved in Africa wrote autobiographies with the same didactic purposes and expectations in mind. Although the experiences of white authors formerly enslaved or held captive were recorded in published reminiscences, the autobiographical writings of black slaves grew out of their own lectures. Once published, the autobiography led to more frequent trips to the lectern as the black's *written* and *spoken* voice moved in easy tandem.[31]

Moses Roper, the former North Carolina slave, illustrated many of the conventions of black autobiographies in his "Introduction" to the successive editions of his *Narrative of the Adventures and Escape of Moses Roper, from American Slavery*. In the first edition published in the United States in 1838, Roper declared that he wrote his autobiography "with the view of exposing the cruel system of slavery" and with the hope that it would become "the instruments of opening the eyes of the ignorant to this system; of convincing the wicked, cruel, and hardened slave-holder; and of befriending generally the cause of oppressed humanity." His decision to publish his life story, Roper assured his readers, "did not arise from any desire to make myself conspicuous." Roper was conscious not only of the possible imputation of vanity to an autobiographer but also of the conventional rules for determining the credibility of such stories. After Thomas Price, the editor of the volume, had quoted from the letters of

---

From Sundown to Sunup: The Making of the Black Community (Westport, Conn., 1972), 179–89; Starling, *Slave Narrative*, 39–50. See also [Olaudah Equiano], *The Interesting Narrative of the Life of Olaudah Equiano, or Gustavus Vassa, the African* (1789; Dublin, 1791), 1–2; Smith, *Where I'm Bound*, 3–27; Charles H. Nichols, *Many Thousand Gone: The Ex-Slaves' Account of Their Bondage and Freedom* (Leiden, Netherlands, 1963); Gilbert Osofsky, ed., *Puttin' On Ole Massa: The Slave Narratives of Henry Bibb, William Wells Brown, and Solomon Northrup* (New York, 1969), 9–44; Frances Smith Foster, *Witnessing Slavery: The Development of Ante-bellum Slave Narratives* (Westport, Conn., 1979); Arna Bontemps, ed., *Great Slave Narratives* (Boston, 1969), vii–xix; John F. Bayliss, ed., *Black Slave Narratives* (London, 1970), 7–21; Butterfield, *Black Autobiography in America*, 11–89; Charles H. Nichols, ed., *Black Men in Chains: Narratives by Escaped Slaves* (New York, 1972), 9–24.

31. Stephen Clissold, *The Barbary Slaves* (London, 1977); Blassingame, *Slave Community*, 367–82; Riley, *Authentic Narrative*, x–xxii; Blassingame, *Slave Testimony*, xxxiv–xxxvii, 145–64.

introduction written by American abolitionists that Roper brought to England and noted the narrative's "internal evidence of truth," the former slave confronted directly the possibility that many readers might feel that his account was "somewhat at variance with the dictates of humanity." Roper assured his readers that he did not present facts "unsubstantiated by collateral evidence, nor highly colored to the disadvantage of cruel task-masters." Finally, Roper observed that his master and other slaveholders would have an opportunity to read and contradict any aspect of his autobiography.[32]

Usually, autobiographers present their views of the genre in the prefaces of their life stories. Unfortunately, during the antebellum period autobiographers often had friends and acquaintances write prefaces, and Douglass followed this route in 1845. Only later in his speeches did Douglass publicly explain why he had written his autobiography. Essentially, Douglass contended, he wrote the autobiography to authenticate his antislavery speeches—and thus his voice. Douglass delivered a typical exposition of this theme in his speech of 18 May 1846 in London in which he pointed out that after delivering antislavery lectures for four years

> my manner was such as to create a suspicion that I was not a runaway slave, but some educated free negro, whom the abolitionists had sent forth to attract attention to what was called there a faltering cause. They said, he appears to have no fear of white people. How can he ever have been in bondage? But one strong reason for this doubt was, the fact that I never made known to the people to whom I spoke where I came from . . . But it became necessary to set myself right before the public in the United States, and to reveal the whole facts of my case. I did not feel it safe to do so till last spring, when I was solicited to it by a number of anti-slavery friends, who assured me that it would be safe to do so. I then published a narrative of my experience in slavery, in which I detailed the cruelties of it as I had myself felt them.[33]

Douglass knew well that perhaps the central problem he faced was to establish his credibility. To do so, he adopted several strategies. First, he placed a daguerreotype of himself on the book's frontispiece and signed his name below it. Before the reader had even begun the *Narrative,* they had seen a reproduction of the author and of his handwriting, evidence of his

32. Moses Roper, *A Narrative of the Adventures and Escape of Moses Roper, From American Slavery* (Philadelphia, 1838), 5, 7–8.
33. Blassingame, *Douglass Papers,* 1 : 37–38, 82, 88–89, 132–33.

literacy. Next he preceded his text with letters from William Lloyd Garrison and Wendell Phillips, who served as witnesses to his veracity. Finally, in the text of the *Narrative* Douglass used real names when referring to people and places and described how he came to know Garrison and Phillips.[34]

The letters of Garrison and Phillips afforded powerful confirmation of Douglass's "many sufferings" and his several attainments. Acknowledging the popular misconception of slavery in Maryland as being less severe than in the Deep South, Garrison proclaimed that Douglass's lived experience belied that stereotype and proved that slavery in whatever form still degraded blacks, leaving nothing "undone to cripple their intellects, darken their minds, debase their moral nature, obliterate all traces of their relationship to mankind." Garrison further asserted that he was deeply moved by the way Douglass had emerged from this prison house to "consecrate" his life as an antislavery lecturer with an "intellect richly endowed" and a character filled with "gentleness," "meekness," "manliness." Douglass had passed through all that he claimed. Reiterating some of the points Garrison made, Phillips wrote of his personal acquaintance with Douglass and emphasized his "truth, candor, and sincerity." The *Narrative,* Phillips argued, gave "a fair specimen of the whole truth. No one-sided portrait,—no wholesale complaints,—but strict justice done."[35]

But Douglass did not rest even here in promoting his authenticity. Soon after the publication of the *Narrative,* he took a bold and unprecedented step: he mailed a copy of the *Narrative* to his master Thomas Auld, and thereby challenged him publicly to refute it. Auld obviously had the greatest motive and was in the best position to disprove Douglass's *Narrative* if it were untrue. Although Douglass relished this gesture, he also compounded his risk of realizing the fugitive's greatest fear—recapture. At a time when many of his fellow fugitives recounted the story of their lives only on condition that their anonymity be maintained by suppressing their true names, those of their masters, and the places of their enslavement, Douglass's revelations of such details in the face of the obvious threat their publication posed represented the greatest authentication of his text.[36]

---

34. Stepto, *From Behind the Veil,* 4–5, 17–26.

35. *Narrative* (Boston, 1845), iii, iv, v, vi, vii, xiv.

36. On kidnappings and renditions of fugitive slaves, see: *NASS,* 29 October 1840, 25 November 1841, 3 February, 15 August, 29 September, 13 October, 17, 24 November, 8, 15 December 1842, 2 February 1843, 9 May, 25 July, 26 September, 7 November 1844, 22 May 1845.

The swift acclaim Douglass's work achieved attested to the success of these verifying methods. Of all of the other twenty-seven black autobiographies published before 1846, only six went through four or more editions during the nineteenth century and only three of these were translated into foreign languages. The most successful of them were the narratives of Charles Ball (six English-language editions), James A. Gronnisaw (six English-language and one Swedish edition), Moses Roper (seven English-language and one Celtic edition), and Olaudah Equiano (twelve English-language, one Dutch, and one German edition).

The *Narrative* far outstripped any of its predecessors. Between its appearance in May and September 1845, more than 4,500 copies of the *Narrative* had been sold. Three years later it had been translated into French, German, and Dutch. Between 1845 and 1847, two Irish and four English editions were published. According to Douglass, the *Narrative* had "passed through nine editions in England" by January 1848. Nine American editions had been published by 1850. In six years a total of twenty-one editions of the book had been published in the United States, the United Kingdom, and Europe. By 1853, at least 30,000 copies of the book had been sold. The price of the American editions varied between 25 and 35 cents.[37]

The *Narrative* served several extraliterary purposes. Published just as Douglass was leaving the United States for an extended tour of England, Scotland, and Ireland, the *Narrative* promoted his lectures. Sales of the book before and after his appearance in a town helped him meet his expenses. To the extent that readers in the United Kingdom believed the *Narrative,* they were that much more prepared to accept Douglass's lectures castigating America and American slavery. Douglass added further drama to his highly publicized "flight" to Great Britain to avoid the certain recapture assured by the publication of his *Narrative* by constantly alluding to this threat in his speeches.[38]

At the beginning of his tour of the United Kingdom, references to the *Narrative* became stock rhetorical devices in Douglass's speeches. Doug-

---

37. *NS,* 7 January, 21 April, 29 September 1848; *NASS,* 29 April 1847; *Lib.,* 20 June 6, 12, 19 September, 24, 31 October 1845, 2 January 1846, 12 November 1847, 24 May 1850. The foreign-language editions were: *Levensverhaal van Frederik Douglass, een' gewezen' slaaf (door hem zelven geschreven); Uit het Engelsch* (Rotterdam: H. A. Kramers, 1846); *Vie de Frédéric Douglass, esclave americain, écrite par lui-même, traduite de l'anglais par S.-K. Parkes* (Paris: Pagnerre, 1848).

38. *Lib.,* 25 July 1845, 10 July 1846; Cork *Examiner,* 22 October 1845; *NASS,* 4 December 1845; *British Friend,* 3 : 191 (December 1845); Bristol *Mercury,* 6 January 1846; *ASB,* 9 January 1846; *Littell's Living Age,* 9 : 50 (4 April 1846); Newcastle *Guardian,* 11 July 1846.

lass frequently emphasized the threat of recapture when he began a speech. Typical was his assertion in a speech in Cork, Ireland, in October 1845 that although publication of the *Narrative* removed doubts that he had been a slave, it produced some excitement in the South, endangering his safety: "The excitement at last increased so much that it was thought better for me to get out of the way lest my master might use some stratagems to get me back into his clutches. I am here then in order to avoid the scent of the blood hounds of America, and of spreading light on the subject of her slave system."[39]

The *Narrative* was the most widely reviewed of all antebellum black autobiographies. Dozens of newspapers and magazines published in the United States, the United Kingdom, and Europe praised the book, and reviews exceeding three thousand words were not unusual. Varying from long summaries containing numerous extracts to thoughtful essays on the nature of black autobiographies, the reviews generally accepted Douglass's self-portrait as true, interesting, and instructive.[40]

Reviewers in the antislavery press flocked to celebrate the *Narrative*. The *Liberator* inaugurated the campaign while the *Narrative* was still being printed. Announcing the forthcoming book in a lead editorial on 9 May 1845, the *Liberator* stressed that Douglass alone wrote the account. The acting editor of the newspaper then reprinted in full Garrison's preface. The reviewer for the *National Anti-Slavery Standard* attested that the book was "illustrated by a remarkably good engraving of the author" and buttressed this authenticating device with an indication of his personal acquaintance with the author. The *Liberator* added that the *Narrative* "was written entirely by Mr. Douglass, and reveals all the facts in regard to his birthplace,—the names of his mother, master, overseer, &c &c."[41]

The May 1845 annual meeting of the New England Anti-Slavery Society was also used to advance the *Narrative*. Attended by Garrison, Phillips, and Douglass, the convention was extensively covered in the press. Quickly taking advantage of free advertising, the first motion of the business committee offered by Wendell Phillips on 27 May welcomed the *Narrative* as "The new Anti-Slavery lecturer" and commended it to "all

39. Blassingame, *Douglass Papers*, 1: 37–45, 76, 81–90, 109, 128, 132–33, 291, 399.

40. For an overview of critical reception of books by nineteenth-century black authors, see: Julian D. Mason, "The Critical Reception of American Negro Authors in American Magazines, 1800–1885" (Ph.D. diss., University of North Carolina, 1962).

41. *Lib.*, 23 May 1845; *NASS*, 12 June 1845. See also: Concord (N.H.) *Herald of Freedom*, 9 May 1845; Chicago *Western Citizen*, 19 June 1845.

those who believe the slaves of the South to be either well treated, or happy, or ignorant of their right to freedom, or in need of preparation to make them fit for freedom; and that we urge upon the friends of the cause the duty of circulating it among all classes."[42]

Abolitionist critics contended the *Narrative* exposed slavery where it was allegedly "mildest" and that it would be an important "auxiliary" in the abolition crusade. The *Liberator* review of 23 May 1845, asserted that the *Narrative* "cannot fail to produce a great sensation wherever it may happen to circulate, especially among the slavocracy. . . . What a lifting of the veil is this, to convince the skeptical that it is impossible to exaggerate the horrors and enormities of that impious system!"[43]

The *Narrative* substantiated the intellectual capacity of African Americans for many critics. The growth of moral sensibilities, acquisition of a rudimentary education, and evidence of courage in the midst of slavery's degradation recounted by Douglass indicated that he was an exceptional man and that all blacks freed of the slave's fetters could improve themselves. The abolitionist editor of the Oberlin *Evangelist* found in Douglass's autobiography an expression of "some of the noblest sentiments of the human heart," a harbinger that "the days of Oppression are numbered," and an example of the potentiality of blacks once emancipated. Abolitionist Mary Howitt in her review of 1847 in London's *People's Journal* described Douglass as "a noble human being" and viewed his *Narrative* as an incomparable catalog of slavery's horrors: "If we were to write ten volumes on the atrocities and miseries of slavery in the abstract, we could say nothing half so impressive and conclusive as is the simple, honest narrative of a real slave, written by himself."[44]

Several critics declared how instructive the book would be to all classes or readers. "This little book taught by examples the cruel workings of the systems of Slavery, in a region where its burden is comparatively light, and the plainness of the narration and the simplicity of the style made it attractive to all classes of readers." One of the most enthusiastic critiques was in the *National Anti-Slavery Standard* of 12 June 1845. Contending that the book would enlighten even slavery's defenders, the reviewer observed: "This book ought to be read by all before whose mental blindness visions of happy slaves continually dance. It is the story of the life of a man of great

42. *Lib.*, 6 June 1845; *NASS*, 26 June 1845.
43. *Lib.*, 9, 23, 30 May 1845; *NASS*, 5 June 1845.
44. Oberlin *Evangelist*, 29 April 1846; (London) *People's Journal*, 2 : 302 (1847).

intellectual power, in the very circumstances of Slavery,—in the North-ernmost of the slave states, and under kind masters."[45]

Nonabolitionist journals, especially those published in the United Kingdom, upheld the work's didactic purpose for a European audience distant from American slavery. The Cork *Examiner* on 22 October 1845 asserted that the *Narrative* "gives an insight into the slave system in Amer-ica, which cannot elsewhere be obtained in so concise and interesting a form." Similarly, *Chamber's Edinburgh Journal* published a review of the *Narrative* on 24 January 1846 in which the author declared that it would "help considerably to disseminate correct ideas respecting slavery and its attendant evils. Some of the passages present a dismal picture of what is endured by the negro race in the slave-holding states of the union." The review in England's Newcastle *Guardian* looked upon the *Narrative* pri-marily as a revelation about American religion and as a corrective to many previously published accounts of American slavery.[46]

Writers for nonabolitionist journals tended to be more skeptical than the abolitionist reviewers and were anxious to determine the credibility of Douglass's account. Generally assuming "that Frederick Douglass is what he professes," the London *Spectator* reviewer thought it "improb-able" that Douglass fought with a slaveholder or learned to read in the manner he described in the *Narrative*. Doubt about Douglass's author-ship lingered until the end and the reviewer concluded: "If this narrative is really true in its basis, and untouched by any one save Douglass him-self, it is a singular book, and he is a more singular man. Even if it is of the nature of the true stories of De Foe, it is curious as a picture of slav-ery, and worth reading."[47]

Most critics had fewer doubts about Douglass's credibility than the *Spectator* reviewer. The Boston *Transcript,* for example, contended that the *Narrative* "bears throughout the indelible marks of truth." The Boston *Courier* asserted that the book contained "many descriptions of scenes at the South, which, if true, bear sufficient witness against the 'peculiar insti-tution,' to make every honest man to wish its downfall soon, and by almost any means. And there seems to be no reason for believing that more than the

45. Massachusetts Anti-Slavery Society, *Fourteenth Annual Report* (Boston, 1846), 44; *NASS,* 12 June 1845.

46. Cork *Examiner,* 22 October 1845; *Chamber's Edinburgh Journal,* new ser., 5 : 56 (24 January 1846); Newcastle *Guardian,* 11 July 1846. See also: *New York Evangelist,* 26 June 1845; *Christian Freeman,* 29 May 1845.

47. Quoted in *Littell's Living Age,* 8 : 65 (10 January 1846).

truth is told." In November 1845, the *British Friend* declared that "Truth seems stamped on every page of this narrative."[48]

For a few critics, the prefatory letters enhanced the credibility of Douglass's autobiography. The London *League* referred, for instance, to the book's being "certified by highly respectable persons" as "authentic." William Howitt, reviewing the first Irish edition of the book for the London *Atlas,* commented on Douglass's authenticating prefaces because readers might well ask, "Who is this FREDERICK DOUGLASS? And what guarantee have we that he is what he represents himself to be? In answer to this, we have only to say that his book is prefaced by two admirable letters from the well-known champions of American freedom, WILLIAM LLOYD GARRISON and WENDELL PHILLIPS, bearing the highest testimonies to his character and to his services in the abolition cause."[49]

Other critics distrusted the letters. The most extreme reaction came from the *Religious Spectator* reviewer, who felt their endorsement of the book was reason enough not to read it: "We might possibly have laid it aside without reading it, from perceiving that it was published under the patronage of several individuals, whose course on the subject of slavery we have never regarded as either politic or right." The New York *Tribune* found Phillips's letter to be neutral but Garrison's remarks counterproductive. The *Tribune* was highly critical of the "noble and generous" Garrison and contended that the tone of his comments made Douglass's seem "very just and temperate" in contrast. Beyond this, the *Tribune* argued the prefatory comments did little to authenticate Douglass's account. Phillips, at least, did not invalidate the account. By contrast, Garrison's comments were, the *Tribune* charged, "in his usual over emphatic style . . . he has indulged in violent invective and denunciation till he has spoiled the temper of his mind. Like a man who has been in the habit of screaming himself hoarse to make the deaf hear, he can no longer pitch his voice on a key agreeable to common ears."[50]

Many commented on Douglass's use of personal and place names. The Bristol *Mercury* asserted that Douglass had done much to remove doubt about his identity in the book by "giving the names of the masters under

48. *Courier* and *Transcript* quoted in *Narrative* (Dublin, 1846), cxxi; *Lib.,* 6 June 1845; *British Friend,* 3 : 191 (December 1845). See also *Lib.,* 26 December 1845.

49. Quoted in *Lib.,* 28 November 1845; *Narrative* (Dublin, 1846), cxxx–cxxxi. See also: *British Friend,* 3 : 191 (December 1845).

50. *Religious Spectator,* n.d., as quoted in *PaF,* 31 July 1845, *NASS,* 7 August 1845; New York *Tribune,* 10 June 1845.

whom he had lived, and dates and events which would at once prove the correctness of his account." Specificity represented a major part of the *Tribune*'s reason for accepting the validity of the *Narrative:* "He has had the courage to name the persons, times and places, thus exposing himself to obvious danger, and setting the seal on his deep convictions as to the religious need of speaking the whole truth."[51]

But most critics looked beyond specificity for additional evidence to show that Douglass had written his autobiography and that it was a faithful account of his life. Ironically, they found confirmation of Douglass's written words in his spoken words. A thoughtful and very skeptical reviewer for the *Religious Spectator,* upon being given a copy of the book, initially cast it aside because it had been published by the American Anti-Slavery Society. With such an imprimatur on the book, he doubted that Douglass had either written it or was a fugitive slave until he learned "upon good authority, that his lectures are characterized by as able reasoning, as genuine wit, and as bold and stirring appeals, as we almost ever find in connexion with the highest intellectual culture."[52]

Skeptical critics in the United Kingdom often delayed the publication of reviews of the *Narrative* until they had an opportunity to hear Douglass speak. In his speeches they found proof that he had written his autobiography. Typical of such critics was the Irish abolitionist Isaac Nelson, who declared in January 1846:

> I looked forward with much interest and some incredulity to a meeting with the author of this unique piece of autobiography, doubting whether any man reared a slave, and so recently escaped from bonds, could, under the circumstances, produce such a work. My meeting with Frederick Douglass dispelled my doubts; he is indeed an extraordinary man—the type of a class—such an intellectual phenomenon as only appears at times in the republic of letters. I have had opportunities of observing his mind in several attitudes, and applied to various subjects during his stay in Belfast, and I take leave to say that not only do I consider him adequate to the task of writing such a book as the one before us, but also of achieving more Herculean feats.[53]

51. Bristol *Mercury,* 6 January 1846, as quoted in *NASS,* 5 March 1846; New York *Tribune,* 10 June 1845.

52. Quoted in *PaF,* 31 July 1845, *NASS,* 7 August 1845. See also: *New York Evangelist,* 26 June 1845.

53. Quoted in *Narrative* (Dublin, 1846), cxxxii.

A number of reviewers found it impossible to separate Douglass the antislavery orator from Douglass the autobiographer. Identifying Douglass as an escaped slave and "itinerant lecturer" of the American Anti-Slavery Society, a reviewer for the London *Spectator* declared that Douglass, "having a natural force and fluency of language, and dealing with things within his own experience, . . . appears to have spoken with so much acceptance as to have been stimulated to commit to paper the autobiographical portion of his addresses." The New York *Tribune* reacted in a similar fashion in an 1845 review. Douglass, the *Tribune* reported, "is said to be an excellent speaker—can speak from a thorough personal experience—and has upon the audience, beside, the influence of a strong character and uncommon talents. In the book before us he has put into the story of his life the thoughts, the feelings and the adventures that have been so affecting through the living voice; nor are they less so from the printed page."[54]

Some of the most significant reviews concentrated on Douglass's revelations about the development of his interior character. The *British Friend* in its November 1845 assessment of the style and content of the "plain, but eloquent narrative" declared: "In reading it, one sees before him the fearful tossings and heavings of an immortal soul, herded with beasts, and compelled to grope about, feeling after God among reptiles. The reader feels himself in communion with immortality—sunk to a thing—with the image of God turned into a brute." Similarly, the review in an issue of the Newcastle *Guardian* noted the revelations about Douglass's character contained in "his simple yet spirit-stirring narration" of his life and especially "the risings of noble and generous feelings of his soul, and of the exertions which he made for the acquisition of knowledge, despite the almost insuperable obstacles which were thrown in his way." Abolitionist Ralph Varian, writing in the December 1845 issue of the *British Friend,* asserted that the book was "a revelation of the wondrous power which a highly gifted nature possesses, to triumph over brute force, and circumstances the most disheartening."[55]

The work's plainness of style suggested an absence of guile and thus advanced its credibility for the critics. The Lynn, Massachusetts, *Pioneer* argued that the *Narrative* was "evidently drawn with a nice eye, and the coloring is chaste and subdued, rather than extravagant or overwrought.

---

54. Quoted in *Littell's Living Age,* 8 : 64–65 (10 January 1846); New York *Tribune, 10* June 1845.

55. *British Friend,* 3 : 174 (November 1845), 3 : 191 (December 1845); Newcastle *Guardian,* 11 July 1846. See also *Lib.,* 26 December 1845.

Thrilling as it is, and full of the most burning eloquence, it is yet simple and unimpassioned. Its eloquence is the eloquence of truth, and so is as simple and touching as the impulses of childhood." In his January 1846 review of the *Narrative,* the Reverend Isaac Nelson of Belfast, Ireland, informed his compatriots: "I regard the narrative of FREDERICK DOUGLASS as a literary wonder. The incidents of his life are of such a kind as to hold the reader spell-bound, while they are related in a style simple, perspicuous, and eloquent." Similarly, while viewing the *Narrative* as a "curiosity" focused too heavily on the "incredible brutality" of some individuals, the London *League*'s reviewer concluded: "But even as a literary production, this book possesses no ordinary claims. The author, though uneducated, or rather self-educated, displays great natural powers: he utters his thoughts always lucidly, and often with a polished and vigorous eloquence." The New York *Tribune* was less reserved in its praise of the style of the book than the *League*. In its long critique, the *Tribune* asserted: "Considered merely as a narrative, we have never read one more simple, true, coherent, and warm with genuine feeling. It is an excellent piece of writing."[56]

The pathos and metaphorical flights in the *Narrative* elicited comments from several reviewers. Douglass's autobiography was, they argued, "affecting," "touching," "unspeakably affecting" and filled with passages demonstrating "simple pathos," "deep pathos," or "pathos and sublimity." Wilson Armistead, reviewing the book in 1848, asserted that "the narrative of Douglass contains many affecting incidents, many passages of great eloquence and power." "A.M.," a *Liberator* correspondent, illustrated most fully the pathetic elements of the *Narrative* when she wrote from Albany, New York: "I have wept over the pages of Dickens' 'Oliver Twist' — I have moistened with my tears whole chapters of Eugene Sue's mysteries of Paris—but Douglass's history of the wrongs of the American Slave, brought, not tears—no, tears refused me their comfort—its horrible truths crowded in such quick succession, and entered so deep into the chambers of my soul, as to entirely close the relief valve. . . . I groaned in the agony of my spirit." According to the critics, the passages demonstrating Douglass's masterful use of pathos included those describing his relationship with his mother, the songs of the slaves, his acquisition of an education, and the treatment of aged slaves. The most frequent comments on the use of meta-

---

56. Lynn (Mass.) *Pioneer,* n.d., as quoted in *Lib.,* 30 May 1845; London *League,* n.d., as quoted in *Lib.,* 28 November 1845; Isaac Nelson, as quoted in *Narrative* (Dublin, 1846), cxxxii; New York *Tribune,* 10 June 1845.

phors in the *Narrative* centered on Douglass's apostrophe to freedom as he watched ships in the Chesapeake Bay.[57]

The reception accorded the *Narrative* in the South ironically verified its details and lent authority to it. The American Anti-Slavery Society apparently exhausted every means to push the book in Maryland and was relatively successful. The early reactions of Marylanders to the *Narrative* boosted sales because they testified to its credibility. For example, the editor of a Philadelphia newspaper, the *Elevator,* while reviewing Douglass's "exceedingly interesting" autobiography, reported that on a trip to Maryland he encountered several blacks who knew Douglass "by his assumed as well as by his real name, and related to us many interesting incidents about their former companion."[58]

More direct testimony validating the *Narrative* came from the pens of white Marylanders personally acquainted with slavery on the Eastern Shore and Douglass's owners. This valuable testimony began when a white resident of Baltimore reported in September 1845 that Douglass's *Narrative* "is now circulating and being read in this city, and five hundred copies are still wanted here. They would be read with avidity, and do much good." Signing his letter "A Citizen of Maryland," the writer then assessed the credibility of Douglass's account: "I have made some inquiry, and have reason to believe his statements are true. Col. Edward Lloyd's relatives are my relatives! Let this suffice for the present." Another white native of Maryland and acquaintance of the Lloyds read Douglass's account in the spring of 1846 and wrote "from my knowledge of slavery as it really exists . . . I am fully prepared to bear a decided testimony to the truth of all his assertions, with regard to the discipline upon the plantations of Maryland, as well as his descriptions of cruelty and murder."[59]

Unfavorable southern responses to the *Narrative,* however, far outstripped the favorable ones over the next several years. Whether it was true or false, most southern whites felt that the *Narrative* was an incendiary document inciting slaves to rebel. As late as the spring of 1849 a grand jury in Grayson County, Virginia, indicted Jarvis C. Bacon for "feloniously and knowingly circulating" the *Narrative* because the jurors felt the book was

57. Wilson Armistead, *A Tribute for the Negro* (Manchester, Eng., 1848), 455; *Lib.,* 6 June 1845. See also *NASS,* 12 June 1845; New York *Tribune,* 10 June 1845; (London) *People's Journal,* 2 : 302–305 (1847).

58. Philadelphia *Elevator,* n.d., as quoted in *Lib.,* 15 August 1845.

59. Ibid., 26 September 1845, 15 May 1846.

"intended to cause slaves to rebel and make insurrection, and denying the right of property of masters in their slaves."[60]

However much Douglass may have sympathized with Jarvis Bacon, he first had to confront the persistent challenge of A. C. C. Thompson of Delaware. Apparently prompted by Douglass's former owner Thomas Auld, Thompson wrote a long review essay of the *Narrative* for the *Delaware Republican*. Describing Douglass's autobiography variously as "dirty," "false," "infamous libel," and a "ridiculous publication," Thompson contended that it was filled with "glaring falsehoods" and declared "the whole to be a budget of falsehoods from beginning to end." While refuting Douglass's claim that slave children were customarily separated from their mothers in Maryland, Thompson concentrated on correcting the *Narrative*'s unflattering characterization of Edward Lloyd, Aaron Anthony, Giles Hicks, Austin Gore, Thomas Lambdin, Edward Covey, and Thomas Auld. From what he knew of these men and Douglass when he was a slave, Thompson concluded that Douglass did not write the book, which, he argued, bore "the glaring impress of falsehood on every page."[61]

This was just the challenge Douglass had been awaiting. Writing to Thompson from England in 1846, Douglass thanked him profusely for proving that he had been a slave and that the people he wrote about were not fictitious. To Thompson's charge that he had maligned good masters and Christian men with charitable feelings, Douglass restated his complaints concerning his treatment and observed, "The cowskin makes as deep a gash in my flesh, when wielded by a professed saint, as it does when wielded by an open sinner." The chief focus of Douglass's response was, however, on Thompson's "triumphant vindication of the truth" of this *Narrative:* "your testimony is direct and perfect—just what I have long wanted . . . you . . . brush away the miserable insinuation of my northern pro-slavery enemies, that I have used fictitious not real names." Douglass promised to add Thompson's letter as an appendix to the second Irish edition of his *Narrative*.[62]

Thompson launched a second and more systematic attack on Douglass's autobiography after some northern journalists expressed doubts about the *Delaware Republican* review. As the basis for his second attack, Thompson collected letters from Thomas Auld, James Dawson, Dr. A. C. C.

60. Ibid., 18 May 1849.
61. Wilmington *Delaware Republican*, n.d., as quoted in *NASS*, 25 December 1845.
62. *Lib.*, 27 February 1846.

xlii   INTRODUCTION TO VOLUME ONE

Thompson, L. Dodson, and Thomas Graham denying the validity of Douglass's autobiography. The central focus of the letters was the character of Thomas Auld. Auld's neighbors and acquaintances contended that Douglass's portrayal of Auld was "a base and villainous fabrication," "basely false," and "palpably untrue." A number of Thompson's witnesses claimed that Auld's "conduct to his servants was more like an indulgent father than a master." Auld himself denied that he had ever flogged Douglass and claimed that Douglass had suppressed information about his promise that "when he was 25 years old I would emancipate him; . . . He does not say one word about this in his Narrative, as it would not have answered to have mentioned so much truth." Thompson argued that the testimony of Auld and his neighbors demonstrated that "the assertions of this negro Douglass are nothing more than gross misrepresentations."[63]

On 6 February 1846, when Douglass wrote the preface to the second Irish edition of his autobiography, he kept his promise to Thompson. In spite of the confident tone of his earlier response to Thompson, Douglass nevertheless repeated in his preface sections of the report of his farewell meeting in Lynn, Massachusetts, and the resolutions passed at that meeting testifying to his fugitive status. He also reprinted the declaration of a committee of the Hibernian Anti-Slavery Society that Douglass "has long been known to us by reputation, and is now introduced to us by letters from some of the most distinguished and faithful friends of the Anti-Slavery cause in the United States."

Douglass's central focus in the four-page preface, however, was Thompson. Conceding that the two naturally "differ in our details," Douglass began his references to Thompson by declaring: "He agrees with me at least in the important fact, that I am what I proclaim myself to be, an ungrateful fugitive from the 'patriarchal institutions' of the Slave States; and he certifies that many of the heroes of my Narrative are still living and doing well, as 'honored and worthy members of the Methodist Episcopal Church.'" The Thompson-Douglass exchange maintained interest in the *Narrative* for years after its publication. Douglass fueled the fires by repeatedly referring to it in his speeches, letters, and editorials.[64]

What concerned Douglass most, however, about Thompson's charges was the allegation that he had misrepresented the character of his master Thomas Auld. Since Auld had specifically denied that Douglass's portrayal

63. Ibid., 20 February 1846.
64. *Narrative* (Dublin, 1846), ii–vi; Blassingame, *Douglass Papers,* 1 : 200–201.

of him was accurate, Douglass concentrated more and more on Auld in his speeches and writings. With consummate skill, Douglass transformed Auld, in the public mind, into the archetypal vindictive slaveholder desperate to recapture and punish his former slave. Speaking in London in May 1846, Douglass gave a characteristic presentation when he said that his master, after trying unsuccessfully to refute the *Narrative,* had transferred title in him to his brother, who "resolves that if ever I touch American soil, I shall be instantly reduced to a state of slavery. However, it is not to a state of slavery that they wish now to have me reduced. They have a feeling of revenge to gratify."[65]

Thomas Auld's actions after Douglass arrived in England highlighted and exaggerated the danger the fugitive slave faced. By giving the impression that Douglass would be immediately reenslaved if he returned to the United States, Auld created greater sympathy for Douglass in the United Kingdom that eventually led abolitionists there to raise money to purchase the fugitive so they could manumit him. Long before the inauguration of this manumission effort, however, Douglass began a literary and oratorical campaign to neutralize Thomas Auld's assault on the credibility of his *Narrative.* Even in responding to attacks from third parties, Douglass tried, whenever possible, to allude to Auld's letter to Thompson. The earliest opportunity Douglass had for a full response to Auld came in 1846, when an American in the United Kingdom declared that Douglass lied about slavery in his speeches. Writing a response from Glasgow in April 1846, Douglass concentrated on Auld and contended that Auld felt so keenly Douglass's "exposures" and "severe goadings" that his "old master is in a state of mind quite favorable to an attempt at re-capture . . . to feed his revenge." According to Douglass, Auld told "a positive lie," when he swore "he never struck me, or told any one else to do so." Recalling an occasion when Auld beat him "until he wearied himself," Douglass declared: "My memory in such matters, is better than his."[66]

Two years later Douglass began using Auld's denial of the validity of the *Narrative* in an attempt to goad his former master into a public debate. He inaugurated the campaign by writing his first public letter to his master on 3 September 1848, the anniversary of his escape from slavery. Receiving no reply from Auld, Douglass then reprinted his response of 1846 to A. C. C. Thompson in the 13 October 1848 issue of the *North Star.* Then, on 3

---

65. Blassingame, *Douglass Papers,* 1 : 252.
66. *Lib.,* 15 May 1846; Benjamin Quarles, *Frederick Douglass* (Washington, D.C., 1948), 51.

September 1849, Douglass wrote his second letter to Auld. Although other fugitive slaves wrote public letters to their masters, few tried to use their correspondence as Douglass did to shore up the credibility of their auto-biographies. Douglass, for example, began his second "friendly epistle" to Auld by denying that he would "wilfully malign the character even of a slaveholder" and asserted: "I can say, with a clear conscience, in all that I have ever written or spoken respecting yourself, I have tried to remember that, though I am beyond your power and control, I am still accountable to our common Father and Judge,—in the sight of whom I believe that I stand acquitted of all intentional misrepresentation against you. Of course, I have said many hard things respecting yourself; but all has been based upon what I knew of you at the time I was a slave in your family."[67]

Three other critics agreed, in part, with the claims of Thomas Auld and A. C. C. Thompson. The most important of such reviews of the *Narrative* appeared in July 1849 when the Reverend Ephraim Peabody included it in his thirty-two-page *Christian Examiner* essay, "Narratives of Fugitive Slaves." Peabody's review of the autobiographies of Henry Watson, Lewis and Milton Clarke, William Wells Brown, Josiah Henson, and Douglass was important for two reasons. First, Peabody was one of the few ante-bellum critics to concentrate on black autobiographies as literature. Second, Frederick Douglass published a response to Peabody's essay. In his oft-quoted opening paragraph, Peabody declared: "AMERICA has the mournful honor of adding a new department to the literature of civiliza-tion,—the autobiographies of escaped slaves." Viewing such works as "remarkable as being pictures of slavery by the slave" revealing the black's "native love of freedom" and sense of poetry and romance, they contained, Peabody asserted, adventures comparable to the *Iliad* and the *Odyssey*.[68]

Peabody was most impressed with the autobiography of Josiah Henson and spent fourteen pages summarizing it because, he asserted, his readers would "be interested in the efforts of one who, without noise or pretension, without bitterness towards the whites, without extravagant claims in behalf of the blacks, has patiently, wisely, and devotedly given himself to the improvement of the large body of his wretched countrymen amongst whom his lot has been cast." Writing approvingly of Henson's attempt to purchase his freedom, his religious convictions, his "fidelity," "freedom from exag-

67. *NS*, 8 September, 13 October 1848, 7 September 1849; *Lib.*, 14 September 1849; Blassingame, *Slave Testimony*, 48–57, 114–15.
68. (Boston) *Christian Examiner*, 47 : 61–62 (July 1849).

geration," "absence of personal bitterness," and "commiseration for all classes," Peabody declared that Henson's narrative presented "the best picture of the evils incident to slave life on the plantations which can be found."[69]

All of the other autobiographies, and especially Douglass's, suffered in comparison to Henson's. Indeed, from Peabody's perspective, beside Henson's account, the other autobiographies

> possess no especial interest beyond what must belong to the life of almost any fugitive slave. They are records of degradation on the part of both blacks and whites,—of suffering and wrong and moral corruption. They give, doubtless, a just idea of what slavery is to the slave. But, on the other hand, while we have no reason to question the truth of particular facts representing individuals, we have no doubt that they convey an altogether erroneous idea of the general character of the masters. The best qualities of the master are likely to appear anywhere rather than in his connection with the slave. And except it be an easy kindness, the slave is in no position to estimate aright the virtues of one who, towards himself, appears simply as a power whom he cannot resist. They stand in such utterly false relations to each other, that their whole intercourse must necessarily be vitiated, and the worst qualities of each, and these almost exclusively, must be perpetually forced on the attention of the other. But human society could not long exist were the great body of slaveholders like those whom these narratives describe.[70]

Peabody admitted that he was personally acquainted with Douglass and that his narrative "contains the life of a superior man." He then shifted to a critique of Douglass's speaking style. Peabody took special umbrage at Douglass's "severity of judgement and a one-sidedness of view," his "seeing only the evils of slavery," and his "violence and extravagance of expression." Although Peabody acknowledged "the sympathy which his narrative excites, and our respect for the force of character he has shown in rising from the depths of bondage," he let his critical remarks stand in hopes that they would lead Douglass to follow a wiser course.[71]

Douglass responded to Peabody in an editorial in the *North Star* on 3 August 1849. Contending that because Peabody was a northern minister he was "ill qualified" to write his essay, Douglass argued that, contrary to

69. Ibid., 80, 83, 93.
70. Ibid., 69–70.
71. Ibid., 74–75.

Peabody's claims, there were few truly antislavery masters. Northerners had, for too long, been deceived by southern words. Douglass conceded that "slaveholders frequently speak of slavery as an evil . . . in the presence of persons from the North," but rarely in front of slaves, and concluded that "if we judge the slaveholder by his words, it will be difficult to convict him of unkindness to his slaves, or to charge him with the desire to continue the relation of slavery; but the unmistakable language of conduct leaves no doubt of his guilt in both these points. To detest slavery in words, and to cling to it in practice, is a display of hypocrisy that should deceive no one." Rejecting Peabody's advice about the style and content of his lectures, Douglass then turned to his criticisms of the slave autobiographies. In the process he defended the honesty of his portrait of slaveholders:

> Speaking of the Narratives, Mr. Peabody admits, "they give a just idea of what slavery is to the slave," but adds, "they convey an altogether erroneous idea of the character of the masters." Here we think Mr. Peabody's logic at fault. What slavery is to the slave, the slaveholder is to the slave; and the character of the slaveholder may be fairly inferred from his treatment of the slave. It is not by the courtesy and hospitality which slaveholders extend to Northern clergymen and travellers, whose good opinions they think desirable, that we are to learn their true characters. Here they have an end to attain. But it is their conduct towards those over whom they have unlimited power, by which they are to be tried and adjudged. In this relation they act freely and without restraint; in the other case they act from necessity.[72]

Support for, and popularization of, the views Douglass expressed in his *Narrative* and responses to Thompson and Peabody came from Harriet Beecher Stowe. The publication of Stowe's *Uncle Tom's Cabin* in 1852 led to renewed interest in all slave autobiographies, and especially those of Josiah Henson, Lewis Clarke, and Douglass. When reviewers questioned "whether the representations of 'Uncle Tom's Cabin' are a fair representation of slavery as it at present exists," Stowe published in 1853 *The Key to Uncle Tom's Cabin,* which, she claimed, was the factual base for the novel. The *Key* contained a collection of "real incidents,—of actions really performed, of words and expressions really uttered." To prove that George Harris, the intelligent mulatto character, was not overdrawn in her novel, Stowe quoted extracts from the autobiographies of Lewis and Milton

72. *NS,* 3 August 1849.

Clarke, Josiah Henson, and Frederick Douglass because their accounts, she contended, were "related by those who know slavery by the best of all tests—experience; and they are given by men who have earned a character in freedom which makes their word as good as the word of any man living." The central incident that Stowe focused on in Douglass's *Narrative* was his description of his acquisition of an education, which she argued was "a most interesting and affecting parallel" to George's teaching himself to read and write.[73]

Stowe's defense and use of Douglass's *Narrative* and other black autobiographies prompted the *Key*'s critics to comment specifically on the slave testimony section and to publish their reflections on slave autobiographies and Douglass's account. For reviewers in southern newspapers and magazines, the *Key* sometimes led to extended criticism of a body of literature they had previously ignored. The critic in the July 1853 issue of the *Southern Quarterly Review*, for example, found little that was credible in slave autobiographies:

> The runaway narratives are, no doubt, pure inventions of the cunning fugitives, to work upon the charities and sympathies of those who are simple enough to receive their statements as truthful. . . . Such tales of torture of the whites, such pictures of sorrow by the meek and sensitive blacks, would draw tears from eyes of stone. . . . These narratives are now pretty much stereotyped. The runaways have learned their part, and they go through it, on the one key, with great dexterity, and with daily improvement on the music; so that the horrors of poor Frederick Douglass, himself, have been greatly surpassed by later sufferers, who have set up as rivals for Northern favour.[74]

Although there is no evidence that Douglass responded to the essay in the *Southern Quarterly Review*, he did react to similar criticisms of Harriet Beecher Stowe's works in *Graham's Magazine*. The dispute arose over some general comments made by the editor in the course of reviewing *Uncle Tom's Cabin*. He included his severe criticisms of recent writings on slavery in an essay entitled "Black Letters; or Uncle Tom-Foolery in Literature." George Graham complained that the bookshelves "groan under the weight of Sambo's woes, done up in covers! . . . We hate this niggerism, and hope it may be done away with." Graham admonished writers to "turn

---

73. Harriet Beecher Stowe, *A Key to Uncle Tom's Cabin; Presenting the Original Facts and Documents Upon Which the Story Is Founded* (Boston, 1853), 5, 16, 19.
   74. *Southern Quarterly Review*, 24 : 232–33 (July 1853).

to something worthier than these negro subjects" and expressed his displea-
sure over the literary "incursion of blacks." After a scathing attack on *Uncle
Tom's Cabin,* Graham refused to review "the other black books—those
literary nigritudes—those little tadpoles of the press—sable bodies and
stirring tales."[75]

Douglass replied by classing Graham among the "Northern cringers to
the slave power" and arguing that it was an "ungenerous and ungentlemanly
attack (*'miscalled a Review'*)." Graham's attack on Stowe was, however,
understandable: "Recrimination is the favorite artillery of the defenders
and abettors of the slave system." Graham accepted Douglass's challenge
by attacking him specifically in the March issue of his magazine. Graham
contended that although he respected Douglass, "we hate the present negro
literature—especially that of Fred.'s, which by abusing the white, is intended to elevate the black man." Arguing that Graham indicted himself,
Douglass reprinted Graham's March editorial without comment.[76]

Among antebellum critics of Douglass's *Narrative,* George Graham
was in a distinct minority of those claiming that the book had little literary
merit. Along with A. C. C. Thompson, Ephraim Peabody, Thomas Auld,
and the *Southern Quarterly Review,* Graham felt that the book exaggerated
the faults of southern whites, contained more invention than truth, or had
not been written by Douglass. Contrary to these views, the overwhelming
majority of antebellum critics found much to praise in the *Narrative.*

Blazoned, scrutinized, celebrated, excoriated, Frederick Douglass by
the early 1850s was fixed in the American public's mind as a real person
who had earlier passed through the mill of slavery on the Eastern Shore of
Maryland. Subjected to the tough test of credibility leveled against nineteenth-century autobiographers, he had almost singlehandedly restored
vigor to the slave narratives as key weapons in the antislavery crusade. But
Douglass also established that his tremendous gift as a writer was not
limited to political instruments. Douglass proved himself a master of one of
the most American of literary genres—the salvational autobiography.

Embracing the tradition of Puritan conversion narratives, Indian captivity narratives, and especially the secularized yet deeply moral autobiographies best represented by Benjamin Franklin, Douglass so crafted his
work that his positive relationship with them all was unmistakable as he,
too, encountered and renounced the snares of the world and stayed to an

75. *Graham's Magazine,* 42 : 209–14 (January 1853), 42 : 365 (March 1853).
76. *FDP,* 25 February, 4 March 1853.

ever clearer pursuit of moral responsibility, wisdom, and freedom. However black, enslaved, and seemingly other, his affecting and lucid prose argued for oneness with Franklin and his racial brethren. By jeopardizing his very security as a fugitive in order to rebuild the credibility of the American slave narrative, none so dramatically as Douglass integrated both the horror and the great quest of the African-American experience into this deep stream of American autobiography. He advanced and extended that tradition and is rightfully designated one of its greatest practitioners.

Statement on Editorial Method

The method followed in editing Douglass's autobiographical writings reflects modern critical theory regarding the literary genre and the conventional concerns of historians concerning the evidentiary value of such works.[1] As a consequence, the editorial method differs somewhat from that followed in Series One: Speeches, Debates, and Interviews. Essentially, we have been guided in our development of the editorial method by the observation of Erik Erikson that "an item in an autobiography should be judged first for its meaning in the *stage of the recorder's life,* and secondly, for its meaning in the *course of his whole life history.* But this means that at the same time it must be seen also in the immediate *context of contemporary history,* and in the *historical process* of which it is but a stage. Only then can one turn to the remembered item itself, and see what set of criteria would give it a certain convincing probability."[2]

Modern literary scholars regard the concept of a single, stable, unchanging text as invalid. Instead, reprinted and revised editions must be studied to produce a scholarly edition of the work that captures the author's intent. Literary scholars have discovered how dynamic nineteenth-century published works were with authors intervening editorially in various stages of type composition, proofsheets, and subsequent revised editions. For the *Narrative* alone, Douglass participated in the production of twenty-one editions. Collectively, Douglass produced thirty separate editions of his three autobiographies.

Committed to producing accurate and reliable printed versions of Douglass's autobiographies, the project has followed the guidelines laid down by the Modern Language Association's Committee for Scholarly Editions (CSE) on all textual practices. Each volume will supply a precise publication history of its autobiography. In addition, textual appendixes will accompany each volume, identifying all variations in the texts of

1. A useful discussion to the contrasting methodologies of literary and historical editors can be found in Mary-Jo Klein, *A Guide to Documentary Editing* (Baltimore, 1987), 1–29; and in G. Thomas Tanselle, "The Editing of Historical Documents," *Studies in Bibliography,* 31 : 1–56 (January 1978).

2. Eric Erikson, "Gandhi's Autobiography—The Leader as a Child," *American Scholar,* 35 : 639 (Spring 1966).

authoritative manuscript and published editions of the autobiography and certifying Douglass's intention.[3]

Historians of slavery have long debated the credibility of Douglass's autobiographies. Among the most extreme critics of the slave narrative genre was Ulrich B. Phillips, who declared in 1929 in his seminal book *Life and Labor in the Old South* that "ex-slave narratives in general . . . were issued with so much abolitionist editing that as a class their authenticity is doubtful."[4] Although accepting the possibility that Douglass wrote the *Narrative,* many other historians contended that Douglass was such an unusual individual that what he wrote was not characteristic of the lives and feelings of most slaves. Such views prompted a response from historian Gilbert Osofsky in 1969:

> In describing his personal life, the sensitive and creative writer touches a deeper reality that transcends his individuality. Frederick Douglass, for example, was certainly an exceptional man, but his autobiography has much to teach us about the slaves around him, his friends and enemies on the plantation and in the city, and many other typical aspects of American slavery. . . . To exclude the "exceptional" is to eliminate all strong autobiography as a distortion of the events of its time. Yet it is these writers whose books are most likely to interpret reality with insight and clarity.[5]

Barrett John Mandel responds most directly to the historians' concern about autobiographical "facts." Seeking to dispel a number of myths about autobiographies, Mandel argues that such works "emanate

---

3. The guidelines of the Center for Scholarly Editions' have been followed scrupulously. Additional readings of the texts by professional proofreaders and editorial assistants preceded readings by the editors and independent scholars. Center for Editions of American Authors, *An Introductory Statement of Editorial Principles and Procedures,* rev. ed. (New York, 1972); Center for Scholarly Editions, *The Center for Scholarly Editions: An Introductory Statement* (New York, 1977); Committee on Scholarly Editions, "Committee on Scholarly Editions: Aims and Policies," *Publications of the Modern Language Association of America,* 100 : 444–47 (September 1985); Paul Baender, "Reflections upon the CEAA by a Departing Editor," *Resources for American Literary Study,* 4 : 131–44 (Autumn 1974); Klein, *Documentary Editing,* 8–23. Our five independent proofreaders were: Jeffery A. Drobney, Susan E. Lewis, Eva Segert-Tauger, Timothy Sweet, and Betty L. Wiley.

4. Ulrich Bonnell Phillips, *Life and Labor in the Old South* (Boston, 1929), 219; idem, *The American Slave: A Survey of Supply, Employment and Control of Negro Labor as Determined by the Plantation Regime* (New York, 1918), 445n; Blassingame, *Slave Testimony,* xvii; Andrews, *To Tell A Free Story,* 17, 295n; David Thomas Bailey, "A Divided Prism: Two Sources of Black Testimony on Slavery," *Journal of Southern History,* 46 : 182 (August 1980).

5. Osofsky, *Puttin' on Ole Massa,* 10–11.

ultimately from the reality of being." The special order of reality in autobiographies represents considerably more, however, than pictures from
the past; autobiography is not a literal photographic rendition of the past;
autobiographical intent cannot be separated from autobiographical facts:
"At every moment of any true autobiography . . . the author's intention
is to convey the sense that 'this happened to me.' " The autobiography's
angle of vision and subjectivity constitute part of its reality. The essential truth of an autobiography is what it reveals about the author: "Autobiographies are not essentially fabular; they are experiential: an autobiography shares experience as its way of revealing reality. . . . [It]
embodies truth when the reader seeks confirmation of his or her own
perceptions of reality in terms of those experienced by another mortal."
The presence of some apparent inaccuracies need not undermine the essential truth of an autobiography as a representation of an author's life.
Mandel puts it well when he asserts, "The simple truth that autobiography is not fiction is not threatened by the fact that a swatch of autobiography out of context may have the appearance of fiction." The autobiographer uses language to create "the illusion of the past coming to
life" and embodies this in his or her accounts: "The way in which the
illusion of the past is presented is, finally, the meaning of the author's
life: it is the 'form' one's life takes, and it is the only meaning there can
be for a subject." Finally, in words framed for historians and literary
critics, Mandel sums up his views of the truthfulness of autobiographies:
"In my experience most autobiographies are honest . . . with occasional
distortions, honest evasions, discrete pockets of non-communication.
An honest autobiography puts its illusion of the past forward in good
faith."[6]

Historians who have investigated the nature of historical evidence and
have attempted to corroborate autobiographical details by examining independent sources share the views of such literary critics as Mandel. Fore-
most among these scholars are the twentieth-century historians who have

6. Barrett J. Mandel, "Full of Life Now," in Olney, *Autobiography*, 62, 64, 66. See also: Darrel
Mansell, "Unsettling the Colonel's Hash: 'Fact' in Autobiography," *Modern Language Quarterly* 37 :
115–32 (June 1976); Janet Varner Gunn, "Autobiography and the Narrative Experience of Temporality
as Depth," *Soundings* 60 : 194–209 (Summer 1977); Ross Miller, "Autobiography as Fact and Fiction:
Franklin, Adams, Malcolm X," *Centennial Review*, 16 : 221–32 (Summer 1972); Karl J. Weintraub,
"Autobiography and Historical Consciousness," *Critical Inquiry*, 1 : 821–48 (June 1975); Roy Pascal,
Design and Truth in Autobiography (Cambridge, Mass., 1960); and William L. Howarth, "Some
Principles of Autobiography," *New Literary History*, 5 : 363–81 (Winter 1974).

edited nineteenth-century slave narratives.[7] Typical of them is Robin
Winks, who in 1968 called on historians examining slave narratives to try
"to unravel the real from the unreal, and to show the validity of, and the
truth that still lurks behind, that portion we could call unreal." The historian, Winks contends, "must concern himself fully as much with what
people thought to be true, as with the so-called objective data of history,"
because "even though certain historical documents may be proven to be
largely fictitious, or heavily embroidered, these same documents contain
covert evidence of an objective reality."[8]

The concerns of the historian and the literary critic merge in Bruce
Mazlish's exploration of the autobiography situated "between truth and
self-deception." Mazlish views autobiography in psychological and historical perspective and argues that scholarly analysis should focus on "what
must always be at the heart of autobiography: present, form, and content all
help to define autobiography and its reality." Presenting what he calls a
"compacted definition of 'modern' autobiography," Mazlish asserts that it
is "a literary genre . . . , which offers us a picture from a specific present
viewpoint . . . of an individual past, reached by means of introspection and
memory of a special sort, wherein the self is seen as a developing entity,
changing by definable stages, and where knowledge of the self links with
knowledge of the external world, and both together provide us with a deep
and true grasp of reality."[9]

In order to grasp the objective reality of Douglass's life story as embod-
ied in his autobiographies and diary, the historian, somewhat more than the
literary critic and the psychologist, insists on going outside the text for
independent data on the people and events mentioned in it. The editors have
used annotations extensively in this volume to identify all those individuals, places, events, and literary allusions appearing in the texts and to
substantiate Douglass's representation of them as much as possible.

Identification is only provided for an individual, place, or event the
first time the reference appears in the volume. Items having appeared
previously in Series One have been shortened considerably and revised,

7. Robin Winks et al., eds., *Four Fugitive Slave Narratives* (Reading, Mass., 1969), v–xxxiv;
John Brown, *Slave Life in Georgia,* edited by F. N. Boney (Savannah, 1972), vii–xxi; Solomon
Northup, *Twelve Years a Slave,* edited by Sue Eakin and Joseph Logsdon (Baton Rouge, 1968), ix–xxiv;
Osofsky, *Puttin' on Ole Massa,* 9–44.
8. Winks, *Four Fugitive Slave Narratives,* vii, v.
9. Bruce Mazlish, "Autobiography and Psycho-analysis: Between Truth and Self-Deception,"
Encounter, 35 : 28–37 (October 1970). See also: Erikson, "Gandhi's Autobiography," 635.

when necessary, to place the people and events within the context of Douglass's autobiographies. In the annotation of materials appearing for the first time in the diary and autobiographies, the editors have confined themselves, as in Series One, to supplying only that information mandatory for the comprehension of the texts. We have provided the least information about persons, places, and events ordinarily covered in standard textbooks, encyclopedias, and biographical dictionaries, while devoting more space to the most obscure. Because it has not been our intention to settle perennial historical debates or to write a biography of Douglass, we have tried to keep the notes as short as possible. In spite of our best efforts, some casual references have been elusive or impossible to identify with precision. Information on people, places, and events has often been drawn from a variety of sources, and we have cited them at the end of each note as a guide to future researchers. These annotations will be placed in an appendix to follow the text of each autobiography. The textual reference for each note will be indicated by means of the page and line numbers of the Yale edition text.

In addition to the textual appendix and the historical annotation appendix, there will be one or more additional appendixes published following the texts of the autobiographies. In each volume, one appendix will contain the sources and texts of the critical response to the autobiography, including published reviews and letters to Douglass. These critical responses are reprinted in the chronological order of their original publication. The names of "reviewers" are listed whenever they could be identified. Whenever prefaces written by Douglass or introductions written by other individuals appeared in editions of the autobiographies other than that of the chosen copy-text, those prefaces and introductions will be reproduced in an appendix to the volume. Handwritten marginal "annotation" of the texts of the autobiographies by members of his master's family confirming or challenging Douglass's views also will be printed in appendixes. Finally, the travel diary of Douglass's second wife, Helen Pitts Douglass, will be published in an appendix to the volume containing the text of his own travel diary. The texts of all nineteenth-century documents reproduced in these appendixes will be transcribed and verified by the same procedures used for the texts of Douglass's autobiographical writings. The only form of annotation for these documents will be the brief introductions to each of the appendixes.

To help the reader in following Douglass's movements, contemporary maps of Talbot County, Baltimore, and Maryland's Eastern Shore are reproduced in an appendix for each of the antebellum autobiographies. One other type of annotation, contemporary illustrations, has been added to each volume. The frontispieces for each authoritative text will be published with the appropriate volume. For the volume containing *Life and Times,* the autobiography that covers seventy-seven years of Douglass's life, the original published illustrations will be produced.

Fielding Lucas, Jr., The State of Maryland. Detail of the Eastern Shore. (Baltimore, 1840)

Fielding Lucas, Jr., Plan of the City of Baltimore (detail). (Baltimore, 1836)

Frontispiece of *Narrative of the Life of Frederick Douglass, an American Slave* (Boston: Published at the Anti-Slavery Office, 1845).

NARRATIVE

OF THE

LIFE

OF

FREDERICK DOUGLASS,

AN

AMERICAN SLAVE.

WRITTEN BY HIMSELF.

BOSTON:

PUBLISHED AT THE ANTI-SLAVERY OFFICE,

No. 25 CORNHILL

1845.

Title page of *Narrative of the Life of Frederick Douglass, an American Slave* (Boston: Published at the Anti-Slavery Office, 1845).

NARRATIVE

OF THE

LIFE

OF

FREDERICK DOUGLASS,

AN

AMERICAN SLAVE.

WRITTEN BY HIMSELF.

BOSTON:

PUBLISHED AT THE ANTI-SLAVERY OFFICE,

No. 25 Cornhill.

1845.

Entered, according to Act of Congress, in the year 1845,
By Frederick Douglass,
In the Clerk's Office of the District Court of Massachusetts.

PREFACE.

In the month of August, 1841, I attended an anti-slavery convention in Nantucket, at which it was my happiness to become acquainted with FREDERICK DOUGLASS, the writer of the following Narrative. He was a stranger to nearly every member of that body; but, having recently made his escape from the southern prison-house of bondage, and feeling his curiosity excited to ascertain the principles and measures of the abolitionists,—of whom he had heard a somewhat vague description while he was a slave,— he was induced to give his attendance, on the occasion alluded to, though at that time a resident in New Bedford.

Fortunate, most fortunate occurrence!—fortunate for the millions of his manacled brethren, yet panting for deliverance from their awful thraldom!—fortunate for the cause of negro emancipation, and of universal liberty!—fortunate for the land of his birth, which he has already done so much to save and bless!—fortunate for a large circle of friends and acquaintances, whose sympathy and affection he has strongly secured by the many sufferings he has endured, by his virtuous traits of character, by his ever-abiding remembrance of those who are in bonds, as being bound with them!—fortunate for the multitudes, in various parts of our republic, whose minds he has enlightened on the subject of slavery, and who have been melted to tears by his pathos, or roused to virtuous indignation by his stirring eloquence against the enslavers of men!—fortunate for himself, as it at once brought him into the field of public usefulness, "gave the world assurance of a MAN," quickened the slumbering energies of his soul, and consecrated him to the great work of breaking the rod of the oppressor, and letting the oppressed go free!

I shall never forget his first speech at the convention—the extraordinary emotion it excited in my own mind—the powerful impression it created upon a crowded auditory, completely taken by surprise—the applause which followed from the beginning to the end of his felicitous remarks. I think I never hated slavery so intensely as at that moment; certainly, my perception of the enormous outrage which is inflicted by it, on the godlike nature of its victims, was rendered far more clear than ever. There stood one, in physical proportion and stature commanding and exact—in intellect richly endowed—in natural eloquence a prodigy—in soul manifestly "created but a little lower than the angels"—yet a slave, ay, a fugitive slave,— trembling for his safety, hardly daring to believe that on the American soil, a single white person could be found who would befriend him at all hazards, for the love of God and humanity! Capable of high attainments as an intellectual and moral being—needing nothing but a comparatively small amount of cultivation to make him an ornament to society and a blessing to his race—by the law of the land, by the voice of the people, by the terms of the slave code, he was only a piece of property, a beast of burden, a chattel personal, nevertheless!

A beloved friend from New Bedford prevailed on Mr. DOUGLASS to address the convention. He came forward to the platform with a hesitancy and embarrassment, necessarily the attendants of a sensitive mind in such a novel position. After apologizing for his ignorance, and reminding the audience that slavery was a poor school for the human intellect and heart, he proceeded to narrate some of the facts in his own history as a slave, and in the course of his speech gave utterance to many noble thoughts and thrilling reflections. As soon as he had taken his seat, filled with hope and admiration, I rose, and declared that PATRICK HENRY, of revolutionary fame, never made a speech more eloquent in the cause of liberty, than the one we had just listened to from the lips of that hunted fugitive. So I believed at that time—such is my belief now. I reminded the audience of the peril which surrounded this self-emancipated young man at the North,—even in Massachusetts, on the soil of the Pilgrim Fathers, among the descendants of revolutionary sires; and I appealed to them, whether they would ever allow him to be carried back into slavery,—law or no law, constitution or no constitution. The response was unanimous and in thunder-tones—"NO!" "Will you succor and protect him as a brother-man—a resident of the old Bay State?" "YES!" shouted the whole mass, with an energy so startling, that the ruthless tyrants south of Mason and Dixon's line might almost have heard the mighty burst of feeling, and recognized it as the pledge of an invincible determination, on the part of those who gave it, never to betray him that wanders, but to hide the outcast, and firmly to abide the consequences.

It was at once deeply impressed upon my mind, that, if Mr. DOUGLASS could be persuaded to consecrate his time and talents to the promotion of the anti-slavery enterprise, a powerful impetus would be given to it, and a stunning blow at the same time inflicted on northern prejudice against a colored complexion. I therefore endeavored to instil hope and courage into his mind, in order that he might dare to engage in a vocation so anomalous and responsible for a person in his situation; and I was seconded in this effort by warm-hearted friends, especially by the late General Agent of the

Massachusetts Anti-Slavery Society, Mr. JOHN A. COLLINS, whose judgment in this instance entirely coincided with my own. At first, he could give
no encouragement; with unfeigned diffidence, he expressed his conviction
that he was not adequate to the performance of so great a task; the path
marked out was wholly an untrodden one; he was sincerely apprehensive
that he should do more harm than good. After much deliberation, however,
he consented to make a trial; and ever since that period, he has acted as a
lecturing agent, under the auspices either of the American or the Massachusetts Anti-Slavery Society. In labors he has been most abundant; and his
success in combating prejudice, in gaining proselytes, in agitating the public mind, has far surpassed the most sanguine expectations that were raised
at the commencement of his brilliant career. He has borne himself with
gentleness and meekness, yet with true manliness of character. As a public
speaker, he excels in pathos, wit, comparison, imitation, strength of reasoning, and fluency of language. There is in him that union of head and heart,
which is indispensable to an enlightenment of the heads and a winning of
the hearts of others. May his strength continue to be equal to his day! May
he continue to "grow in grace, and in the knowledge of God," that he may
be increasingly serviceable in the cause of bleeding humanity, whether at
home or abroad!

It is certainly a very remarkable fact, that one of the most efficient
advocates of the slave population, now before the public, is a fugitive slave,
in the person of FREDERICK DOUGLASS; and that the free colored population
of the United States are as ably represented by one of their own number, in
the person of CHARLES LENOX REMOND, whose eloquent appeals have
extorted the highest applause of multitudes on both sides of the Atlantic.
Let the calumniators of the colored race despise themselves for their baseness and illiberality of spirit, and henceforth cease to talk of the natural
inferiority of those who require nothing but time and opportunity to attain to
the highest point of human excellence.

It may, perhaps, be fairly questioned, whether any other portion of the
population of the earth could have endured the privations, sufferings and
horrors of slavery, without having become more degraded in the scale of
humanity than the slaves of African descent. Nothing has been left undone
to cripple their intellects, darken their minds, debase their moral nature,
obliterate all traces of their relationship to mankind; and yet how wonder-
fully they have sustained the mighty load of a most frightful bondage, under
which they have been groaning for centuries! To illustrate the effect of
slavery on the white man,—to show that he has no powers of endurance, in

such a condition, superior to those of his black brother,—DANIEL O'CON-
NELL, the distinguished advocate of universal emancipation, and the
mightiest champion of prostrate but not conquered Ireland, relates the
following anecdote in a speech delivered by him in the Conciliation Hall,
Dublin, before the Loyal National Repeal Association, March 31, 1845.
"No matter," said Mr. O'CONNELL, "under what specious term it may
disguise itself, slavery is still hideous. *It has a natural, an inevitable tendency to brutalize every noble faculty of man.* An American sailor, who was
cast away on the shore of Africa, where he was kept in slavery for three
years, was, at the expiration of that period, found to be imbruted and
stultified—he had lost all reasoning power; and having forgotten his native
language, could only utter some savage gibberish between Arabic and
English, which nobody could understand, and which even he himself found
difficulty in pronouncing. So much for the humanizing influence of THE
DOMESTIC INSTITUTION!" Admitting this to have been an extraordinary case
of mental deterioration, it proves at least that the white slave can sink as low
in the scale of humanity as the black one.

Mr. DOUGLASS has very properly chosen to write his own Narrative, in
his own style, and according to the best of his ability, rather than to employ
some one else. It is, therefore, entirely his own production; and, considering
how long and dark was the career he had to run as a slave,—how few have
been his opportunities to improve his mind since he broke his iron fetters,—
it is, in my judgment, highly creditable to his head and heart. He who can
peruse it without a tearful eye, a heaving breast, an afflicted spirit,—
without being filled with an unutterable abhorrence of slavery and all its
abettors, and animated with a determination to seek the immediate overthrow of that execrable system,—without trembling for the fate of this
country in the hands of a righteous God, who is ever on the side of the
oppressed, and whose arm is not shortened that it cannot save,—must have
a flinty heart, and be qualified to act the part of a trafficker "in slaves and the
souls of men." I am confident that it is essentially true in all its statements;
that nothing has been set down in malice, nothing exaggerated, nothing
drawn from the imagination; that it comes short of the reality, rather than
overstates a single fact in regard to SLAVERY AS IT IS. The experience of
FREDERICK DOUGLASS, as a slave, was not a peculiar one; his lot was not
especially a hard one; his case may be regarded as a very fair specimen of
the treatment of slaves in Maryland, in which State it is conceded that they
are better fed and less cruelly treated than in Georgia, Alabama, or Louisiana. Many have suffered incomparably more, while very few on the planta-

tions have suffered less, than himself. Yet how deplorable was his situation! what terrible chastisements were inflicted upon his person! what still more shocking outrages were perpetrated upon his mind! with all his noble powers and sublime aspirations, how like a brute was he treated, even by those professing to have the same mind in them that was in Christ Jesus! to what dreadful liabilities was he continually subjected! how destitute of friendly counsel and aid, even in his greatest extremities! how heavy was the midnight of woe which shrouded in blackness the last ray of hope, and filled the future with terror and gloom! what longings after freedom took possession of his breast, and how his misery augmented, in proportion as he grew reflective and intelligent,—thus demonstrating that a happy slave is an extinct man! how he thought, reasoned, felt, under the lash of the driver, with the chains upon his limbs! what perils he encountered in his endeavors to escape from his horrible doom! and how signal have been his deliverance and preservation in the midst of a nation of pitiless enemies!

This Narrative contains many affecting incidents, many passages of great eloquence and power; but I think the most thrilling one of them all is the description DOUGLASS gives of his feelings, as he stood soliloquizing respecting his fate, and the chances of his one day being a freeman, on the banks of the Chesapeake Bay—viewing the receding vessels as they flew with their white wings before the breeze, and apostrophizing them as animated by the living spirit of freedom. Who can read that passage, and be insensible to its pathos and sublimity? Compressed into it is a whole Alexandrian library of thought, feeling, and sentiment—all that can, all that need be urged, in the form of expostulation, entreaty, rebuke, against that crime of crimes,—making man the property of his fellow-man! O, how accursed is that system, which entombs the godlike mind of man, defaces the divine image, reduces those who by creation were crowned with glory and honor to a level with four-footed beasts, and exalts the dealer in human flesh above all that is called God! Why should its existence be prolonged one hour? Is it not evil, only evil, and that continually? What does its presence imply but the absence of all fear of God, all regard for man, on the part of the people of the United States? Heaven speed its eternal overthrow!

So profoundly ignorant of the nature of slavery are many persons, that they are stubbornly incredulous whenever they read or listen to any recital of the cruelties which are daily inflicted on its victims. They do not deny that the slaves are held as property; but that terrible fact seems to convey to their minds no idea of injustice, exposure to outrage, or savage barbarity. Tell them of cruel scourgings, of mutilations and brandings, of scenes of pollution and blood, of the banishment of all light and knowledge, and they affect to be greatly indignant at such enormous exaggerations, such whole-sale misstatements, such abominable libels on the character of the southern planters! As if all these direful outrages were not the natural results of slavery! As if it were less cruel to reduce a human being to the condition of a thing, than to give him a severe flagellation, or to deprive him of necessary food and clothing! As if whips, chains, thumb-screws, paddles, blood-hounds, overseers, drivers, patrols, were not all indispensable to keep the slaves down, and to give protection to their ruthless oppressors! As if, when the marriage institution is abolished, concubinage, adultery, and incest, must not necessarily abound; when all the rights of humanity are annihi-lated, any barrier remains to protect the victim from the fury of the spoiler; when absolute power is assumed over life and liberty, it will not be wielded with destructive sway! Skeptics of this character abound in society. In some few instances, their incredulity arises from a want of reflection; but, gener-ally, it indicates a hatred of the light, a desire to shield slavery from the assaults of its foes, a contempt of the colored race, whether bond or free. Such will try to discredit the shocking tales of slaveholding cruelty which are recorded in this truthful Narrative; but they will labor in vain. Mr. DOUGLASS has frankly disclosed the place of his birth, the names of those who claimed ownership in his body and soul, and the names also of those who committed the crimes which he has alleged against them. His state-ments, therefore, may easily be disproved, if they are untrue.

In the course of his Narrative, he relates two instances of murderous cruelty,—in one of which a planter deliberately shot a slave belonging to a neighboring plantation, who had unintentionally gotten within his lordly domain in quest of fish; and in the other, an overseer blew out the brains of a slave who had fled to a stream of water to escape a bloody scourging. Mr. DOUGLASS states that in neither of these instances was any thing done by way of legal arrest or judicial investigation. The Baltimore American, of March 17, 1845, relates a similar case of atrocity, perpetrated with similar impunity—as follows:—"*Shooting a Slave.*—We learn, upon the authority of a letter from Charles county, Maryland, received by a gentleman of this city, that a young man, named Matthews, a nephew of General Matthews, and whose father, it is believed, holds an office at Washington, killed one of the slaves upon his father's farm by shooting him. The letter states that young Matthews had been left in charge of the farm; that he gave an order to the servant, which was disobeyed, when he proceeded to the house, *ob-tained a gun, and, returning, shot the servant.* He immediately, the letter continues, fled to his father's residence, where he still remains un-molested."—Let it never be forgotten, that no slaveholder or overseer can be convicted of any outrage perpetrated on the person of a slave, however diabolical it may be, on the testimony of colored witnesses, whether bond or free. By the slave code, they are adjudged to be as incompetent to testify against a white man, as though they were indeed a part of the brute creation. Hence, there is no legal protection in fact, whatever there may be in form, for the slave population; and any amount of cruelty may be inflicted on them with impunity. Is it possible for the human mind to conceive of a more horrible state of society?

The effect of a religious profession on the conduct of southern masters is vividly described in the following Narrative, and shown to be any thing but salutary. In the nature of the case, it must be in the highest degree pernicious. The testimony of Mr. DOUGLASS, on this point, is sustained by a cloud of witnesses, whose veracity is unimpeachable. "A slaveholder's profession of Christianity is a palpable imposture. He is a felon of the highest grade. He is a man-stealer. It is of no importance what you put in the other scale."

Reader! are you with the man-stealers in sympathy and purpose, or on the side of their down-trodden victims? If with the former, then are you the foe of God and man. If with the latter, what are you prepared to do and dare in their behalf? Be faithful, be vigilant, be untiring in your efforts to break every yoke, and let the oppressed go free. Come what may—cost what it may—inscribe on the banner which you unfurl to the breeze, as your religious and political motto—"No COMPROMISE WITH SLAVERY! No UNION WITH SLAVEHOLDERS!"

WM. LLOYD GARRISON.

BOSTON, *May* 1, 1845.

LETTER
FROM WENDELL PHILLIPS, ESQ.

BOSTON, April 22, 1845.

My Dear Friend:

YOU remember the old fable of "The Man and the Lion," where the lion complained that he should not be so misrepresented "when the lions wrote history."

I am glad the time has come when the "lions write history." We have been left long enough to gather the character of slavery from the involuntary evidence of the masters. One might, indeed, rest sufficiently satisfied with what, it is evident, must be, in general, the results of such a relation, without seeking farther to find whether they have followed in every instance. Indeed, those who stare at the half-peck of corn a week, and love to count the lashes on the slave's back, are seldom the "stuff" out of which reformers and abolitionists are to be made. I remember that, in 1838, many were waiting for the results of the West India experiment, before they could come into our ranks. Those "results" have come long ago; but, alas! few of that number have come with them, as converts. A man must be disposed to judge of emancipation by other tests than whether it has increased the produce of sugar,—and to hate slavery for other reasons than because it starves men and whips women,—before he is ready to lay the first stone of his anti-slavery life.

I was glad to learn, in your story, how early the most neglected of God's children waken to a sense of their rights, and of the injustice done them. Experience is a keen teacher; and long before you had mastered your A B C, or knew where the "white sails" of the Chesapeake were bound, you began, I see, to gauge the wretchedness of the slave, not by his hunger and want, not by his lashes and toil, but by the cruel and blighting death which gathers over his soul.

In connection with this, there is one circumstance which makes your recollections peculiarly valuable, and renders your early insight the more remarkable. You come from that part of the country where we are told slavery appears with its fairest features. Let us hear, then, what it is at its best estate—gaze on its bright side, if it has one; and then imagination may task her powers to add dark lines to the picture, as she travels southward to that (for the colored man) Valley of the Shadow of Death, where the Mississippi sweeps along.

Again, we have known you long, and can put the most entire confidence in your truth, candor, and sincerity. Every one who has heard you speak has felt, and, I am confident, every one who reads your book will feel, persuaded that you give them a fair specimen of the whole truth. No one-sided portrait,—no wholesale complaints,—but strict justice done, whenever individual kindliness has neutralized, for a moment, the deadly system with which it was strangely allied. You have been with us, too, some years, and can fairly compare the twilight of rights, which your race enjoy at the North, with that "noon of night" under which they labor south of Mason and Dixon's line. Tell us whether, after all, the half-free colored man of Massachusetts is worse off than the pampered slave of the rice swamps!

In reading your life, no one can say that we have unfairly picked out some rare specimens of cruelty. We know that the bitter drops, which even you have drained from the cup, are no incidental aggravations, no individual ills, but such as must mingle always and necessarily in the lot of every slave. They are the essential ingredients, not the occasional results, of the system.

After all, I shall read your book with trembling for you. Some years ago, when you were beginning to tell me your real name and birthplace, you may remember I stopped you, and preferred to remain ignorant of all. With the exception of a vague description, so I continued, till the other day, when you read me your memoirs. I hardly knew, at the time, whether to thank you or not for the sight of them, when I reflected that it was still dangerous, in Massachusetts, for honest men to tell their names! They say the fathers, in 1776, signed the Declaration of Independence with the halter about their necks. You, too, publish your declaration of freedom with danger compassing you around. In all the broad lands which the Constitution of the United States overshadows, there is no single spot,—however narrow or desolate,—where a fugitive slave can plant himself and say, "I am safe." The whole armory of Northern Law has no shield for you. I am free to say that, in your place, I should throw the MS. into the fire.

You, perhaps, may tell your story in safety, endeared as you are to so many warm hearts by rare gifts, and a still rarer devotion of them to the service of others. But it will be owing only to your labors, and the fearless efforts of those who, trampling the laws and Constitution of the country under their feet, are determined that they will "hide the outcast," and that their hearths shall be, spite of the law, an asylum for the oppressed, if, some time or other, the humblest may stand in our streets, and bear witness in safety against the cruelties of which he has been the victim.

Yet it is sad to think, that these very throbbing hearts which welcome your story, and form your best safeguard in telling it, are all beating contrary to the "statute in such case made and provided." Go on, my dear friend, till you, and those who, like you, have been saved, so as by fire, from the dark prison-house, shall stereotype these free, illegal pulses into statutes; and New England, cutting loose from a blood-stained Union, shall glory in being the house of refuge for the oppressed;—till we no longer merely "*hide* the outcast," or make a merit of standing idly by while he is hunted in our midst; but, consecrating anew the soil of the Pilgrims as an asylum for the oppressed, proclaim our *welcome* to the slave so loudly, that the tones shall reach every hut in the Carolinas, and make the broken-hearted bondman leap up at the thought of old Massachusetts.

God speed the day!

Till then, and ever,

Yours truly,

WENDELL PHILLIPS.

FREDERICK DOUGLASS.

NARRATIVE

OF THE

LIFE OF FREDERICK DOUGLASS.

CHAPTER I.

I WAS born in Tuckahoe, near Hillsborough, and about twelve miles from Easton, in Talbot county, Maryland. I have no accurate knowledge of my age, never having seen any authentic record containing it. By far the larger part of the slaves know as little of their ages as horses know of theirs, and it is the wish of most masters within my knowledge to keep their slaves thus ignorant. I do not remember to have ever met a slave who could tell his birthday. They seldom come nearer to it than planting-time, harvest-time, cherry-time, spring-time, or fall-time. A want of information concerning my own was a source of unhappiness to me even during childhood. The white children could tell their ages. I could not tell why I ought to be deprived of the same privilege. I was not allowed to make any inquiries of my master concerning it. He deemed all such inquiries on the part of a slave improper and impertinent, and evidence of a restless spirit. The nearest estimate I can give makes me now between twenty-seven and twenty-eight years of age. I come to this, from hearing my master say, some time during 1835, I was about seventeen years old.

My mother was named Harriet Bailey. She was the daughter of Isaac and Betsey Bailey, both colored, and quite dark. My mother was of a darker complexion than either my grandmother or grandfather.

My father was a white man. He was admitted to be such by all I ever heard speak of my parentage. The opinion was also whispered that my master was my father; but of the correctness of this opinion, I know nothing; the means of knowing was withheld from me. My mother and I were separated when I was but an infant—before I knew her as my mother. It is a common custom, in the part of Maryland from which I ran away, to part children from their mothers at a very early age. Frequently, before the child has reached its twelfth month, its mother is taken from it, and hired out on some farm a considerable distance off, and the child is placed under the care of an old woman, too old for field labor. For what this separation is done, I do not know, unless it be to hinder the development of the child's affection toward its mother, and to blunt and destroy the natural affection of the mother for the child. This is the inevitable result.

I never saw my mother, to know her as such, more than four or five

times in my life; and each of these times was very short in duration, and
at night. She was hired by a Mr. Stewart, who lived about twelve miles
from my home. She made her journeys to see me in the night, travelling
the whole distance on foot, after the performance of her day's work. She
was a field hand, and a whipping is the penalty of not being in the field at
sunrise, unless a slave has special permission from his or her master to
the contrary—a permission which they seldom get, and one that gives to
him that gives it the proud name of being a kind master. I do not recollect
ever seeing my mother by the light of day. She was with me in the night.
She would lie down with me, and get me to sleep, but long before I
waked she was gone. Very little communication ever took place between
us. Death soon ended what little we could have while she lived, and with
it her hardships and suffering. She died when I was about seven years old,
on one of my master's farms, near Lee's Mill. I was not allowed to be
present during her illness, at her death, or burial. She was gone long before I knew any thing about it. Never having enjoyed, to any considerable
extent, her soothing presence, her tender and watchful care, I received the
tidings of her death with much the same emotions I should have probably
felt at the death of a stranger.

Called thus suddenly away, she left me without the slightest intimation
of who my father was. The whisper that my master was my father, may or
may not be true; and, true or false, it is of but little consequence to my
purpose whilst the fact remains, in all its glaring odiousness, that slaveholders have ordained, and by law established, that the children of slave women
shall in all cases follow the condition of their mothers; and this is done too
obviously to administer to their own lusts, and make a gratification of their
wicked desires profitable as well as pleasurable; for by this cunning arrangement, the slaveholder, in cases not a few, sustains to his slaves the
double relation of master and father.

I know of such cases; and it is worthy of remark that such slaves
invariably suffer greater hardships, and have more to contend with, than
others. They are, in the first place, a constant offence to their mistress. She
is ever disposed to find fault with them; they can seldom do any thing to
please her; she is never better pleased than when she sees them under the
lash, especially when she suspects her husband of showing to his mulatto
children favors which he withholds from his black slaves. The master is
frequently compelled to sell this class of his slaves, out of deference to the
feelings of his white wife; and, cruel as the deed may strike any one to be,
for a man to sell his own children to human flesh-mongers, it is often the

dictate of humanity for him to do so; for, unless he does this, he must not only whip them himself, but must stand by and see one white son tie up his brother, of but few shades darker complexion than himself, and ply the gory lash to his naked back; and if he lisp one word of disapproval, it is set down to his parental partiality, and only makes a bad matter worse, both for himself and the slave whom he would protect and defend.

Every year brings with it multitudes of this class of slaves. It was doubtless in consequence of a knowledge of this fact, that one great statesman of the south predicted the downfall of slavery by the inevitable laws of population. Whether this prophecy is ever fulfilled or not, it is nevertheless plain that a very different-looking class of people are springing up at the south, and are now held in slavery, from those originally brought to this country from Africa; and if their increase will do no other good, it will do away the force of the argument, that God cursed Ham, and therefore American slavery is right. If the lineal descendants of Ham are alone to be scripturally enslaved, it is certain that slavery at the south must soon become unscriptural; for thousands are ushered into the world, annually, who, like myself, owe their existence to white fathers, and those fathers most frequently their own masters.

I have had two masters. My first master's name was Anthony. I do not remember his first name. He was generally called Captain Anthony— a title which, I presume, he acquired by sailing a craft on the Chesapeake Bay. He was not considered a rich slaveholder. He owned two or three farms, and about thirty slaves. His farms and slaves were under the care of an overseer. The overseer's name was Plummer. Mr. Plummer was a miserable drunkard, a profane swearer, and a savage monster. He always went armed with a cowskin and a heavy cudgel. I have known him to cut and slash the women's heads so horribly, that even master would be enraged at his cruelty, and would threaten to whip him if he did not mind himself. Master, however, was not a humane slaveholder. It required extraordinary barbarity on the part of an overseer to affect him. He was a cruel man, hardened by a long life of slaveholding. He would at times seem to take great pleasure in whipping a slave. I have often been awakened at the dawn of day by the most heart-rending shrieks of an own aunt of mine, whom he used to tie up to a joist, and whip upon her naked back till she was literally covered with blood. No words, no tears, no prayers, from his gory victim, seemed to move his iron heart from its bloody purpose. The louder she screamed, the harder he whipped; and where the blood ran fastest, there he whipped longest. He would whip her to make

her scream, and whip her to make her hush; and not until overcome by
fatigue, would he cease to swing the blood-clotted cowskin. I remember
the first time I ever witnessed this horrible exhibition. I was quite a child,
but I well remember it. I never shall forget it whilst I remember any thing.
It was the first of a long series of such outrages, of which I was doomed
to be a witness and a participant. It struck me with awful force. It was the
blood-stained gate, the entrance to the hell of slavery, through which I
was about to pass. It was a most terrible spectacle. I wish I could commit
to paper the feelings with which I beheld it.

This occurrence took place very soon after I went to live with my old
master, and under the following circumstances. Aunt Hester went out one
night,—where or for what I do not know,—and happened to be absent
when my master desired her presence. He had ordered her not to go out
evenings, and warned her that she must never let him catch her in company
with a young man, who was paying attention to her belonging to Colonel
Lloyd. The young man's name was Ned Roberts, generally called Lloyd's
Ned. Why master was so careful of her, may be safely left to conjecture. She
was a woman of noble form, and of graceful proportions, having very few
equals, and fewer superiors, in personal appearance, among the colored or
white women of our neighborhood.

Aunt Hester had not only disobeyed his orders in going out, but had
been found in company with Lloyd's Ned; which circumstance, I found,
from what he said while whipping her, was the chief offence. Had he
been a man of pure morals himself, he might have been thought interested
in protecting the innocence of my aunt; but those who knew him will not
suspect him of any such virtue. Before he commenced whipping Aunt
Hester, he took her into the kitchen, and stripped her from neck to waist,
leaving her neck, shoulders, and back, entirely naked. He then told her to
cross her hands, calling her at the same time a d——d b——h. After
crossing her hands, he tied them with a strong rope, and led her to a stool
under a large hook in the joist, put in for the purpose. He made her get
upon the stool, and tied her hands to the hook. She now stood fair for his
infernal purpose. Her arms were stretched up at their full length, so that
she stood upon the ends of her toes. He then said to her, "Now, you d——d
b——h, I'll learn you how to disobey my orders!" and after rolling up
his sleeves, he commenced to lay on the heavy cowskin, and soon the
warm, red blood (amid heart-rending shrieks from her, and horrid oaths
from him) came dripping to the floor. I was so terrified and horror-
stricken at the sight, that I hid myself in a closet, and dared not venture

out till long after the bloody transaction was over. I expected it would be my turn next. It was all new to me. I had never seen any thing like it before. I had always lived with my grandmother on the outskirts of the plantation, where she was put to raise the children of the younger women. I had therefore been, until now, out of the way of the bloody scenes that often occurred on the plantation.

CHAPTER II.

MY master's family consisted of two sons, Andrew and Richard; one daughter, Lucretia, and her husband, Captain Thomas Auld. They lived in one house, upon the home plantation of Colonel Edward Lloyd. My master was Colonel Lloyd's clerk and superintendent. He was what might be called the overseer of the overseers. I spent two years of childhood on this plantation in my old master's family. It was here that I witnessed the bloody transaction recorded in the first chapter; and as I received my first impressions of slavery on this plantation, I will give some description of it, and of slavery as it there existed. The plantation is about twelve miles north of Easton, in Talbot county, and is situated on the border of Miles River. The principal products raised upon it were tobacco, corn, and wheat. These were raised in great abundance; so that, with the products of this and the other farms belonging to him, he was able to keep in almost constant employment a large sloop, in carrying them to market at Baltimore. This sloop was named Sally Lloyd, in honor of one of the colonel's daughters. My master's son-in-law, Captain Auld, was master of the vessel; she was otherwise manned by the colonel's own slaves. Their names were Peter, Isaac, Rich, and Jake. These were esteemed very highly by the other slaves, and looked upon as the privileged ones of the plantation; for it was no small affair, in the eyes of the slaves, to be allowed to see Baltimore.

Colonel Lloyd kept from three to four hundred slaves on his home plantation, and owned a large number more on the neighboring farms belonging to him. The names of the farms nearest to the home plantation were Wye Town and New Design. "Wye Town" was under the overseership of a man named Noah Willis. New Design was under the overseership of a Mr. Townsend. The overseers of these, and all the rest of the farms, numbering over twenty, received advice and direction from the managers of the home plantation. This was the great business place. It was the seat of government for the whole twenty farms. All disputes among the overseers were settled here. If a slave was convicted of any high misdemeanor, became unmanageable, or evinced a determination to run away, he was brought immediately here, severely whipped, put on board the sloop, carried to Baltimore, and sold to Austin Woolfolk, or some other slave-trader, as a warning to the slaves remaining.

Here, too, the slaves of all the other farms received their monthly allowance of food, and their yearly clothing. The men and women slaves received, as their monthly allowance of food, eight pounds of pork, or its equivalent in fish, and one bushel of corn meal. Their yearly clothing consisted of two coarse linen shirts, one pair of linen trousers, like the shirts, one jacket, one pair of trousers for winter, made of coarse negro cloth, one pair of stockings, and one pair of shoes; the whole of which could not have cost more than seven dollars. The allowance of the slave children was given to their mothers, or the old women having the care of them. The children unable to work in the field had neither shoes, stockings, jackets, nor trousers, given to them; their clothing consisted of two coarse linen shirts per year. When these failed them, they went naked until the next allowance-day. Children from seven to ten years old, of both sexes, almost naked, might be seen at all seasons of the year.

There were no beds given the slaves, unless one coarse blanket be considered such, and none but the men and women had these. This, however, is not considered a very great privation. They find less difficulty from the want of beds, than from the want of time to sleep; for when their day's work in the field is done, the most of them having their washing, mending, and cooking to do, and having few or none of the ordinary facilities for doing either of these, very many of their sleeping hours are consumed in preparing for the field the coming day; and when this is done, old and young, male and female, married and single, drop down side by side, on one common bed,—the cold, damp floor,—each covering himself or herself with their miserable blankets; and here they sleep till they are summoned to the field by the driver's horn. At the sound of this, all must rise, and be off to the field. There must be no halting; every one must be at his or her post; and woe betides them who hear not this morning summons to the field; for if they are not awakened by the sense of hearing, they are by the sense of feeling: no age nor sex finds any favor. Mr. Severe, the overseer, used to stand by the door of the quarter, armed with a large hickory stick and heavy cowskin, ready to whip any one who was so unfortunate as not to hear, or, from any other cause, was prevented from being ready to start for the field at the sound of the horn.

Mr. Severe was rightly named: he was a cruel man. I have seen him whip a woman, causing the blood to run half an hour at the time; and this, too, in the midst of her crying children, pleading for their mother's release. He seemed to take pleasure in manifesting his fiendish barbarity. Added to his cruelty, he was a profane swearer. It was enough to chill the blood and stiffen the hair of an ordinary man to hear him talk. Scarce a sentence escaped him but what was commenced or concluded by some horrid oath. The field was the place to witness his cruelty and profanity. His presence made it both the field of blood and blasphemy. From the rising till the going down of the sun, he was cursing, raving, cutting, and slashing among the slaves of the field, in the most frightful manner. His career was short. He died very soon after I went to Colonel Lloyd's; and he died as he lived, uttering, with his dying groans, bitter curses and horrid oaths. His death was regarded by the slaves as the result of a merciful Providence.

Mr. Severe's place was filled by a Mr. Hopkins. He was a very different man. He was less cruel, less profane, and made less noise, than Mr. Severe. His course was characterized by no extraordinary demonstrations of cruelty. He whipped, but seemed to take no pleasure in it. He was called by the slaves a good overseer.

The home plantation of Colonel Lloyd wore the appearance of a country village. All the mechanical operations for all the farms were performed here. The shoemaking and mending, the blacksmithing, cartwrighting, coopering, weaving, and grain-grinding, were all performed by the slaves on the home plantation. The whole place wore a business-like aspect very unlike the neighboring farms. The number of houses, too, conspired to give it advantage over the neighboring farms. It was called by the slaves the *Great House Farm*. Few privileges were esteemed higher, by the slaves of the out-farms, than that of being selected to do errands at the Great House Farm. It was associated in their minds with greatness. A representative could not be prouder of his election to a seat in the American Congress, than a slave on one of the out-farms would be of his election to do errands at the Great House Farm. They regarded it as evidence of great confidence reposed in them by their overseers; and it was on this account, as well as a constant desire to be out of the field from under the driver's lash, that they esteemed it a high privilege, one worth careful living for. He was called the smartest and most trusty fellow, who had this honor conferred upon him the most frequently. The competitors for this office sought as diligently to please their overseers, as the office-seekers in the political parties seek to please and deceive the people. The same traits of character might be seen in Colonel Lloyd's slaves, as are seen in the slaves of the political parties.

The slaves selected to go to the Great House Farm, for the monthly allowance for themselves and their fellow-slaves, were peculiarly enthusiastic. While on their way, they would make the dense old woods, for miles around, reverberate with their wild songs, revealing at once the highest joy and the deepest sadness. They would compose and sing as they went along, consulting neither time nor tune. The thought that came up, came out—if not in the word, in the sound;—and as frequently in the one as in the other. They would sometimes sing the most pathetic sentiment in the most rapturous tone, and the most rapturous sentiment in the most pathetic tone. Into all of their songs they would manage to weave something of the Great House Farm. Especially would they do this, when leaving home. They would then sing most exultingly the following words:—

> "I am going away to the Great House Farm!
> O, yea! O, yea! O!"

This they would sing, as a chorus, to words which to many would seem unmeaning jargon, but which, nevertheless, were full of meaning to themselves. I have sometimes thought that the mere hearing of those songs would do more to impress some minds with the horrible character of slavery, than the reading of whole volumes of philosophy on the subject could do.

I did not, when a slave, understand the deep meaning of those rude and apparently incoherent songs. I was myself within the circle; so that I neither saw nor heard as those without might see and hear. They told a tale of woe which was then altogether beyond my feeble comprehension; they were tones loud, long, and deep; they breathed the prayer and complaint of souls boiling over with the bitterest anguish. Every tone was a testimony against slavery, and a prayer to God for deliverance from chains. The hearing of those wild notes always depressed my spirit, and filled me with ineffable sadness. I have frequently found myself in tears while hearing them. The mere recurrence to those songs, even now, afflicts me; and while I am writing these lines, an expression of feeling has already found its way down my cheek. To those songs I trace my first glimmering conception of the dehumanizing character of slavery. I can never get rid of that conception. Those songs still follow me, to deepen my hatred of slavery, and quicken my sympathies for my brethren in bonds. If any one wishes to be impressed with the soul-killing effects of slavery, let him go to Colonel Lloyd's plantation, and, on allowance-day, place himself in the deep pine woods, and there let him, in silence, analyze the sounds that shall pass through the chambers of his soul,—and if he is not thus impressed, it will only be because "there is no flesh in his obdurate heart."

I have often been utterly astonished, since I came to the north, to find persons who could speak of the singing, among slaves, as evidence of their contentment and happiness. It is impossible to conceive of a greater mistake. Slaves sing most when they are most unhappy. The songs of the slave represent the sorrows of his heart; and he is relieved by them, only as an aching heart is relieved by its tears. At least, such is my experience. I have often sung to drown my sorrow, but seldom to express my happiness. Crying for joy, and singing for joy, were alike uncommon to me while in the jaws of slavery. The singing of a man cast away upon a desolate island might be as appropriately considered as evidence of contentment and happiness, as the singing of a slave; the songs of the one and of the other are prompted by the same emotion.

CHAPTER III.

COLONEL LLOYD kept a large and finely cultivated garden, which afforded almost constant employment for four men, besides the chief gardener, (Mr. M'Durmond.) This garden was probably the greatest attraction of the place. During the summer months, people came from far and near—from Baltimore, Easton, and Annapolis—to see it. It abounded in fruits of almost every description, from the hardy apple of the north to the delicate orange of the south. This garden was not the least source of trouble on the plantation. Its excellent fruit was quite a temptation to the hungry swarms of boys, as well as the older slaves, belonging to the colonel, few of whom had the virtue to resist it. Scarcely a day passed, during the summer, but that some slave had to take the lash for stealing fruit. The colonel had to resort to all kinds of stratagems to keep his slaves out of the garden. The last and most successful one was that of tarring his fence all around; after which, if a slave was caught with any tar upon his person, it was deemed sufficient proof that he had either been into the garden, or had tried to get in. In either case, he was severely whipped by the chief gardener. This plan worked well; the slaves became as fearful of tar as of the lash. They seemed to realize the impossibility of touching *tar* without being defiled.

The colonel also kept a splendid riding equipage. His stable and carriage-house presented the appearance of some of our large city livery establishments. His horses were of the finest form and noblest blood. His carriage-house contained three splendid coaches, three or four gigs, besides dearborns and barouches of the most fashionable style.

This establishment was under the care of two slaves—Old Barney and Young Barney—father and son. To attend to this establishment was their sole work. But it was by no means an easy employment; for in nothing was Colonel Lloyd more particular than in the management of his horses. The slightest inattention to these was unpardonable, and was visited upon those, under whose care they were placed, with the severest punishment; no excuse could shield them, if the colonel only suspected any want of attention to his horses—a supposition which he frequently indulged, and one which, of course, made the office of Old and Young Barney a very trying one. They never knew when they were safe from punishment. They were frequently whipped when least deserving, and escaped whipping when most deserving it. Every thing depended upon the looks of the horses, and the state of Colonel Lloyd's own mind when his horses were brought to him for use. If a horse did not move fast enough, or hold his head high enough, it was owing to some fault of his keepers. It was painful to stand near the stable-door, and hear the various complaints against the keepers when a horse was taken out for use. "This horse has not had proper attention. He has not been sufficiently rubbed and curried, or he has not been properly fed; his food was too wet or too dry; he got it too soon or too late; he was too hot or too cold; he had too much hay, and not enough of grain; or he had too much grain, and not enough of hay; instead of Old Barney's attending to the horse, he had very improperly left it to his son." To all these complaints, no matter how unjust, the slave must answer never a word. Colonel Lloyd could not brook any contradiction from a slave. When he spoke, a slave must stand, listen, and tremble; and such was literally the case. I have seen Colonel Lloyd make Old Barney, a man between fifty and sixty years of age, uncover his bald head, kneel down upon the cold, damp ground, and receive upon his naked and toil-worn shoulders more than thirty lashes at the time. Colonel Lloyd had three sons—Edward, Murray, and Daniel,— and three sons-in-law, Mr. Winder, Mr. Nicholson, and Mr. Lowndes. All of these lived at the Great House Farm, and enjoyed the luxury of whipping the servants when they pleased, from Old Barney down to William Wilkes, the coach-driver. I have seen Winder make one of the house-servants stand off from him a suitable distance to be touched with the end of his whip, and at every stroke raise great ridges upon his back.

To describe the wealth of Colonel Lloyd would be almost equal to describing the riches of Job. He kept from ten to fifteen house-servants. He was said to own a thousand slaves, and I think this estimate quite within the truth. Colonel Lloyd owned so many that he did not know them when he saw them; nor did all the slaves of the out-farms know him. It is reported of him, that, while riding along the road one day, he met a colored man, and addressed him in the usual manner of speaking to colored people on the public highways of the south: "Well, boy, whom do you belong to?" "To Colonel Lloyd," replied the slave. "Well, does the colonel treat you well?" "No, sir," was the ready reply. "What, does he work you too hard?" "Yes, sir." "Well, don't he give you enough to eat?" "Yes, sir, he gives me enough, such as it is."

The colonel, after ascertaining whom the slave belonged to, rode on; the man also went on about his business, not dreaming that he had been conversing with his master. He thought, said, and heard nothing more of the matter, until two or three weeks afterwards. The poor man was then informed by his overseer that, for having found fault with his master, he was now to be sold to a Georgia trader. He was immediately chained and handcuffed; and thus, without a moment's warning, he was snatched away, and forever sundered, from his family and friends, by a hand more unrelenting than death. This is the penalty of telling the truth, of telling the simple truth, in answer to a series of plain questions.

It is partly in consequence of such facts, that slaves, when inquired of as to their condition and the character of their masters, almost universally say they are contented, and that their masters are kind. The slaveholders have been known to send in spies among their slaves, to ascertain their views and feelings in regard to their condition. The frequency of this has had the effect to establish among the slaves the maxim, that a still tongue makes a wise head. They suppress the truth rather than take the consequences of telling it, and in so doing prove themselves a part of the human family. If they have any thing to say of their masters, it is generally in their masters' favor, especially when speaking to an untried man. I have been frequently asked, when a slave, if I had a kind master, and do not remember ever to have given a negative answer; nor did I, in pursuing this course, consider myself as uttering what was absolutely false; for I always measured the kindness of my master by the standard of kindness set up among slaveholders around us. Moreover, slaves are like other people, and imbibe prejudices quite common to others. They think their own better than that of others. Many, under the influence of this prejudice, think their own masters are better than the masters of other slaves; and this, too, in some cases, when the very reverse is true. Indeed, it is not uncommon for slaves even to fall out and quarrel among themselves about the relative goodness of their masters, each contending for the superior goodness of his own over that of the others. At the very same time, they mutually execrate their masters when viewed separately. It was so on our plantation. When Colonel Lloyd's slaves met the slaves of Jacob Jepson, they seldom parted without a quarrel about their masters; Colonel Lloyd's slaves contending that he was the richest, and Mr. Jepson's slaves that he was the smartest, and most of a man. Colonel Lloyd's slaves would boast his ability to buy and sell Jacob Jepson. Mr. Jepson's slaves would boast his ability to whip Colonel Lloyd. These quarrels would almost always end in a fight between the parties, and those that whipped were supposed to have gained the point at issue. They seemed to think that the greatness of their masters was transferable to themselves. It was considered as being bad enough to be a slave; but to be a poor man's slave was deemed a disgrace indeed!

CHAPTER IV.

MR. HOPKINS remained but a short time in the office of overseer. Why his career was so short, I do not know, but suppose he lacked the necessary severity to suit Colonel Lloyd. Mr. Hopkins was succeeded by Mr. Austin Gore, a man possessing, in an eminent degree, all those traits of character indispensable to what is called a first-rate overseer. Mr. Gore had served Colonel Lloyd, in the capacity of overseer, upon one of the out-farms, and had shown himself worthy of the high station of overseer upon the home or Great House Farm.

Mr. Gore was proud, ambitious, and persevering. He was artful, cruel, and obdurate. He was just the man for such a place, and it was just the place for such a man. It afforded scope for the full exercise of all his powers, and he seemed to be perfectly at home in it. He was one of those who could torture the slightest look, word, or gesture, on the part of the slave, into impudence, and would treat it accordingly. There must be no answering back to him; no explanation was allowed a slave, showing himself to have been wrongfully accused. Mr. Gore acted fully up to the maxim laid down by slaveholders,—"It is better that a dozen slaves suffer under the lash, than that the overseer should be convicted, in the presence of the slaves, of having been at fault." No matter how innocent a slave might be—it availed him nothing, when accused by Mr. Gore of any misdemeanor. To be accused was to be convicted, and to be convicted was to be punished; the one always following the other with immutable certainty. To escape punishment was to escape accusation; and few slaves had the fortune to do either, under the overseership of Mr. Gore. He was just proud enough to demand the most debasing homage of the slave, and quite servile enough to crouch, himself, at the feet of the master. He was ambitious enough to be contented with nothing short of the highest rank of overseers, and persevering enough to reach the height of his ambition. He was cruel enough to inflict the severest punishment, artful enough to descend to the lowest trickery, and obdurate enough to be insensible to the voice of a reproving conscience. He was, of all the overseers, the most dreaded by the slaves. His presence was painful; his eye flashed confusion; and seldom was his sharp, shrill voice heard, without producing horror and trembling in their ranks.

Mr. Gore was a grave man, and, though a young man, he indulged in no jokes, said no funny words, seldom smiled. His words were in perfect keeping with his looks, and his looks were in perfect keeping with his words. Overseers will sometimes indulge in a witty word, even with the slaves; not so with Mr. Gore. He spoke but to command, and commanded but to be obeyed; he dealt sparingly with his words, and bountifully with his whip, never using the former where the latter would answer as well. When he whipped, he seemed to do so from a sense of duty, and feared no consequences. He did nothing reluctantly, no matter how disagreeable; always at his post, never inconsistent. He never promised but to fulfil. He was, in a word, a man of the most inflexible firmness and stone-like coolness.

His savage barbarity was equalled only by the consummate coolness with which he committed the grossest and most savage deeds upon the slaves under his charge. Mr. Gore once undertook to whip one of Colonel Lloyd's slaves, by the name of Demby. He had given Demby but few stripes, when, to get rid of the scourging, he ran and plunged himself into a creek, and stood there at the depth of his shoulders, refusing to come out. Mr. Gore told him that he would give him three calls, and that, if he did not come out at the third call, he would shoot him. The first call was given. Demby made no response, but stood his ground. The second and third calls were given with the same result. Mr. Gore then, without consultation or deliberation with any one, not even giving Demby an additional call, raised his musket to his face, taking deadly aim at his standing victim, and in an instant poor Demby was no more. His mangled body sank out of sight, and blood and brains marked the water where he had stood.

A thrill of horror flashed through every soul upon the plantation, excepting Mr. Gore. He alone seemed cool and collected. He was asked by

Colonel Lloyd and my old master, why he resorted to this extraordinary expedient. His reply was, (as well as I can remember,) that Demby had become unmanageable. He was setting a dangerous example to the other slaves,—one which, if suffered to pass without some such demonstration on his part, would finally lead to the total subversion of all rule and order upon the plantation. He argued that if one slave refused to be corrected, and escaped with his life, the other slaves would soon copy the example; the result of which would be, the freedom of the slaves, and the enslavement of the whites. Mr. Gore's defence was satisfactory. He was continued in his station as overseer upon the home plantation. His fame as an overseer went abroad. His horrid crime was not even submitted to judicial investigation. It was committed in the presence of slaves, and they of course could neither institute a suit, nor testify against him; and thus the guilty perpetrator of one of the bloodiest and most foul murders goes unwhipped of justice, and uncensured by the community in which he lives. Mr. Gore lived in St. Michael's, Talbot county, Maryland, when I left there; and if he is still alive, he very probably lives there now; and if so, he is now, as he was then, as highly esteemed and as much respected as though his guilty soul had not been stained with his brother's blood.

I speak advisedly when I say this,—that killing a slave, or any colored person, in Talbot county, Maryland, is not treated as a crime, either by the courts or the community. Mr. Thomas Lanman, of St. Michael's, killed two slaves, one of whom he killed with a hatchet, by knocking his brains out. He used to boast of the commission of the awful and bloody deed. I have heard him do so laughingly, saying, among other things, that he was the only benefactor of his country in the company, and that when others would do as much as he had done, we should be relieved of "the d——d niggers."

The wife of Mr. Giles Hicks, living but a short distance from where I used to live, murdered my wife's cousin, a young girl between fifteen and sixteen years of age, mangling her person in the most horrible manner, breaking her nose and breastbone with a stick, so that the poor girl expired in a few hours afterward. She was immediately buried, but had not been in her untimely grave but a few hours before she was taken up and examined by the coroner, who decided that she had come to her death by severe beating. The offence for which this girl was thus murdered was this:—She had been set that night to mind Mrs. Hicks' baby, and during the night she fell asleep, and the baby cried. She, having lost her rest for several nights previous, did not hear the crying. They were both in the room with Mrs. Hicks. Mrs. Hicks, finding the girl slow to move, jumped from her bed, seized an oak stick of wood by the fireplace, and with it broke the girl's nose and breastbone, and thus ended her life. I will not say that this most horrid murder produced no sensation in the community. It did produce sensation, but not enough to bring the murderess to punishment. There was a warrant issued for her arrest, but it was never served. Thus she escaped not only punishment, but even the pain of being arraigned before a court for her horrid crime.

Whilst I am detailing bloody deeds which took place during my stay on Colonel Lloyd's plantation, I will briefly narrate another, which occurred about the same time as the murder of Demby by Mr. Gore.

Colonel Lloyd's slaves were in the habit of spending a part of their nights and Sundays in fishing for oysters, and in this way made up the deficiency of their scanty allowance. An old man belonging to Colonel Lloyd, while thus engaged, happened to get beyond the limits of Colonel Lloyd's, and on the premises of Mr. Beal Bondly. At this trespass, Mr. Bondly took offence, and with his musket came down to the shore, and blew its deadly contents into the poor old man.

Mr. Bondly came over to see Colonel Lloyd the next day, whether to pay him for his property, or to justify himself in what he had done, I know not. At any rate, this whole fiendish transaction was soon hushed up. There was very little said about it at all, and nothing done. It was a common saying, even among little white boys, that it was worth a half-cent to kill a "nigger," and a half-cent to bury one.

CHAPTER V.

As to my own treatment while I lived on Colonel Lloyd's plantation, it was very similar to that of the other slave children. I was not old enough to work in the field, and there being little else than field work to do, I had a great deal of leisure time. The most I had to do was to drive up the cows at evening, keep the fowls out of the garden, keep the front yard clean, and run of errands for my old master's daughter, Mrs. Lucretia Auld. The most of my leisure time I spent in helping Master Daniel Lloyd in finding his birds, after he had shot them. My connection with Master Daniel was of some advantage to me. He became quite attached to me, and was a sort of protector of me. He would not allow the older boys to impose upon me, and would divide his cakes with me.

I was seldom whipped by my old master, and suffered little from any thing else than hunger and cold. I suffered much from hunger, but much more from cold. In hottest summer and coldest winter, I was kept almost naked—no shoes, no stockings, no jacket, no trousers, nothing on but a coarse tow linen shirt, reaching only to my knees. I had no bed. I must have perished with cold, but that, the coldest nights, I used to steal a bag which was used for carrying corn to the mill. I would crawl into this bag, and there sleep on the cold, damp, clay floor, with my head in and feet out. My feet have been so cracked with the frost, that the pen with which I am writing might be laid in the gashes.

We were not regularly allowanced. Our food was coarse corn meal boiled. This was called *mush*. It was put into a large wooden tray or trough, and set down upon the ground. The children were then called, like so many pigs, and like so many pigs they would come and devour the mush; some with oyster-shells, others with pieces of shingle, some with naked hands, and none with spoons. He that ate fastest got most; he that was strongest secured the best place; and few left the trough satisfied.

I was probably seven or eight years old when I left Colonel Lloyd's plantation. I left it with joy. I shall never forget the ecstasy with which I received the intelligence that my old master (Anthony) had determined to let me go to Baltimore, to live with Mr. Hugh Auld, brother to my old master's son-in-law, Captain Thomas Auld. I received this information about three days before my departure. They were three of the happiest days I ever enjoyed. I spent the most part of all these three days in the creek, washing off the plantation scurf, and preparing myself for my departure.

The pride of appearance which this would indicate was not my own. I spent the time in washing, not so much because I wished to, but because Mrs. Lucretia had told me I must get all the dead skin off my feet and knees before I could go to Baltimore; for the people in Baltimore were very cleanly, and would laugh at me if I looked dirty. Besides, she was going to give me a pair of trousers, which I should not put on unless I got all the dirt off me. The thought of owning a pair of trousers was great indeed! It was almost a sufficient motive, not only to make me take off what would be called by pig-drovers the mange, but the skin itself. I went at it in good earnest, working for the first time with the hope of reward.

The ties that ordinarily bind children to their homes were all suspended in my case. I found no severe trial in my departure. My home was charmless; it was not home to me; on parting from it, I could not feel that I was leaving any thing which I could have enjoyed by staying. My mother was dead, my grandmother lived far off, so that I seldom saw her. I had two sisters and one brother, that lived in the same house with me; but the early separation of us from our mother had well nigh blotted the fact of our relationship from our memories. I looked for home elsewhere, and was confident of finding none which I should relish less than the one which I was leaving. If, however, I found in my new home hardship, hunger, whipping, and nakedness, I had the consolation that I should not have escaped any one of them by staying. Having already had more than a taste of them in the house of my old master, and having endured them there, I very naturally inferred my ability to endure them elsewhere, and especially at Baltimore; for I had something of the feeling about Baltimore that is expressed in the proverb, that "being hanged in England is preferable to dying a natural death in Ireland." I had the strongest desire to see Baltimore. Cousin Tom, though not fluent in speech, had inspired me with that desire by his eloquent description of the place. I could never point out any thing at the Great House, no matter how beautiful or powerful, but that he had seen something at Baltimore far exceeding, both in beauty and strength, the object which I pointed out to him. Even the Great House itself, with all its pictures, was far inferior to many buildings in Baltimore. So strong was my desire, that I thought a gratification of it would fully compensate for whatever loss of comfort I should sustain by the exchange. I left without a regret, and with the highest hopes of future happiness.

We sailed out of Miles River for Baltimore on a Saturday morning. I remember only the day of the week, for at that time I had no knowledge of the days of the month, nor the months of the year. On setting sail, I walked aft, and gave to Colonel Lloyd's plantation what I hoped would be the last look. I then placed myself in the bows of the sloop, and there spent the remainder of the day in looking ahead, interesting myself in what was in the distance rather than in things near by or behind.

In the afternoon of that day, we reached Annapolis, the capital of the State. We stopped but a few moments, so that I had no time to go on shore. It was the first large town that I had ever seen, and though it would look small compared with some of our New England factory villages, I thought it a wonderful place for its size—more imposing even than the Great House Farm!

We arrived at Baltimore early on Sunday morning, landing at Smith's Wharf, not far from Bowley's Wharf. We had on board the sloop a large flock of sheep; and after aiding in driving them to the slaughter-house of Mr. Curtis on Loudon Slater's Hill, I was conducted by Rich, one of the hands belonging on board of the sloop, to my new home in Alliciana Street, near Mr. Gardner's ship-yard, on Fell's Point.

'Mr. and Mrs. Auld were both at home, and met me at the door with their little son Thomas, to take care of whom I had been given. And here I saw what I had never seen before; it was a white face beaming with the most kindly emotions; it was the face of my new mistress, Sophia Auld. I wish I could describe the rapture that flashed through my soul as I beheld it. It was a new and strange sight to me, brightening up my pathway with the light of happiness. Little Thomas was told, there was his Freddy,—and I was told to take care of little Thomas; and thus I entered upon the duties of my new home with the most cheering prospect ahead.

I look upon my departure from Colonel Lloyd's plantation as one of the most interesting events of my life. It is possible, and even quite probable, that but for the mere circumstance of being removed from that plantation to Baltimore, I should have to-day, instead of being here seated by my own table, in the enjoyment of freedom and the happiness of home, writing this Narrative, been confined in the galling chains of slavery. Going to live at Baltimore laid the foundation, and opened the gateway, to all my subsequent prosperity. I have ever regarded it as the first plain manifestation of that kind Providence which has ever since attended me, and marked my life with so many favors. I regarded the selection of myself as being somewhat remarkable. There were a number of slave children that might have been sent from the plantation to Baltimore. There were those younger, those older, and those of the same age. I was chosen from among them all, and was the first, last, and only choice.

I may be deemed superstitious, and even egotistical, in regarding this event as a special interposition of divine Providence in my favor. But I should be false to the earliest sentiments of my soul, if I suppressed the opinion. I prefer to be true to myself, even at the hazard of incurring the ridicule of others, rather than to be false, and incur my own abhorrence. From my earliest recollection, I date the entertainment of a deep conviction that slavery would not always be able to hold me within its foul embrace; and in the darkest hours of my career in slavery, this living word of faith and spirit of hope departed not from me, but remained like ministering angels to cheer me through the gloom. This good spirit was from God, and to him I offer thanksgiving and praise.

CHAPTER VI.

MY new mistress proved to be all she appeared when I first met her at the door,—a woman of the kindest heart and finest feelings. She had never had a slave under her control previously to myself, and prior to her marriage she had been dependent upon her own industry for a living. She was by trade a weaver; and by constant application to her business, she had been in a good degree preserved from the blighting and dehumanizing effects of slavery. I was utterly astonished at her goodness. I scarcely knew how to behave towards her. She was entirely unlike any other white woman I had ever seen. I could not approach her as I was accustomed to approach other white ladies. My early instruction was all out of place. The crouching servility, usually so acceptable a quality in a slave, did not answer when manifested towards her. Her favor was not gained by it; she seemed to be disturbed by it. She did not deem it impudent or unmannerly for a slave to look her in the face. The meanest slave was put fully at ease in her presence, and none left without feeling better for having seen her. Her face was made of heavenly smiles, and her voice of tranquil music.

But, alas! this kind heart had but a short time to remain such. The fatal poison of irresponsible power was already in her hands, and gradually commenced its infernal work. That cheerful eye, under the influence of slavery, eventually became red with rage; that voice, made all of sweet accord, changed to one of harsh and horrid discord; and that angelic face gave place to that of a demon. Thus is slavery the enemy of both the slave and the slaveholder.

Very soon after I went to live with Mr. and Mrs. Auld, she very kindly commenced to teach me the A, B, C. After I had learned this, she assisted me in learning to spell words of three or four letters. Just at this point of my progress, Mr. Auld found out what was going on, and at once forbade Mrs. Auld to instruct me further, telling her, among other things, that it was unlawful, as well as unsafe, to teach a slave to read. To use his own words, further, he said, "If you give a nigger an inch, he will take an ell. A nigger should know nothing but to obey his master—to do as he is told to do. Learning would *spoil* the best nigger in the world. Now," said he, "if you teach that nigger (speaking of myself) how to read, there would be no keeping him. It would forever unfit him to be a slave. He would at once become unmanageable, and of no value to his master. As to himself, it could do him no good, but a great deal of harm. It would make him discontented and unhappy." These words sank deep into my heart, stirred up sentiments within that lay slumbering, and called into existence an entirely new train of thought. It was a new and special revelation, explaining dark and mysterious things, with which my youthful understanding had struggled, but struggled in vain. I now understood what had been to me a most perplexing difficulty—to wit, the white man's power to enslave the black man. It was a grand achievement, and I prized it highly. From that moment, I understood the pathway from slavery to freedom. It was just what I wanted, and I got it at a time when I the least expected it. Whilst I was saddened by the thought of losing the aid of my kind mistress, I was gladdened by the invaluable instruction which, by the merest accident, I had gained from my master. Though conscious of the difficulty of learning without a teacher, I set out with high hope, and a fixed purpose, at whatever cost of trouble, to learn how to read. The very decided manner with which he spoke, and strove to impress his wife with the evil consequences of giving me instruction, served to convince me that he was deeply sensible of the truths he was uttering. It gave me the best assurance that I might rely with the utmost confidence on the results which, he said, would flow from teaching me to read. What he most dreaded, that I most desired. What he most loved, that I most hated. That which to him was a great evil, to be carefully shunned, was to me a great good, to be diligently sought; and the argument which he so warmly urged, against my learning to read, only served to inspire me with a desire and determination to learn. In learning to read, I owe almost as much to the bitter opposition of my master, as to the kindly aid of my mistress. I acknowledge the benefit of both.

I had resided but a short time in Baltimore before I observed a marked difference, in the treatment of slaves, from that which I had witnessed in the country. A city slave is almost a freeman, compared with a slave on the plantation. He is much better fed and clothed, and enjoys privileges altogether unknown to the slave on the plantation. There is a vestige of decency, a sense of shame, that does much to curb and check those outbreaks of atrocious cruelty so commonly enacted upon the plantation. He is a desperate slaveholder, who will shock the humanity of his non-slaveholding neighbors with the cries of his lacerated slave. Few are willing to incur the odium attaching to the reputation of being a cruel master; and above all things, they would not be known as not giving a slave enough to eat. Every city slaveholder is anxious to have it known of him, that he feeds his slaves well; and it is due to them to say, that most of them do give their slaves enough to eat. There are, however, some painful exceptions to this rule. Directly opposite to us, on Philpot Street, lived Mr. Thomas Hamilton. He owned two slaves. Their names were Henrietta and Mary. Henrietta was about twenty-two years of age, Mary was about fourteen; and of all the mangled and emaciated creatures I ever looked upon, these two were the most so. His heart must be harder than stone, that could look at these unmoved. The head, neck, and shoulders of Mary were literally cut to pieces. I have frequently felt her head, and found it nearly covered with festering sores, caused by the lash of her cruel mistress. I do not know that her master ever whipped her, but I have been an eye-witness to the cruelty of Mrs. Hamilton. I used to be in Mr. Hamilton's house nearly every day. Mrs. Hamilton used to sit in a large chair in the middle of the room, with a heavy cowskin always by her side, and scarce an hour passed during the day but was marked by the blood of one of these slaves. The girls seldom passed her without her saying, "Move faster, you *black gip!*" at the same time giving them a blow with the cowskin over the head or shoulders, often drawing the blood. She would then say, "Take that, you *black gip!*"— continuing, "If you don't move faster, I'll move you!" Added to the cruel lashings to which these slaves were subjected, they were kept nearly half-starved. They seldom knew what it was to eat a full meal. I have seen Mary contending with the pigs for the offal thrown into the street. So much was Mary kicked and cut to pieces, that she was oftener called *"pecked"* than by her name.

CHAPTER VII.

I LIVED in Master Hugh's family about seven years. During this time, I succeeded in learning to read and write. In accomplishing this, I was compelled to resort to various stratagems. I had no regular teacher. My mistress, who had kindly commenced to instruct me, had, in compliance with the advice and direction of her husband, not only ceased to instruct, but had set her face against my being instructed by any one else. It is due, however, to my mistress to say of her, that she did not adopt this course of treatment immediately. She at first lacked the depravity indispensable to shutting me up in mental darkness. It was at least necessary for her to have some training in the exercise of irresponsible power, to make her equal to the task of treating me as though I were a brute.

My mistress was, as I have said, a kind and tender-hearted woman; and in the simplicity of her soul she commenced, when I first went to live with her, to treat me as she supposed one human being ought to treat another. In entering upon the duties of a slaveholder, she did not seem to perceive that I sustained to her the relation of a mere chattel, and that for her to treat me as a human being was not only wrong, but dangerously so. Slavery proved as injurious to her as it did to me. When I went there, she was a pious, warm, and tender-hearted woman. There was no sorrow or suffering for which she had not a tear. She had bread for the hungry, clothes for the naked, and comfort for every mourner that came within her reach. Slavery soon proved its ability to divest her of these heavenly qualities. Under its influence, the tender heart became stone, and the lamb-like disposition gave way to one of tiger-like fierceness. The first step in her downward course was in her ceasing to instruct me. She now commenced to practise her husband's precepts. She finally became even more violent in her opposition than her husband himself. She was not satisfied with simply doing as well as he had commanded; she seemed anxious to do better. Nothing seemed to make her more angry than to see me with a newspaper. She seemed to think that here lay the danger. I have had her rush at me with a face made all up of fury, and snatch from me a newspaper, in a manner that fully revealed her apprehension. She was an apt woman; and a little experience soon demonstrated, to her satisfaction, that education and slavery were incompatible with each other.

From this time I was most narrowly watched. If I was in a separate room any considerable length of time, I was sure to be suspected of having a book, and was at once called to give an account of myself. All this, however, was too late. The first step had been taken. Mistress, in teaching me the alphabet, had given me the *inch,* and no precaution could prevent me from taking the *ell.*

The plan which I adopted, and the one by which I was most successful, was that of making friends of all the little white boys whom I met in the street. As many of these as I could, I converted into teachers. With their kindly aid, obtained at different times and in different places, I finally succeeded in learning to read. When I was sent of errands, I always took my book with me, and by going one part of my errand quickly, I found time to get a lesson before my return. I used also to carry bread with me, enough of which was always in the house, and to which I was always welcome; for I was much better off in this regard than many of the poor white children in the neighborhood. This bread I used to bestow on the hungry little urchins, who, in return, would give me the more valuable bread of knowledge. I am strongly tempted to give the names of two or three of those little boys, as a testimonial of the gratitude and affection I bear them; but prudence forbids;—not that it would injure me, but it might embarrass them; for it is almost an unpardonable offence to teach slaves to read in this Christian country. It is enough to say of the dear little fellows, that they lived on Philpot Street, very near Durgin and Bailey's ship-yard. I used to talk this matter of slavery over with them. I would sometimes say to them, I wished I could be as free as they would be when they got to be men. "You will be free as soon as you are twenty-one, *but I am a slave for life!* Have not I as good a right to be free as you have?" These words used to trouble them; they would express for me the liveliest sympathy, and console me with the hope that something would occur by which I might be free.

I was now about twelve years old, and the thought of being *a slave for life* began to bear heavily upon my heart. Just about this time, I got hold of a book entitled "The Columbian Orator." Every opportunity I got, I used to read this book. Among much of other interesting matter, I found in it a dialogue between a master and his slave. The slave was represented as having run away from his master three times. The dialogue represented the conversation which took place between them, when the slave was retaken the third time. In this dialogue, the whole argument in behalf of slavery was brought forward by the master, all of which was disposed of by the slave. The slave was made to say some very smart as well as impressive things in reply to his master—things which had the desired though unexpected effect; for the conversation resulted in the voluntary emancipation of the slave on the part of the master.

In the same book, I met with one of Sheridan's mighty speeches on and in behalf of Catholic emancipation. These were choice documents to me. I read them over and over again with unabated interest. They gave tongue to interesting thoughts of my own soul, which had frequently flashed through my mind, and died away for want of utterance. The moral which I gained from the dialogue was the power of truth over the conscience of even a slaveholder. What I got from Sheridan was a bold denunciation of slavery, and a powerful vindication of human rights. The reading of these documents enabled me to utter my thoughts, and to meet the arguments brought forward to sustain slavery; but while they relieved me of one difficulty, they brought on another even more painful than the one of which I was relieved. The more I read, the more I was led to abhor and detest my enslavers. I could regard them in no other light than a band of successful robbers, who had left their homes, and gone to Africa, and stolen us from our homes, and in a strange land reduced us to slavery. I loathed them as being the meanest as well as the most wicked of men. As I read and contemplated the subject, behold! that very discontentment which Master Hugh had predicted would follow my learning to read had already come, to torment and sting my soul to unutterable anguish. As I writhed under it, I would at times feel that learning to read had been a curse rather than a blessing. It had given me a view of my wretched condition, without the remedy. It opened my eyes to the horrible pit, but to no ladder upon which to get out. In moments of agony, I envied my fellow-slaves for their stupidity. I have often wished myself a beast. I preferred the condition of the meanest reptile to my own. Any thing, no matter what, to get rid of thinking! It was this everlasting thinking of my condition that tormented me. There was no getting rid of it. It was pressed upon me by every object within sight or hearing, animate or inanimate. The silver trump of freedom had roused my soul to eternal wakefulness. Freedom now appeared, to disappear no more forever. It was heard in every sound, and seen in every thing. It was ever present to torment me with a sense of my wretched condition. I saw nothing without seeing it, I heard nothing without hearing it, and felt nothing without feeling it. It looked from every star, it smiled in every calm, breathed in every wind, and moved in every storm.

I often found myself regretting my own existence, and wished myself dead; and but for the hope of being free, I have no doubt but that I should have killed myself, or done something for which I should have been killed. While in this state of mind, I was eager to hear any one speak of slavery. I was a ready listener. Every little while, I could hear something about the abolitionists. It was some time before I found what the word meant. It was always used in such connections as to make it an interesting word to me. If a slave ran away and succeeded in getting clear, or if a slave killed his master, set fire to a barn, or did any thing very wrong in the mind of a slaveholder, it was spoken of as the fruit of *abolition*. Hearing the word in this connection very often, I set about learning what it meant. The dictionary afforded me little or no help. I found it was "the act of abolishing;" but then I did not know what was to be abolished. Here I was perplexed. I did not dare to ask any one about its meaning, for I was satisfied that it was something they wanted me to know very little about. After a patient waiting, I got one of our city papers, containing an account of the number of petitions from the north, praying for the abolition of slavery in the District of Columbia, and of the slave trade between the States. From this time I understood the words *abolition* and *abolitionist,* and always drew near when that word was spoken, expecting to hear something of importance to myself and fellow-slaves. The light broke in upon me by degrees. I went one day down on the wharf of Mr. Waters; and seeing two Irishmen unloading a scow of stone, I went, unasked, and helped them. When we had finished, one of them came to me and asked me if I were a slave. I told him I was. He asked, "Are ye a slave for life?" I told him that I was. The good Irishman seemed to be deeply affected by the statement. He said to the other that it was a pity so fine a little fellow as myself should be a slave for life. He said it was a shame to hold me. They both advised me to run away to the north; that I should find friends there, and that I should be free. I pretended not to be interested in what they said, and treated them as if I did not understand them; for I feared they might be treacherous. White men have been known to encourage slaves to escape, and then, to get the reward, catch them and return them to their masters. I was afraid that these seemingly good men might use me so; but I nevertheless remembered their advice, and from that time I resolved to run away. I looked forward to a time at which it would be safe for me to escape. I was too young to think of doing so immediately; besides, I wished to learn how to write, as I might have occasion to write my own pass. I consoled myself with the hope that I should one day find a good chance. Meanwhile, I would learn to write.

The idea as to how I might learn to write was suggested to me by being in Durgin and Bailey's ship-yard, and frequently seeing the ship carpenters, after hewing, and getting a piece of timber ready for use, write on the timber the name of that part of the ship for which it was intended. When a piece of timber was intended for the larboard side, it would be marked thus—"L." When a piece was for the starboard side, it would be marked thus—"S." A piece for the larboard side forward, would be marked thus—"L.F." When a piece was for starboard side forward, it would be marked thus—"S.F." For larboard aft, it would be marked thus—"L.A." For starboard aft, it would be marked thus—"S.A." I soon learned the names of these letters, and for what they were intended when placed upon a piece of timber in the ship-yard. I immediately commenced copying them, and in a short time was able to make the four letters named. After that, when I met with any boy who I knew could write, I would tell him I could write as well as he. The next word would be, "I don't believe you. Let me see you try it." I would then make the letters which I had been so fortunate as to learn, and ask him to beat that. In this way I got a good many lessons in writing, which it is quite possible I should never have gotten in any other way. During this time, my copy-book was the board fence, brick wall, and pavement; my pen and ink was a lump of chalk. With these, I learned mainly how to write. I then commenced and continued copying the italics in Webster's Spelling Book, until I could make them all without looking on the book. By this time, my little Master Thomas had gone to school, and learned how to write, and had written over a number of copy-books. These had been brought home, and shown to some of our near neighbors, and then laid aside. My mistress used to go to class meeting at the Wilk Street meeting-house every Monday afternoon, and leave me to take care of the house. When left thus, I used to spend the time in writing in the spaces left in Master Thomas's copy-book, copying what he had written. I continued to do this until I could write a hand very similar to that of Master Thomas. Thus, after a long, tedious effort for years, I finally succeeded in learning how to write.

CHAPTER VIII.

IN a very short time after I went to live at Baltimore, my old master's youngest son, Richard, died; and in about three years and six months after his death, my old master, Captain Anthony, died, leaving only his son, Andrew, and daughter, Lucretia, to share his estate. He died while on a visit to see his daughter at Hillsborough. Cut off thus unexpectedly, he left no will as to the disposal of his property. It was therefore necessary to have a valuation of the property, that it might be equally divided between Mrs. Lucretia and Master Andrew. I was immediately sent for, to be valued with the other property. Here again my feelings rose up in detestation of slavery. I had now a new conception of my degraded condition. Prior to this, I had become, if not insensible to my lot, at least partly so. I left Baltimore with a young heart overborne with sadness, and a soul full of apprehension. I took passage with Captain Rowe, in the schooner Wild Cat, and, after a sail of about twenty-four hours, I found myself near the place of my birth. I had now been absent from it almost, if not quite, five years. I, however, remembered the place very well. I was only about five years old when I left it, to go and live with my old master on Colonel Lloyd's plantation; so that I was now between ten and eleven years old.

We were all ranked together at the valuation. Men and women, old and young, married and single, were ranked with horses, sheep, and swine. There were horses and men, cattle and women, pigs and children, all holding the same rank in the scale of being, and all were subjected to the same narrow examination. Silvery-headed age and sprightly youth, maids and matrons, had to undergo the same indelicate inspection. At this moment, I saw more clearly than ever the brutalizing effects of slavery upon both slave and slaveholder.

After the valuation, then came the division. I have no language to express the high excitement and deep anxiety which were felt among us poor slaves during this time. Our fate for life was now to be decided. We had no more voice in that decision than the brutes among whom we were ranked. A single word from the white men was enough—against all our wishes, prayers, and entreaties—to sunder forever the dearest friends, dearest kindred, and strongest ties known to human beings. In addition to the pain of separation, there was the horrid dread of falling into the hands of Master Andrew. He was known to us all as being a most cruel wretch,—a common drunkard, who had, by his reckless mismanagement and profligate dissipation, already wasted a large portion of his father's property. We all felt that we might as well be sold at once to the Georgia traders, as to pass into his hands; for we knew that that would be our inevitable condition,—a condition held by us all in the utmost horror and dread.

I suffered more anxiety than most of my fellow-slaves. I had known what it was to be kindly treated; they had known nothing of the kind. They had seen little or nothing of the world. They were in very deed men and women of sorrow, and acquainted with grief. Their backs had been made familiar with the bloody lash, so that they had become callous; mine was yet tender; for while at Baltimore I got few whippings, and few slaves could boast of a kinder master and mistress than myself; and the thought of passing out of their hands into those of Master Andrew—a man who, but a few days before, to give me a sample of his bloody disposition, took my little brother by the throat, threw him on the ground, and with the heel of his boot stamped upon his head till the blood gushed from his nose and ears— was well calculated to make me anxious as to my fate. After he had committed this savage outrage upon my brother, he turned to me, and said that was the way he meant to serve me one of these days,—meaning, I suppose, when I came into his possession.

Thanks to a kind Providence, I fell to the portion of Mrs. Lucretia, and was sent immediately back to Baltimore, to live again in the family of Master Hugh. Their joy at my return equalled their sorrow at my departure. It was a glad day to me. I had escaped a fate worse than lion's jaws. I was absent from Baltimore, for the purpose of valuation and division, just about one month, and it seemed to have been six.

Very soon after my return to Baltimore, my mistress, Lucretia, died, leaving her husband and one child, Amanda; and in a very short time after her death, Master Andrew died. Now all the property of my old master, slaves included, was in the hands of strangers,—strangers who had nothing to do with accumulating it. Not a slave was left free. All remained slaves, from the youngest to the oldest. If any one thing in my experience, more than another, served to deepen my conviction of the infernal character of slavery, and to fill me with unutterable loathing of slaveholders, it was their base ingratitude to my poor old grandmother. She had served my old master faithfully from youth to old age. She had been the source of all his wealth; she had peopled his plantation with slaves; she had become a great grand-mother in his service. She had rocked him in infancy, attended him in childhood, served him through life, and at his death wiped from his icy brow the cold death-sweat, and closed his eyes forever. She was neverthe-less left a slave—a slave for life—a slave in the hands of strangers; and in their hands she saw her children, her grandchildren, and her great-grand-children, divided, like so many sheep, without being gratified with the small privilege of a single word, as to their or her own destiny. And, to cap the climax of their base ingratitude and fiendish barbarity, my grandmother, who was now very old, having outlived my old master and all his children, having seen the beginning and end of all of them, and her present owners finding she was of but little value, her frame already racked with the pains of old age, and complete helplessness fast stealing over her once active limbs, they took her to the woods, built her a little hut, put up a little mud-chimney, and then made her welcome to the privilege of supporting herself there in perfect loneliness; thus virtually turning her out to die! If my poor old grandmother now lives, she lives to suffer in utter loneliness; she lives to remember and mourn over the loss of children, the loss of grandchildren, and the loss of great-grandchildren. They are, in the language of the slave's poet, Whittier,—

> "Gone, gone, sold and gone
> To the rice swamp dank and lone,
> Where the slave-whip ceaseless swings,
> Where the noisome insect stings,
> Where the fever-demon strews
> Poison with the falling dews,
> Where the sickly sunbeams glare
> Through the hot and misty air:—
>   Gone, gone, sold and gone
>   To the rice swamp dank and lone,
>   From Virginia's hills and waters—
>   Woe is me, my stolen daughters!"

The hearth is desolate. The children, the unconscious children, who once sang and danced in her presence, are gone. She gropes her way, in the darkness of age, for a drink of water. Instead of the voices of her children, she hears by day the moans of the dove, and by night the screams of the hideous owl. All is gloom. The grave is at the door. And now, when weighed down by the pains and aches of old age, when the head inclines to the feet, when the beginning and ending of human existence meet, and helpless infancy and painful old age combine together—at this time, this most needful time, the time for the exercise of that tenderness and affection which children only can exercise towards a declining parent—my poor old grandmother, the devoted mother of twelve children, is left all alone, in yonder little hut, before a few dim embers. She stands—she sits—she staggers—she falls—she groans—she dies—and there are none of her children or grandchildren present, to wipe from her wrinkled brow the cold sweat of death, or to place beneath the sod her fallen remains. Will not a righteous God visit for these things?

In about two years after the death of Mrs. Lucretia, Master Thomas married his second wife. Her name was Rowena Hamilton. She was the eldest daughter of Mr. William Hamilton. Master now lived in St. Michael's. Not long after his marriage, a misunderstanding took place between himself and Master Hugh; and as a means of punishing his brother, he took me from him to live with himself at St. Michael's. Here I underwent another most painful separation. It, however, was not so severe as the one I dreaded at the division of property; for, during this interval, a great change had taken place in Master Hugh and his once kind and affectionate wife. The influence of brandy upon him, and of slavery upon her, had effected a disastrous change in the characters of both; so that, as far as they were concerned, I thought I had little to lose by the change. But it was not to them that I was attached. It was to those little Baltimore boys that I felt the strongest attachment. I had received many good lessons from them, and was still receiving them, and the thought of leaving them was painful indeed. I was leaving, too, without the hope of ever being allowed to return. Master Thomas had said he would never let me return again. The barrier betwixt himself and his brother he considered impassable.

I then had to regret that I did not at least make the attempt to carry out my resolution to run away; for the chances of success are tenfold greater from the city than from the country.

I sailed from Baltimore for St. Michael's in the sloop Amanda, Captain Edward Dodson. On my passage, I paid particular attention to the direction which the steamboats took to go to Philadelphia. I found, instead of going down, on reaching North Point they went up the bay, in a north-easterly direction. I deemed this knowledge of the utmost importance. My determination to run away was again revived. I resolved to wait only so long as the offering of a favorable opportunity. When that came, I was determined to be off.

CHAPTER IX.

I HAVE now reached a period of my life when I can give dates. I left Baltimore, and went to live with Master Thomas Auld, at St. Michael's, in March, 1832. It was now more than seven years since I lived with him in the family of my old master, on Colonel Lloyd's plantation. We of course were now almost entire strangers to each other. He was to me a new master, and I to him a new slave. I was ignorant of his temper and disposition; he was equally so of mine. A very short time, however, brought us into full acquaintance with each other. I was made acquainted with his wife not less than with himself. They were well matched, being equally mean and cruel. I was now, for the first time during a space of more than seven years, made to feel the painful gnawings of hunger—a something which I had not experienced before since I left Colonel Lloyd's plantation. It went hard enough with me then, when I could look back to no period at which I had enjoyed a sufficiency. It was tenfold harder after living in Master Hugh's family, where I had always had enough to eat, and of that which was good. I have said Master Thomas was a mean man. He was so. Not to give a slave enough to eat, is regarded as the most aggravated development of meanness even among slaveholders. The rule is, no matter how coarse the food, only let there be enough of it. This is the theory; and in the part of Maryland from which I came, it is the general practice,—though there are many exceptions. Master Thomas gave us enough of neither coarse nor fine food. There were four slaves of us in the kitchen—my sister Eliza, my aunt Priscilla, Henny, and myself; and we were allowed less than half of a bushel of corn-meal per week, and very little else, either in the shape of meat or vegetables. It was not enough for us to subsist upon. We were therefore reduced to the wretched necessity of living at the expense of our neighbors. This we did by begging and stealing, whichever came handy in the time of need, the one being considered as legitimate as the other. A great many times have we poor creatures been nearly perishing with hunger, when food in abundance lay mouldering in the safe and smoke-house, and our pious mistress was aware of the fact; and yet that mistress and her husband would kneel every morning, and pray that God would bless them in basket and store!

Bad as all slaveholders are, we seldom meet one destitute of every element of character commanding respect. My master was one of this rare sort. I do not know of one single noble act ever performed by him. The leading trait in his character was meanness; and if there were any other element in his nature, it was made subject to this. He was mean; and, like most other mean men, he lacked the ability to conceal his meanness. Captain Auld was not born a slaveholder. He had been a poor man, master only of a Bay craft. He came into possession of all his slaves by marriage; and of all men, adopted slaveholders are the worst. He was cruel, but cowardly. He commanded without firmness. In the enforcement of his rules, he was at times rigid, and at times lax. At times, he spoke to his slaves with the firmness of Napoleon and the fury of a demon; at other times, he might well be mistaken for an inquirer who had lost his way. He did nothing of himself. He might have passed for a lion, but for his ears. In all things noble which he attempted, his own meanness shone most conspicuous. His airs, words, and actions, were the airs, words, and actions of born slaveholders, and, being assumed, were awkward enough. He was not even a good imitator. He possessed all the disposition to deceive, but wanted the power. Having no resources within himself, he was compelled to be the copyist of many, and being such, he was forever the victim of inconsistency; and of consequence he was an object of contempt, and was held as such even by his slaves. The luxury of having slaves of his own to wait upon him was something new and unprepared for. He was a slaveholder without the ability to hold slaves. He found himself incapable of managing his slaves either by force, fear, or fraud. We seldom called him "master;" we generally called him "Captain Auld," and were hardly disposed to title him at all. I doubt not that our conduct had much to do with making him appear awkward, and of consequence fretful. Our want of reverence for him must have perplexed him greatly. He wished to have us call him master, but lacked the firmness necessary to command us to do so. His wife used to insist upon our calling him so, but to no purpose. In August, 1832, my master attended a Methodist camp-meeting held in the Bay-side, Talbot county, and there experienced religion. I indulged a faint hope that his conversion would lead him to emancipate his slaves, and that, if he did not do this, it would, at any rate, make him more kind and humane. I was disappointed in both these respects. It neither made him to be humane to his slaves, nor to emancipate them. If it had any effect on his character, it made him more cruel and hateful in all his ways; for I believe him to have been a much worse man after his conversion than before. Prior to his conversion, he relied upon his own depravity to shield and sustain him in his savage barbarity; but after his conversion, he found religious sanction and support for his slaveholding cruelty. He made the greatest pretensions to piety. His house was the house of prayer. He prayed morning, noon, and night. He very soon distinguished himself among his brethren, and was soon made a class-leader and exhorter. His activity in revivals was great, and he proved himself an instrument in the hands of the church in converting many souls. His house was the preachers' home. They used to take great pleasure in coming there to put up; for while he starved us, he stuffed them. We have had three or four preachers there at a time. The names of those who used to come most frequently while I lived there, were Mr. Storks, Mr. Ewery, Mr. Humphry, and Mr. Hickey. I have also seen Mr. George Cookman at our house. We slaves loved Mr. Cookman. We believed him to be a good man. We thought him instrumental in getting Mr. Samuel Harrison, a very rich slaveholder, to emancipate his slaves; and by some means got the impression that he was laboring to effect the emancipation of all the slaves. When he was at our house, we were sure to be called in to prayers. When the others were there, we were sometimes called in and sometimes not. Mr. Cookman took more notice of us than either of the other ministers. He could not come among us without betraying his sympathy for us, and, stupid as we were, we had the sagacity to see it.

While I lived with my master in St. Michael's, there was a white young man, a Mr. Wilson, who proposed to keep a Sabbath school for the instruction of such slaves as might be disposed to learn to read the New Testament. We met but three times, when Mr. West and Mr. Fairbanks, both class-leaders, with many others, came upon us with sticks and other missiles, drove us off, and forbade us to meet again. Thus ended our little Sabbath school in the pious town of St. Michael's.

I have said my master found religious sanction for his cruelty. As an example, I will state one of many facts going to prove the charge. I have seen him tie up a lame young woman, and whip her with a heavy cowskin upon her naked shoulders, causing the warm red blood to drip; and, in justification of the bloody deed, he would quote this passage of Scripture— "He that knoweth his master's will, and doeth it not, shall be beaten with many stripes."

Master would keep this lacerated young woman tied up in this horrid situation four or five hours at a time. I have known him to tie her up early in the morning, and whip her before breakfast; leave her, go to his store, return at dinner, and whip her again, cutting her in the places already made raw with his cruel lash. The secret of master's cruelty toward "Henny" is found in the fact of her being almost helpless. When quite a child, she fell into the fire, and burned herself horribly. Her hands were so burnt that she never got the use of them. She could do very little but bear heavy burdens. She was to master a bill of expense; and as he was a mean man, she was a constant offence to him. He seemed desirous of getting the poor girl out of existence. He gave her away once to his sister; but, being a poor gift, she was not disposed to keep her. Finally, my benevolent master, to use his own words, "set her adrift to take care of herself." Here was a recently-converted man, holding on upon the mother, and at the same time turning out her helpless child, to starve and die! Master Thomas was one of the many pious slave-holders who hold slaves for the very charitable purpose of taking care of them.

My master and myself had quite a number of differences. He found me unsuitable to his purpose. My city life, he said, had had a very pernicious effect upon me. It had almost ruined me for every good purpose, and fitted me for every thing which was bad. One of my greatest faults was that of letting his horse run away, and go down to his father-in-law's farm, which was about five miles from St. Michael's. I would then have to go after it. My reason for this kind of carelessness, or carefulness, was, that I could always get something to eat when I went there. Master William Hamilton, my master's father-in-law, always gave his slaves enough to eat. I never left there hungry, no matter how great the need of my speedy return. Master Thomas at length said he would stand it no longer. I had lived with him nine months, during which time he had given me a number of severe whippings, all to no good purpose. He resolved to put me out, as he said, to be broken; and, for this purpose, he let me for one year to a man named Edward Covey. Mr. Covey was a poor man, a farm-renter. He rented the place upon which he lived, as also the hands with which he tilled it. Mr. Covey had acquired a very high reputation for breaking young slaves, and this reputation was of immense value to him. It enabled him to get his farm tilled with much less expense to himself than he could have had it done without such a reputation. Some slaveholders thought it not much loss to allow Mr. Covey to have their slaves one year, for the sake of the training to which they were subjected, without any other compensation. He could hire young help with great ease, in consequence of this reputation. Added to the natural good qualities of Mr. Covey, he was a professor of religion—a pious soul—a member and a class-leader in the Methodist church. All of this added weight to his reputation as a "nigger-breaker." I was aware of all the facts, having been made acquainted with them by a young man who had lived there. I nevertheless made the change gladly; for I was sure of getting enough to eat, which is not the smallest consideration to a hungry man.

CHAPTER X.

I LEFT Master Thomas's house, and went to live with Mr. Covey, on the 1st of January, 1833. I was now, for the first time in my life, a field hand. In my new employment, I found myself even more awkward than a country boy appeared to be in a large city. I had been at my new home but one week before Mr. Covey gave me a very severe whipping, cutting my back, causing the blood to run, and raising ridges on my flesh as large as my little finger. The details of this affair are as follows: Mr. Covey sent me, very early in the morning of one of our coldest days in the month of January, to the woods, to get a load of wood. He gave me a team of unbroken oxen. He told me which was the in-hand ox, and which the off-hand one. He then tied the end of a large rope around the horns of the in-hand ox, and gave me the other end of it, and told me, if the oxen started to run, that I must hold on upon the rope. I had never driven oxen before, and of course I was very awkward. I, however, succeeded in getting to the edge of the woods with little difficulty; but I had got a very few rods into the woods, when the oxen took fright, and started full tilt, carrying the cart against trees, and over stumps, in the most frightful manner. I expected every moment that my brains would be dashed out against the trees. After running thus for a considerable distance, they finally upset the cart, dashing it with great force against a tree, and threw themselves into a dense thicket. How I escaped death, I do not know. There I was, entirely alone, in a thick wood, in a place new to me. My cart was upset and shattered, my oxen were entangled among the young trees, and there was none to help me. After a long spell of effort, I succeeded in getting my cart righted, my oxen disentangled, and again yoked to the cart. I now proceeded with my team to the place where I had, the day before, been chopping wood, and loaded my cart pretty heavily, thinking in this way to tame my oxen. I then proceeded on my way home. I had now consumed one half of the day. I got out of the woods safely, and now felt out of danger. I stopped my oxen to open the gate; and just as I did so, before I could get hold of my ox-rope, the oxen again started, rushed through the gate, catching it between the wheel and the body of the cart, tearing it to pieces, and coming within a few inches of crushing me against the gate-post. Thus twice, in one short day, I escaped death by the merest chance. On my return, I told Mr. Covey what had happened, and how it happened. He ordered me to return to the woods again immediately. I did so, and he followed on after me. Just as I got into the woods, he came up and told me to stop my cart, and that he would teach me how to trifle away my time, and break gates. He then went to a large gum-tree, and with his axe cut three large switches, and, after trimming them up neatly with his pocket-knife, he ordered me to take off my clothes. I made him no answer, but stood with my clothes on. He repeated his order. I still made him no answer, nor did I move to strip myself. Upon this he rushed at me with the fierceness of a tiger, tore off my clothes, and lashed me till he had worn out his switches, cutting me so savagely as to leave the marks visible for a long time after. This whipping was the first of a number just like it, and for similar offences.

I lived with Mr. Covey one year. During the first six months, of that year, scarce a week passed without his whipping me. I was seldom free from a sore back. My awkwardness was almost always his excuse for whipping me. We were worked fully up to the point of endurance. Long before day we were up, our horses fed, and by the first approach of day we were off to the field with our hoes and ploughing teams. Mr. Covey gave us enough to eat, but scarce time to eat it. We were often less than five minutes taking our meals. We were often in the field from the first approach of day till its last lingering ray had left us; and at saving-fodder time, midnight often caught us in the field binding blades.

Covey would be out with us. The way he used to stand it, was this. He would spend the most of his afternoons in bed. He would then come out fresh in the evening, ready to urge us on with his word, example, and frequently with the whip. Mr. Covey was one of the few slaveholders who could and did work with his hands. He was a hard-working man. He knew by himself just what a man or a boy could do. There was no deceiving him. His work went on in his absence almost as well as in his presence; and he had the faculty of making us feel that he was ever present with us. This he did by surprising us. He seldom approached the spot where we were at work openly, if he could do it secretly. He always aimed at taking us by surprise. Such was his cunning, that we used to call him, among ourselves, "the snake." When we were at work in the cornfield, he would sometimes crawl on his hands and knees to avoid detection, and all at once he would rise nearly in our midst, and scream out, "Ha, ha! Come, come! Dash on, dash on!" This being his mode of attack, it was never safe to stop a single minute. His comings were like a thief in the night. He appeared to us as being ever at hand. He was under every tree, behind every stump, in every bush, and at every window, on the plantation. He would sometimes mount his horse, as if bound to St. Michael's, a distance of seven miles, and in half an hour afterwards you would see him coiled up in the corner of the wood-fence, watching every motion of the slaves. He would, for this purpose, leave his horse tied up in the woods. Again, he would sometimes walk up to us, and give us orders as though he was upon the point of starting on a long journey, turn his back upon us, and make as though he was going to the house to get ready; and, before he would get half way thither, he would turn short and crawl into a fence-corner, or behind some tree, and there watch us till the going down of the sun.

Mr. Covey's *forte* consisted in his power to deceive. His life was devoted to planning and perpetrating the grossest deceptions. Every thing he possessed in the shape of learning or religion, he made conform to his disposition to deceive. He seemed to think himself equal to deceiving the Almighty. He would make a short prayer in the morning, and a long prayer at night; and, strange as it may seem, few men would at times appear more devotional than he. The exercises of his family devotions were always commenced with singing; and, as he was a very poor singer himself, the duty of raising the hymn generally came upon me. He would read his hymn, and nod at me to commence. I would at times do so; at others, I would not. My non-compliance would almost always produce much confusion. To show himself independent of me, he would start and stagger through with his hymn in the most discordant manner. In this state of mind, he prayed with more than ordinary spirit. Poor man! such was his disposition, and success at deceiving, I do verily believe that he sometimes deceived himself into the solemn belief, that he was a sincere worshipper of the most high God; and this, too, at a time when he may be said to have been guilty of compelling his woman slave to commit the sin of adultery. The facts in the case are these: Mr. Covey was a poor man; he was just commencing in life; he was only able to buy one slave; and, shocking as is the fact, he bought her, as he said, for *a breeder*. This woman was named Caroline. Mr. Covey bought her from Mr. Thomas Lowe, about six miles from St. Michael's. She was a large, able-bodied woman, about twenty years old. She had already given birth to one child, which proved her to be just what he wanted. After buying her, he hired a married man of Mr. Samuel Harrison, to live with him one year; and him he used to fasten up with her every night! The result was, that, at the end of the year, the miserable woman gave birth to twins. At this result Mr. Covey seemed to be highly pleased, both with the man and the wretched woman. Such was his joy, and that of his wife, that nothing they could do for Caroline during her confinement was too good, or too hard, to be done. The children were regarded as being quite an addition to his wealth.

If at any one time of my life more than another, I was made to drink the bitterest dregs of slavery, that time was during the first six months of my stay with Mr. Covey. We were worked in all weathers. It was never too hot or too cold; it could never rain, blow, hail, or snow, too hard for us to work in the field. Work, work, work, was scarcely more the order of the day than of the night. The longest days were too short for him, and the shortest nights too long for him. I was somewhat unmanageable when I first went there, but a few months of this discipline tamed me. Mr. Covey succeeded in breaking me. I was broken in body, soul, and spirit. My natural elasticity was crushed, my intellect languished, the disposition to read departed, the cheerful spark that lingered about my eye died; the dark night of slavery closed in upon me; and behold a man transformed into a brute!

Sunday was my only leisure time. I spent this in a sort of beast-like stupor, between sleep and wake, under some large tree. At times I would rise up, a flash of energetic freedom would dart through my soul, accompanied with a faint beam of hope, that flickered for a moment, and then vanished. I sank down again, mourning over my wretched condition. I was sometimes prompted to take my life, and that of Covey, but was prevented by a combination of hope and fear. My sufferings on this plantation seem now like a dream rather than a stern reality.

Our house stood within a few rods of the Chesapeake Bay, whose broad bosom was ever white with sails from every quarter of the habitable globe. Those beautiful vessels, robed in purest white, so delightful to the eye of freemen, were to me so many shrouded ghosts, to terrify and torment me with thoughts of my wretched condition. I have often, in the deep stillness of a summer's Sabbath, stood all alone upon the lofty banks of that noble bay, and traced, with saddened heart and tearful eye, the countless number of sails moving off to the mighty ocean. The sight of these always affected me powerfully. My thoughts would compel utterance; and there, with no audience but the Almighty, I would pour out my soul's complaint, in my rude way, with an apostrophe to the moving multitude of ships:—

"You are loosed from your moorings, and are free; I am fast in my chains, and am a slave! You move merrily before the gentle gale, and I sadly before the bloody whip! You are freedom's swift-winged angels, that fly round the world; I am confined in bands of iron! O that I were free! O, that I were on one of your gallant decks, and under your protecting wing! Alas! betwixt me and you, the turbid waters roll. Go on, go on. O that I could also go! Could I but swim! If I could fly! O, why was I born a man, of whom to make a brute! The glad ship is gone; she hides in the dim distance. I am left in the hottest hell of unending slavery. O God, save me! God, deliver me! Let me be free! Is there any God? Why am I a slave? I will run away. I will not stand it. Get caught, or get clear, I'll try it. I had as well die with ague as the fever. I have only one life to lose. I had as well be killed running as die standing. Only think of it; one hundred miles straight north, and I am free! Try it? Yes! God helping me, I will. It cannot be that I shall live and die a slave. I will take to the water. This very bay shall yet bear me into freedom. The steamboats steered in a north-east course from North Point. I will do the same; and when I get to the head of the bay, I will turn my canoe adrift, and walk straight through Delaware into Pennsylvania. When I get there, I shall not be required to have a pass; I can travel without being disturbed. Let but the first opportunity offer, and, come what will, I am off. Meanwhile, I will try to bear up under the yoke. I am not the only slave in the world. Why should I fret? I can bear as much as any of them. Besides, I am but a boy, and all boys are bound to some one. It may be that my misery in slavery will only increase my happiness when I get free. There is a better day coming."

Thus I used to think, and thus I used to speak to myself; goaded almost to madness at one moment, and at the next reconciling myself to my wretched lot.

I have already intimated that my condition was much worse, during the first six months of my stay at Mr. Covey's, than in the last six. The circumstances leading to the change in Mr. Covey's course toward me form an epoch in my humble history. You have seen how a man was made a slave; you shall see how a slave was made a man. On one of the hottest days of the month of August, 1833, Bill Smith, William Hughes, a slave named Eli, and myself, were engaged in fanning wheat. Hughes was clearing the fanned wheat from before the fan, Eli was turning, Smith was feeding, and I was carrying wheat to the fan. The work was simple, requiring strength rather than intellect; yet, to one entirely unused to such work, it came very hard. About three o'clock of that day, I broke down; my strength failed me; I was seized with a violent aching of the head, attended with extreme dizziness; I trembled in every limb. Finding what was coming, I nerved myself up, feeling it would never do to stop work. I stood as long as I could stagger to the hopper with grain. When I could stand no longer, I fell, and felt as if held down by some immense weight. The fan of course stopped; every one had his own work to do; and no one could do the work of the other, and have his own go on at the same time.

Mr. Covey was at the house, about one hundred yards from the tread-ing-yard where we were fanning. On hearing the fan stop, he left imme-diately, and came to the spot where we were. He hastily inquired what the matter was. Bill answered that I was sick, and there was no one to bring wheat to the fan. I had by this time crawled away under the side of the post and rail-fence by which the yard was enclosed, hoping to find relief by getting out of the sun. He then asked where I was. He was told by one of the hands. He came to the spot, and, after looking at me awhile, asked me what was the matter. I told him as well as I could, for I scarce had strength to speak. He then gave me a savage kick in the side, and told me to get up. I tried to do so, but fell back in the attempt. He gave me another kick, and again told me to rise. I again tried, and succeeded in gaining my feet; but, stooping to get to the tub with which I was feeding the fan, I again staggered and fell. While down in this situation, Mr. Covey took up the hickory slat with which Hughes had been striking off the half-bushel measure, and with it gave me a heavy blow upon the head, making a large wound, and the blood ran freely; and with this again told me to get up. I made no effort to comply, having now made up my mind to let him do his worst. In a short time after receiving this blow, my head grew better. Mr. Covey had now left me to my fate. At this moment I resolved, for the first time, to go to my master, enter a complaint, and ask his protection. In order to do this, I must that afternoon walk seven miles; and this, under the circumstances, was truly a severe undertaking. I was exceedingly feeble; made so as much by the kicks and blows which I received, as by the severe fit of sickness to which I had been subjected. I, however, watched my chance, while Covey was looking in an opposite direction, and started for St. Michael's. I suc-ceeded in getting a considerable distance on my way to the woods, when Covey discovered me, and called after me to come back, threatening what he would do if I did not come. I disregarded both his calls and his threats, and made my way to the woods as fast as my feeble state would allow; and thinking I might be overhauled by him if I kept the road, I walked through the woods, keeping far enough from the road to avoid detection, and near enough to prevent losing my way. I had not gone far before my little strength again failed me. I could go no farther. I fell down, and lay for a considerable time. The blood was yet oozing from the wound on my head. For a time I thought I should bleed to death; and think now that I should have done so, but that the blood so matted my hair as to stop the wound. After lying there about three quarters of an hour, I nerved myself up again, and started on my way, through bogs and briers, barefooted and bare-

headed, tearing my feet sometimes at nearly every step; and after a journey
of about seven miles, occupying some five hours to perform it, I arrived at
master's store. I then presented an appearance enough to affect any but a
heart of iron. From the crown of my head to my feet, I was covered with
blood. My hair was all clotted with dust and blood; my shirt was stiff with
blood. My legs and feet were torn in sundry places with briers and thorns,
and were also covered with blood. I suppose I looked like a man who had
escaped a den of wild beasts, and barely escaped them. In this state I
appeared before my master, humbly entreating him to interpose his authority for my protection. I told him all the circumstances as well as I could, and
it seemed, as I spoke, at times to affect him. He would then walk the floor,
and seek to justify Covey by saying he expected I deserved it. He asked me
what I wanted. I told him, to let me get a new home; that as sure as I lived
with Mr. Covey again, I should live with but to die with him; that Covey
would surely kill me; he was in a fair way for it. Master Thomas ridiculed
the idea that there was any danger of Mr. Covey's killing me, and said that
he knew Mr. Covey; that he was a good man, and that he could not think of
taking me from him; that, should he do so, he would lose the whole year's
wages; that I belonged to Mr. Covey for one year, and that I must go back to
him, come what might; and that I must not trouble him with any more
stories, or that he would himself *get hold of me*. After threatening me thus,
he gave me a very large dose of salts, telling me that I might remain in St.
Michael's that night, (it being quite late,) but that I must be off back to Mr.
Covey's early in the morning; and that if I did not, he would *get hold of me,*
which meant that he would whip me. I remained all night, and, according to
his orders, I started off to Covey's in the morning, (Saturday morning,)
wearied in body and broken in spirit. I got no supper that night, or breakfast
that morning. I reached Covey's about nine o'clock; and just as I was
getting over the fence that divided Mrs. Kemp's fields from ours, out ran
Covey with his cowskin, to give me another whipping. Before he could
reach me, I succeeded in getting to the cornfield; and as the corn was very
high, it afforded me the means of hiding. He seemed very angry, and
searched for me a long time. My behavior was altogether unaccountable.
He finally gave up the chase, thinking, I suppose, that I must come home for
something to eat; he would give himself no further trouble in looking for
me. I spent that day mostly in the woods, having the alternative before
me,—to go home and be whipped to death, or stay in the woods and be
starved to death. That night, I fell in with Sandy Jenkins, a slave with whom
I was somewhat acquainted. Sandy had a free wife who lived about four

miles from Mr. Covey's; and it being Saturday, he was on his way to see her. I told him my circumstances, and he very kindly invited me to go home with him. I went home with him, and talked this whole matter over, and got his advice as to what course it was best for me to pursue. I found Sandy an old adviser. He told me, with great solemnity, I must go back to Covey; but that before I went, I must go with him into another part of the woods, where there was a certain *root,* which, if I would take some of it with me, carrying it *always on my right side,* would render it impossible for Mr. Covey, or any other white man, to whip me. He said he had carried it for years; and since he had done so, he had never received a blow, and never expected to while he carried it. I at first rejected the idea, that the simple carrying of a root in my pocket would have any such effect as he had said, and was not disposed to take it; but Sandy impressed the necessity with much earnestness, telling me it could do no harm, if it did no good. To please him, I at length took the root, and, according to his direction, carried it upon my right side. This was Sunday morning. I immediately started for home; and upon entering the yard gate, out came Mr. Covey on his way to meeting. He spoke to me very kindly, bade me drive the pigs from a lot near by, and passed on towards the church. Now, this singular conduct of Mr. Covey really made me begin to think that there was something in the *root* which Sandy had given me; and had it been on any other day than Sunday, I could have attributed the conduct to no other cause than the influence of that root; and as it was, I was half inclined to think the *root* to be something more than I at first had taken it to be. All went well till Monday morning. On this morning, the virtue of the *root* was fully tested. Long before daylight, I was called to go and rub, curry, and feed, the horses. I obeyed, and was glad to obey. But whilst thus engaged, whilst in the act of throwing down some blades from the loft, Mr. Covey entered the stable with a long rope; and just as I was half out of the loft, he caught hold of my legs, and was about tying me. As soon as I found what he was up to, I gave a sudden spring, and as I did so, he holding to my legs, I was brought sprawling on the stable floor. Mr. Covey seemed now to think he had me, and could do what he pleased; but at this moment—from whence came the spirit I don't know—I resolved to fight; and, suiting my action to the resolution, I seized Covey hard by the throat; and as I did so, I rose. He held on to me, and I to him. My resistance was so entirely unexpected, that Covey seemed taken all aback. He trembled like a leaf. This gave me assurance, and I held him uneasy, causing the blood to run where I touched him with the ends of my fingers. Mr. Covey soon called out to Hughes for help. Hughes came, and, while Covey held me, attempted to tie my right hand. While he was in the act of doing so, I watched my chance, and gave him a heavy kick close under the ribs. This kick fairly sickened Hughes, so that he left me in the hands of Mr. Covey. This kick had the effect of not only weakening Hughes, but Covey also. When he saw Hughes bending over with pain, his courage quailed. He asked me if I meant to persist in my resistance. I told him I did, come what might; that he had used me like a brute for six months, and that I was determined to be used so no longer. With that, he strove to drag me to a stick that was lying just out of the stable door. He meant to knock me down. But just as he was leaning over to get the stick, I seized him with both hands by his collar, and brought him by a sudden snatch to the ground. By this time, Bill came. Covey called upon him for assistance. Bill wanted to know what he could do. Covey said, "Take hold of him, take hold of him!" Bill said his master hired him out to work, and not to help to whip me; so he left Covey and myself to fight our own battle out. We were at it for nearly two hours. Covey at length let me go, puffing and blowing at a great rate, saying that if I had not resisted, he would not have whipped me half so much. The truth was, that he had not whipped me at all. I considered him as getting entirely the worst end of the bargain; for he had drawn no blood from me, but I had from him. The whole six months afterwards, that I spent with Mr. Covey, he never laid the weight of his finger upon me in anger. He would occasionally say, he didn't want to get hold of me again. "No," thought I, "you need not; for you will come off worse than you did before."

This battle with Mr. Covey was the turning-point in my career as a slave. It rekindled the few expiring embers of freedom, and revived within me a sense of my own manhood. It recalled the departed self-confidence, and inspired me again with a determination to be free. The gratification afforded by the triumph was a full compensation for whatever else might follow, even death itself. He only can understand the deep satisfaction which I experienced, who has himself repelled by force the bloody arm of slavery. I felt as I never felt before. It was a glorious resurrection, from the tomb of slavery, to the heaven of freedom. My long-crushed spirit rose, cowardice departed, bold defiance took its place; and I now resolved that, however long I might remain a slave in form, the day had passed forever when I could be a slave in fact. I did not hesitate to let it be known of me, that the white man who expected to succeed in whipping, must also succeed in killing me.

From this time I was never again what might be called fairly whipped, though I remained a slave four years afterwards. I had several fights, but was never whipped.

It was for a long time a matter of surprise to me why Mr. Covey did not immediately have me taken by the constable to the whipping-post, and there regularly whipped for the crime of raising my hand against a white man in defence of myself. And the only explanation I can now think of does not entirely satisfy me; but such as it is, I will give it. Mr. Covey enjoyed the most unbounded reputation for being a first-rate overseer and negro-breaker. It was of considerable importance to him. That reputation was at stake; and had he sent me—a boy about sixteen years old—to the public whipping-post, his reputation would have been lost; so, to save his reputation, he suffered me to go unpunished.

My term of actual service to Mr. Edward Covey ended on Christmas day, 1833. The days between Christmas and New Year's day are allowed as holidays; and, accordingly, we were not required to perform any labor, more than to feed and take care of the stock. This time we regarded as our own, by the grace of our masters; and we therefore used or abused it nearly as we pleased. Those of us who had families at a distance, were generally allowed to spend the whole six days in their society. This time, however, was spent in various ways. The sober, staid, thinking and industrious ones of our number would employ themselves in making corn-brooms, mats, horse-collars, and baskets; and another class of us would spend the time in hunting opossums, hares, and coons. But by far the larger part engaged in such sports and merriments as ball playing, wrestling, running foot-races, fiddling, dancing, and drinking whisky; and this latter mode of spending the time was by far the most agreeable to the feelings of our masters. A slave who would work during the holidays was considered by our masters as scarcely deserving them. He was regarded as one who rejected the favor of his master. It was deemed a disgrace not to get drunk at Christmas; and he was regarded as lazy indeed, who had not provided himself with the necessary means, during the year, to get whisky enough to last him through Christmas.

From what I know of the effect of these holidays upon the slave, I believe them to be among the most effective means in the hands of the slaveholder in keeping down the spirit of insurrection. Were the slaveholders at once to abandon this practice, I have not the slightest doubt it would lead to an immediate insurrection among the slaves. These holidays serve as conductors, or safety-valves, to carry off the rebellious spirit of enslaved humanity. But for these, the slave would be forced up to the wildest desperation; and woe betide the slaveholder, the day he ventures to remove or hinder the operation of those conductors! I warn him that, in such an event, a spirit will go forth in their midst, more to be dreaded than the most appalling earthquake.

The holidays are part and parcel of the gross fraud, wrong, and inhumanity of slavery. They are professedly a custom established by the benevolence of the slaveholders; but I undertake to say, it is the result of selfishness, and one of the grossest frauds committed upon the down-trodden slave. They do not give the slaves this time because they would not like to have their work during its continuance, but because they know it would be unsafe to deprive them of it. This will be seen by the fact, that the slaveholders like to have their slaves spend those days just in such a manner as to make them as glad of their ending as of their beginning. Their object seems to be, to disgust their slaves with freedom, by plunging them into the lowest depths of dissipation. For instance, the slaveholders not only like to see the slave drink of his own accord, but will adopt various plans to make him drunk. One plan is, to make bets on their slaves, as to who can drink the most whisky without getting drunk; and in this way they succeed in getting whole multitudes to drink to excess. Thus, when the slave asks for virtuous freedom, the cunning slaveholder, knowing his ignorance, cheats him with a dose of vicious dissipation, artfully labelled with the name of liberty. The most of us used to drink it down, and the result was just what might be supposed: many of us were led to think that there was little to choose between liberty and slavery. We felt, and very properly too, that we had almost as well be slaves to man as to rum. So, when the holidays ended, we staggered up from the filth of our wallowing, took a long breath, and marched to the field,—feeling, upon the whole, rather glad to go, from what our master had deceived us into a belief was freedom, back to the arms of slavery.

I have said that this mode of treatment is a part of the whole system of fraud and inhumanity of slavery. It is so. The mode here adopted to disgust the slave with freedom, by allowing him to see only the abuse of it, is carried out in other things. For instance, a slave loves molasses; he steals some. His master, in many cases, goes off to town, and buys a large quantity; he returns, takes his whip, and commands the slave to eat the molasses, until the poor fellow is made sick at the very mention of it. The same mode is sometimes adopted to make the slaves refrain from asking for more food than their regular allowance. A slave runs through his allowance, and applies for more. His master is enraged at him; but, not willing to send him off without food, gives him more than is necessary, and compels him to eat it within a given time. Then, if he complains that he cannot eat it, he is said to be satisfied neither full nor fasting, and is whipped for being hard to please! I have an abundance of such illustrations of the same principle, drawn from my own observation, but think the cases I have cited sufficient. The practice is a very common one.

On the first of January, 1834, I left Mr. Covey, and went to live with Mr. William Freeland, who lived about three miles from St. Michael's. I soon found Mr. Freeland a very different man from Mr. Covey. Though not rich, he was what would be called an educated southern gentleman. Mr. Covey, as I have shown, was a well-trained negro-breaker and slave-driver. The former (slaveholder though he was) seemed to possess some regard for honor, some reverence for justice, and some respect for humanity. The latter seemed totally insensible to all such sentiments. Mr. Freeland had many of the faults peculiar to slaveholders, such as being very passionate and fretful; but I must do him the justice to say, that he was exceedingly free from those degrading vices to which Mr. Covey was constantly addicted. The one was open and frank, and we always knew where to find him. The other was a most artful deceiver, and could be understood only by such as were skilful enough to detect his cunningly-devised frauds. Another advantage I gained in my new master was, he made no pretensions to, or profession of, religion; and this, in my opinion, was truly a great advantage. I assert most unhesitatingly, that the religion of the south is a mere covering for the most horrid crimes,—a justifier of the most appalling barbarity,—a sanctifier of the most hateful frauds,—and a dark shelter, under which the darkest, foulest, grossest, and most infernal deeds of slaveholders find the strongest protection. Were I to be again reduced to the chains of slavery, next to that enslavement, I should regard being the slave of a religious master the greatest calamity that could befall me. For of all slaveholders with whom I have ever met, religious slaveholders are the worst. I have ever found them the meanest and basest, the most cruel and cowardly, of all others. It was my unhappy lot not only to belong to a religious slaveholder, but to live in a community of such religionists. Very near Mr. Freeland lived the Rev. Daniel Weeden, and in the same neighborhood lived the Rev. Rigby Hopkins. These were members and ministers in the Reformed Methodist Church. Mr. Weeden owned, among others, a woman slave, whose name I have forgotten. This woman's back, for weeks, was kept literally raw, made so by the lash of this merciless, *religious* wretch. He used to hire hands. His maxim was, Behave well or behave ill, it is the duty of a master occasionally to whip a slave, to remind him of his master's authority. Such was his theory, and such his practice.

Mr. Hopkins was even worse than Mr. Weeden. His chief boast was his ability to manage slaves. The peculiar feature of his government was that of whipping slaves in advance of deserving it. He always managed to have one or more of his slaves to whip every Monday morning. He did this to alarm their fears, and strike terror into those who escaped. His plan was to whip for the smallest offences, to prevent the commission of large ones. Mr. Hopkins could always find some excuse for whipping a slave. It would astonish one, unaccustomed to a slaveholding life, to see with what wonderful ease a slaveholder can find things, of which to make occasion to whip a slave. A mere look, word, or motion,—a mistake, accident, or want of power,—are all matters for which a slave may be whipped at any time. Does a slave look dissatisfied? It is said, he has the devil in him, and it must be whipped out. Does he speak loudly when spoken to by his master? Then he is getting high-minded, and should be taken down a button-hole lower. Does he forget to pull off his hat at the approach of a white person? Then he is wanting in reverence, and should be whipped for it. Does he ever venture to vindicate his conduct, when censured for it? Then he is guilty of impudence,—one of the greatest crimes of which a slave can be guilty. Does he ever venture to suggest a different mode of doing things from that pointed out by his master? He is indeed presumptuous, and getting above himself; and nothing less than a flogging will do for him. Does he, while ploughing, break a plough,—or, while hoeing, break a hoe? It is owing to his carelessness, and for it a slave must always be whipped. Mr. Hopkins could always find something of this sort to justify the use of the lash, and he seldom failed to embrace such opportunities. There was not a man in the whole county, with whom the slaves who had the privilege of getting their own home, would not prefer to live, rather than with this Rev. Mr. Hopkins. And yet there was not a man any where round, who made higher professions of religion, or was more active in revivals,—more attentive to the class, love-feast, prayer and preaching meetings, or more devotional in his family,— who prayed earlier, later, louder, and longer,—than this same reverend slave-driver, Rigby Hopkins.

But to return to Mr. Freeland, and to my experience while in his employment. He, like Mr. Covey, gave us enough to eat; but, unlike Mr. Covey, he also gave us sufficient time to take our meals. He worked us hard, but always between sunrise and sunset. He required a good deal of work to be done, but gave us good tools with which to work. His farm was large, but he employed hands enough to work it, and with ease, compared with many of his neighbors. My treatment, while in his employment, was heavenly, compared with what I experienced at the hands of Mr. Edward Covey.

Mr. Freeland was himself the owner of but two slaves. Their names were Henry Harris and John Harris. The rest of his hands he hired. These consisted of myself, Sandy Jenkins,* and Handy Caldwell. Henry and John were quite intelligent, and in a very little while after I went there, I succeeded in creating in them a strong desire to learn how to read. This desire soon sprang up in the others also. They very soon mustered up some old spelling-books, and nothing would do but that I must keep a Sabbath school. I agreed to do so, and accordingly devoted my Sundays to teaching these my loved fellow-slaves how to read. Neither of them knew his letters when I went there. Some of the slaves of the neighboring farms found what was going on, and also availed themselves of this little opportunity to learn to read. It was understood, among all who came, that there must be as little display about it as possible. It was necessary to keep our religious masters at St. Michael's unacquainted with the fact, that, instead of spending the Sabbath in wrestling, boxing, and drinking whisky, we were trying to learn how to read the will of God; for they had much rather see us engaged in those degrading sports, than to see us behaving like intellectual, moral, and accountable beings. My blood boils as I think of the bloody manner in which Messrs. Wright Fairbanks and Garrison West, both class-leaders, in connection with many others, rushed in upon us with sticks and stones, and broke up our virtuous little Sabbath school, at St. Michael's—all calling themselves Christians! humble followers of the Lord Jesus Christ! But I am again digressing.

I held my Sabbath school at the house of a free colored man, whose name I deem it imprudent to mention; for should it be known, it might embarrass him greatly, though the crime of holding the school was committed ten years ago. I had at one time over forty scholars, and those of the right sort, ardently desiring to learn. They were of all ages, though mostly men and women. I look back to those Sundays with an amount of pleasure not to be expressed. They were great days to my soul. The work of instructing my dear fellow-slaves was the sweetest engagement with which I was ever blessed. We loved each other, and to leave them at the close of the Sabbath was a severe cross indeed. When I think that these precious souls are to-day

---

* This is the same man who gave me the roots to prevent my being whipped by Mr. Covey. He was "a clever soul." We used frequently to talk about the fight with Covey, and as often as we did so, he would claim my success as the result of the roots which he gave me. This superstition is very common among the more ignorant slaves. A slave seldom dies but that his death is attributed to trickery.

shut up in the prison-house of slavery, my feelings overcome me, and I am almost ready to ask, "Does a righteous God govern the universe? and for what does he hold the thunders in his right hand, if not to smite the oppressor, and deliver the spoiled out of the hand of the spoiler?" These dear souls came not to Sabbath school because it was popular to do so, nor did I teach them because it was reputable to be thus engaged. Every moment they spent in that school, they were liable to be taken up, and given thirty-nine lashes. They came because they wished to learn. Their minds had been starved by their cruel masters. They had been shut up in mental darkness. I taught them, because it was the delight of my soul to be doing something that looked like bettering the condition of my race. I kept up my school nearly the whole year I lived with Mr. Freeland; and, beside my Sabbath school, I devoted three evenings in the week, during the winter, to teaching the slaves at home. And I have the happiness to know, that several of those who came to the Sabbath school learned how to read; and that one, at least, is now free through my agency.

The year passed off smoothly. It seemed only about half as long as the year which preceded it. I went through it without receiving a single blow. I will give Mr. Freeland the credit of being the best master I ever had, *till I became my own master*. For the ease with which I passed the year, I was, however, somewhat indebted to the society of my fellow-slaves. They were noble souls; they not only possessed loving hearts, but brave ones. We were linked and interlinked with each other. I loved them with a love stronger than any thing I have experienced since. It is sometimes said that we slaves do not love and confide in each other. In answer to this assertion, I can say, I never loved any or confided in any people more than my fellow-slaves, and especially those with whom I lived at Mr. Freeland's. I believe we would have died for each other. We never undertook to do any thing, of any importance, without a mutual consultation. We never moved separately. We were one; and as much so by our tempers and dispositions, as by the mutual hardships to which we were necessarily subjected by our condition as slaves.

At the close of the year 1834, Mr. Freeland again hired me of my master, for the year 1835. But, by this time, I began to want to live *upon free land* as well as *with Freeland;* and I was no longer content, therefore, to live with him or any other slaveholder. I began, with the commencement of the year, to prepare myself for a final struggle, which should decide my fate one way or the other. My tendency was upward. I was fast approaching manhood, and year after year had passed, and I was still a slave. These thoughts roused me—I must do something. I therefore resolved that 1835 should not pass without witnessing an attempt, on my part, to secure my liberty. But I was not willing to cherish this determination alone. My fellow-slaves were dear to me. I was anxious to have them participate with me in this, my life-giving determination. I therefore, though with great prudence, commenced early to ascertain their views and feelings in regard to their condition, and to imbue their minds with thoughts of freedom. I bent myself to devising ways and means for our escape, and meanwhile strove, on all fitting occasions, to impress them with the gross fraud and inhumanity of slavery. I went first to Henry, next to John, then to the others. I found, in them all, warm hearts and noble spirits. They were ready to hear, and ready to act when a feasible plan should be proposed. This was what I wanted. I talked to them of our want of manhood, if we submitted to our enslavement without at least one noble effort to be free. We met often, and consulted frequently, and told our hopes and fears, recounted the difficulties, real and imagined, which we should be called on to meet. At times we were almost disposed to give up, and try to content ourselves with our wretched lot; at others, we were firm and un-bending in our determination to go. Whenever we suggested any plan, there was shrinking—the odds were fearful. Our path was beset with the greatest obstacles; and if we succeeded in gaining the end of it, our right to be free was yet questionable—we were yet liable to be returned to bondage. We could see no spot, this side of the ocean, where we could be free. We knew nothing about Canada. Our knowledge of the north did not extend farther than New York; and to go there, and be forever harassed with the frightful liability of being returned to slavery—with the certainty of being treated tenfold worse than before—the thought was truly a horrible one, and one which it was not easy to overcome. The case sometimes stood thus: At every gate through which we were to pass, we saw a watchman—at every ferry a guard—on every bridge a sentinel—and in every wood a patrol. We were hemmed in upon every side. Here were the difficulties, real or imag-ined—the good to be sought, and the evil to be shunned. On the one hand, there stood slavery, a stern reality, glaring frightfully upon us,—its robes already crimsoned with the blood of millions, and even now feasting itself greedily upon our own flesh. On the other hand, away back in the dim distance, under the flickering light of the north star, behind some craggy hill or snow-covered mountain, stood a doubtful freedom—half frozen—beck-oning us to come and share its hospitality. This in itself was sometimes enough to stagger us; but when we permitted ourselves to survey the road, we were frequently appalled. Upon either side we saw grim death, assuming the most horrid shapes. Now it was starvation, causing us to eat our own flesh;—now we were contending with the waves, and were drowned;—now we were overtaken, and torn to pieces by the fangs of the terrible bloodhound. We were stung by scorpions, chased by wild beasts, bitten by snakes, and finally, after having nearly reached the desired spot,—after swimming rivers, encountering wild beasts, sleeping in the woods, suffering hunger and nakedness,—we were overtaken by our pursuers, and, in our resistance, we were shot dead upon the spot! I say, this picture sometimes appalled us, and made us

> "rather bear those ills we had,
> Than fly to others, that we knew not of."

In coming to a fixed determination to run away, we did more than Patrick Henry, when he resolved upon liberty or death. With us it was a doubtful liberty at most, and almost certain death if we failed. For my part, I should prefer death to hopeless bondage.

Sandy, one of our number, gave up the notion, but still encouraged us. Our company then consisted of Henry Harris, John Harris, Henry Bailey, Charles Roberts, and myself. Henry Bailey was my uncle, and belonged to my master. Charles married my aunt: he belonged to my master's father-in-law, Mr. William Hamilton.

The plan we finally concluded upon was, to get a large canoe belonging to Mr. Hamilton, and upon the Saturday night previous to Easter holidays, paddle directly up the Chesapeake Bay. On our arrival at the head of the bay, a distance of seventy or eighty miles from where we lived, it was our purpose to turn our canoe adrift, and follow the guidance of the north star till we got beyond the limits of Maryland. Our reason for taking the water route was, that we were less liable to be suspected as runaways; we hoped to be regarded as fishermen; whereas, if we should take the land route, we should be subjected to interruptions of almost every kind. Any one having a white face, and being so disposed, could stop us, and subject us to examination.

The week before our intended start, I wrote several protections, one for each of us. As well as I can remember, they were in the following words:—

> "THIS is to certify that I, the undersigned, have given the bearer, my servant, full liberty to go to Baltimore, and spend the Easter holidays. Written with mine own hand, &c., 1835.
>   "WILLIAM HAMILTON,
>   "Near St. Michael's, in Talbot County, Maryland."

We were not going to Baltimore; but, in going up the bay, we went toward Baltimore, and these protections were only intended to protect us while on the bay.

As the time drew near for our departure, our anxiety became more and more intense. It was truly a matter of life and death with us. The strength of our determination was about to be fully tested. At this time, I was very active in explaining every difficulty, removing every doubt, dispelling every fear, and inspiring all with the firmness indispensable to success in our undertaking; assuring them that half was gained the instant we made the move; we had talked long enough; we were now ready to move; if not now, we never should be; and if we did not intend to move now, we had as well fold our arms, sit down, and acknowledge ourselves fit only to be slaves. This, none of us were prepared to acknowledge. Every man stood firm; and at our last meeting, we pledged ourselves afresh, and in the most solemn manner, that, at the time appointed, we would certainly start in pursuit of freedom. This was in the middle of the week, at the end of which we were to be off. We went, as usual, to our several fields of labor, but with bosoms highly agitated with thoughts of our truly hazardous undertaking. We tried to conceal our feelings as much as possible; and I think we succeeded very well.

After a painful waiting, the Saturday morning, whose night was to witness our departure, came. I hailed it with joy, bring what of sadness it might. Friday night was a sleepless one for me. I probably felt more anxious than the rest, because I was, by common consent, at the head of the whole affair. The responsibility of success or failure lay heavily upon me. The glory of the one, and the confusion of the other, were alike mine. The first two hours of that morning were such as I never experienced before, and hope never to again. Early in the morning, we went, as usual, to the field. We were spreading the manure; and all at once, while thus engaged, I was overwhelmed with an indescribable feeling, in the fulness of which I turned to Sandy, who was near by, and said, "We are betrayed!" "Well," said he, "that thought has this moment struck me." We said no more. I was never more certain of any thing.

The horn was blown as usual, and we went up from the field to the house for breakfast. I went for the form, more than for want of any thing to eat that morning. Just as I got to the house, in looking out at the lane gate, I saw four white men, with two colored men. The white men were on horseback, and the colored ones were walking behind, as if tied. I watched them a few moments till they got up to our lane gate. Here they halted, and tied the colored men to the gate-post. I was not yet certain as to what the matter was. In a few moments, in rode Mr. Hamilton, with a speed betokening great excitement. He came to the door, and inquired if Master William was in. He was told he was at the barn. Mr. Hamilton, without dismounting, rode up to the barn with extraordinary speed. In a few moments, he and Mr. Freeland returned to the house. By this time, the three constables rode up, and in great haste dismounted, tied their horses, and met Master William and Mr. Hamilton returning from the barn; and after talking awhile, they all walked up to the kitchen door. There was no one in the kitchen but myself and John. Henry and Sandy were up at the barn. Mr. Freeland put his head in at the door, and called me by my name, saying, there were some gentlemen at the door who wished to see me. I stepped to the door, and inquired what they wanted. They at once seized me, and, without giving me any satisfaction, tied me—lashing my hands closely together. I insisted upon knowing what the matter was. They at length said, that they had learned I had been in a "scrape," and that I was to be examined before my master; and if their information proved false, I should not be hurt.

In a few moments, they succeeded in tying John. They then turned to Henry, who had by this time returned, and commanded him to cross his hands. "I won't!" said Henry, in a firm tone, indicating his readiness to meet the consequences of his refusal. "Won't you?" said Tom Graham, the constable. "No, I won't!" said Henry, in a still stronger tone. With this, two of the constables pulled out their shining pistols, and swore, by their Creator, that they would make him cross his hands or kill him. Each cocked his pistol, and, with fingers on the trigger, walked up to Henry, saying, at the same time, if he did not cross his hands, they would blow his damned heart out. "Shoot me, shoot me!" said Henry; "you can't kill me but once. Shoot, shoot,—and be damned! *I won't be tied!*" This he said in a tone of loud defiance; and at the same time, with a motion as quick as lightning, he with one single stroke dashed the pistols from the hand of each constable. As he did this, all hands fell upon him, and, after beating him some time, they finally overpowered him, and got him tied.

During the scuffle, I managed, I know not how, to get my pass out, and, without being discovered, put it into the fire. We were all now tied; and just as we were to leave for Easton jail, Betsy Freeland, mother of William Freeland, came to the door with her hands full of biscuits, and divided them between Henry and John. She then delivered herself of a speech, to the following effect:—addressing herself to me, she said, *"You devil! You yellow devil!* it was you that put it into the heads of Henry and John to run away. But for you, you long-legged mulatto devil! Henry nor John would never have thought of such a thing." I made no reply, and was immediately hurried off towards St. Michael's. Just a moment previous to the scuffle with Henry, Mr. Hamilton suggested the propriety of making a search for the protections which he had understood Frederick had written for himself and the rest. But, just at the moment he was about carrying his proposal into effect, his aid was needed in helping to tie Henry; and the excitement attending the scuffle caused them either to forget, or to deem it unsafe, under the circumstances, to search. So we were not yet convicted of the intention to run away.

When we got about half way to St. Michael's, while the constables having us in charge were looking ahead, Henry inquired of me what he should do with his pass. I told him to eat it with his biscuit, and own nothing; and we passed the word around, *"Own nothing;"* and *"Own nothing!"* said we all. Our confidence in each other was unshaken. We were resolved to succeed or fail together, after the calamity had befallen us as much as before. We were now prepared for any thing. We were to be dragged that morning fifteen miles behind horses, and then to be placed in the Easton jail. When we reached St. Michael's, we underwent a sort of examination. We all denied that we ever intended to run away. We did this more to bring out the evidence against us, than from any hope of getting clear of being sold; for, as I have said, we were ready for that. The fact was, we cared but little where we went, so we went together. Our greatest concern was about separation. We dreaded that more than any thing this side of death. We found the evidence against us to be the testimony of one person; our master would not tell who it was; but we came to a unanimous decision among ourselves as to who their informant was. We were sent off to the jail at Easton. When we got there, we were delivered up to the sheriff, Mr. Joseph Graham, and by him placed in jail. Henry, John, and myself, were placed in one room together—Charles, and Henry Bailey, in another. Their object in separating us was to hinder concert.

We had been in jail scarcely twenty minutes, when a swarm of slave traders, and agents for slave traders, flocked into jail to look at us, and to ascertain if we were for sale. Such a set of beings I never saw before! I felt myself surrounded by so many fiends from perdition. A band of pirates never looked more like their father, the devil. They laughed and grinned over us, saying, "Ah, my boys! we have got you, haven't we?" And after taunting us in various ways, they one by one went into an examination of us, with intent to ascertain our value. They would impudently ask us if we would not like to have them for our masters. We would make them no answer, and leave them to find out as best they could. Then they would curse and swear at us, telling us that they could take the devil out of us in a very little while, if we were only in their hands.

While in jail, we found ourselves in much more comfortable quarters than we expected when we went there. We did not get much to eat, nor that which was very good; but we had a good clean room, from the windows of which we could see what was going on in the street, which was very much better than if we had been placed in one of the dark, damp cells. Upon the whole, we got along very well, so far as the jail and its keeper were concerned. Immediately after the holidays were over, contrary to all our expectations, Mr. Hamilton and Mr. Freeland came up to Easton, and took Charles, the two Henrys, and John, out of jail, and carried them home, leaving me alone. I regarded this separation as a final one. It caused me more pain than any thing else in the whole transaction. I was ready for any thing rather than separation. I supposed that they had consulted together, and had decided that, as I was the whole cause of the intention of the others to run away, it was hard to make the innocent suffer with the guilty; and that they had, therefore, concluded to take the others home, and sell me, as a warning to the others that remained. It is due to the noble Henry to say, he seemed almost as reluctant at leaving the prison as at leaving home to come to the prison. But we knew we should, in all probability, be separated, if we were sold; and since he was in their hands, he concluded to go peaceably home.

I was now left to my fate. I was all alone, and within the walls of a stone prison. But a few days before, and I was full of hope. I expected to have been safe in a land of freedom; but now I was covered with gloom, sunk down to the utmost despair. I thought the possibility of freedom was gone. I was kept in this way about one week, at the end of which, Captain Auld, my master, to my surprise and utter astonishment, came up, and took me out, with the intention of sending me, with a gentleman of his acquaintance, into Alabama. But, from some cause or other, he did not send me to Alabama, but concluded to send me back to Baltimore, to live again with his brother Hugh, and to learn a trade.

Thus, after an absence of three years and one month, I was once more permitted to return to my old home at Baltimore. My master sent me away, because there existed against me a very great prejudice in the community, and he feared I might be killed.

In a few weeks after I went to Baltimore, Master Hugh hired me to Mr.

William Gardner, an extensive ship-builder, on Fell's Point. I was put there to learn how to calk. It, however, proved a very unfavorable place for the accomplishment of this object. Mr. Gardner was engaged that spring in building two large man-of-war brigs, professedly for the Mexican government. The vessels were to be launched in the July of that year, and in failure thereof, Mr. Gardner was to lose a considerable sum; so that when I entered, all was hurry. There was no time to learn any thing. Every man had to do that which he knew how to do. In entering the ship-yard, my orders from Mr. Gardner were, to do whatever the carpenters commanded me to do. This was placing me at the beck and call of about seventy-five men. I was to regard all these as masters. Their word was to be my law. My situation was a most trying one. At times I needed a dozen pair of hands. I was called a dozen ways in the space of a single minute. Three or four voices would strike my ear at the same moment. It was—"Fred., come help me to cant this timber here."—"Fred., come carry this timber yonder."—"Fred., bring that roller here."—"Fred., go get a fresh can of water."—"Fred., come help saw off the end of this timber."—"Fred., go quick, and get the crowbar."—"Fred., hold on the end of this fall."—"Fred., go to the blacksmith's shop, and get a new punch."—"Hurra, Fred.! run and bring me a cold chisel."—"I say, Fred., bear a hand, and get up a fire as quick as lightning under that steam-box."—"Halloo, nigger! come, turn this grindstone."—"Come, come! move, move! and *bowse* this timber forward."—"I say, darky, blast your eyes, why don't you heat up some pitch?"—"Halloo! halloo! halloo!" (Three voices at the same time.) "Come here!—Go there!—Hold on where you are! Damn you, if you move, I'll knock your brains out!"

This was my school for eight months; and I might have remained there longer, but for a most horrid fight I had with four of the white apprentices, in which my left eye was nearly knocked out, and I was horribly mangled in other respects. The facts in the case were these: Until a very little while after I went there, white and black ship-carpenters worked side by side, and no one seemed to see any impropriety in it. All hands seemed to be very well satisfied. Many of the black carpenters were freemen. Things seemed to be going on very well. All at once, the white carpenters knocked off, and said they would not work with free colored workmen. Their reason for this, as alleged, was, that if free colored carpenters were encouraged, they would soon take the trade into their own hands, and poor white men would be thrown out of employment. They therefore felt called upon at once to put a stop to it. And, taking advantage of Mr. Gardner's necessities, they broke off, swearing they would work no longer, unless he would discharge his black carpenters. Now, though this did not extend to me in form, it did reach me in fact. My fellow-apprentices very soon began to feel it degrading to them to work with me. They began to put on airs, and talk about the "niggers" taking the country, saying we all ought to be killed; and, being encouraged by the journeymen, they commenced making my condition as hard as they could, by hectoring me around, and sometimes striking me. I, of course, kept the vow I made after the fight with Mr. Covey, and struck back again, regardless of consequences; and while I kept them from combining, I succeeded very well; for I could whip the whole of them, taking them separately. They, however, at length combined, and came upon me, armed with sticks, stones, and heavy handspikes. One came in front with a half brick. There was one at each side of me, and one behind me. While I was attending to those in front, and on either side, the one behind ran up with the handspike, and struck me a heavy blow upon the head. It stunned me. I fell, and with this they all ran upon me, and fell to beating me with their fists. I let them lay on for a while, gathering strength. In an instant, I gave a sudden surge, and rose to my hands and knees. Just as I did that, one of their number gave me, with his heavy boot, a powerful kick in the left eye. My eyeball seemed to have burst. When they saw my eye closed, and badly swollen, they left me. With this I seized the handspike, and for a time pursued them. But here the carpenters interfered, and I thought I might as well give it up. It was impossible to stand my hand against so many. All this took place in sight of not less than fifty white ship-carpenters, and not one interposed a friendly word; but some cried, "Kill the damned nigger! Kill him! kill him! He struck a white person." I found my only chance for life was in flight. I succeeded in getting away without an additional blow, and barely so; for to strike a white man is death by Lynch law,—and that was the law in Mr. Gardner's ship-yard; nor is there much of any other out of Mr. Gardner's ship-yard, within the bounds of the Slave States.

I went directly home, and told the story of my wrongs to Master Hugh; and I am happy to say of him, irreligious as he was, his conduct was heavenly, compared with that of his brother Thomas under similar circumstances. He listened attentively to my narration of the circumstances leading to the savage outrage, and gave many proofs of his strong indignation at it. The heart of my once overkind mistress was again melted into pity. My puffed-out eye and blood-covered face moved her to tears. She took a chair by me, washed the blood from my face, and, with a mother's tenderness, bound up my head, covering the wounded eye with a lean piece of fresh beef. It was almost compensation for my sufferings to witness, once more, a manifestation of kindness from this, my once affectionate old mistress. Master Hugh was very much enraged. He gave expression to his feelings by pouring out curses upon the heads of those who did the deed. As soon as I got a little the better of my bruises, he took me with him to Esquire Watson's, on Bond Street, to see what could be done about the matter. Mr. Watson inquired who saw the assault committed. Master Hugh told him it was done in Mr. Gardner's ship-yard, at mid-day, where there was a large company of men at work. "As to that," he said, "the deed was done, and there was no question as to who did it." His answer was, he could do nothing in the case, unless some white man would come forward and testify. He could issue no warrant on my word. If I had been killed in the presence of a thousand colored people, their testimony combined would have been insufficient to have arrested one of the murderers. Master Hugh, for once, was compelled to say this state of things was too bad. Of course, it was impossible to get any white man to volunteer his testimony in my behalf, and against the white young men. Even those who may have sympathized with me were not prepared to do this. It required a degree of courage unknown to them to do so; for just at that time, the slightest manifestation of humanity towards a colored person was denounced as abolitionism, and that name subjected its bearer to frightful liabilities. The watchwords of the bloody-minded in that region, and in those days, were, "Damn the abolitionists!" and "Damn the niggers!" There was nothing done, and probably nothing would have been done if I had been killed. Such was, and such remains, the state of things in the Christian city of Baltimore.

Master Hugh, finding he could get no redress, refused to let me go back again to Mr. Gardner. He kept me himself, and his wife dressed my wound till I was again restored to health. He then took me into the ship-yard of which he was foreman, in the employment of Mr. Walter Price. There I was immediately set to calking, and very soon learned the art of using my mallet and irons. In the course of one year from the time I left Mr. Gardner's, I was able to command the highest wages given to the most experienced calkers. I was now of some importance to my master. I was bringing him from six to seven dollars per week. I sometimes brought him nine dollars per week: my wages were a dollar and a half a day. After learning how to calk, I sought my own employment, made my own contracts, and collected the money which I earned. My pathway became much more smooth than before; my condition was now much more comfortable. When I could get no calking to do, I did nothing. During these leisure times, those old notions about freedom would steal over me again. When in Mr. Gardner's employment, I was kept in such a perpetual whirl of excitement, I could think of nothing, scarcely, but my life; and in thinking of my life, I almost forgot my liberty. I have observed this in my experience of slavery,—that whenever my condition was improved, instead of its increasing my contentment, it only increased my desire to be free, and set me to thinking of plans to gain my freedom. I have found that, to make a contented slave, it is necessary to make a thoughtless one. It is necessary to darken his moral and mental vision, and, as far as possible, to annihilate the power of reason. He must be able to detect no inconsistencies in slavery; he must be made to feel that slavery is right; and he can be brought to that only when he ceases to be a man.

I was now getting, as I have said, one dollar and fifty cents per day. I contracted for it; I earned it; it was paid to me; it was rightfully my own; yet, upon each returning Saturday night, I was compelled to deliver every cent of that money to Master Hugh. And why? Not because he earned it,—not because he had any hand in earning it,—not because I owed it to him,—nor because he possessed the slightest shadow of a right to it; but solely because he had the power to compel me to give it up. The right of the grim-visaged pirate upon the high seas is exactly the same.

CHAPTER XI.

I NOW come to that part of my life during which I planned, and finally succeeded in making, my escape from slavery. But before narrating any of the peculiar circumstances, I deem it proper to make known my intention not to state all the facts connected with the transaction. My reasons for pursuing this course may be understood from the following: First, were I to give a minute statement of all the facts, it is not only possible, but quite probable, that others would thereby be involved in the most embarrassing difficulties. Secondly, such a statement would most undoubtedly induce greater vigilance on the part of slaveholders than has existed heretofore among them; which would, of course, be the means of guarding a door whereby some dear brother bondman might escape his galling chains. I deeply regret the necessity that impels me to suppress any thing of importance connected with my experience in slavery. It would afford me great pleasure indeed, as well as materially add to the interest of my narrative, were I at liberty to gratify a curiosity, which I know exists in the minds of many, by an accurate statement of all the facts pertaining to my most fortunate escape. But I must deprive myself of this pleasure, and the curious of the gratification which such a statement would afford. I would allow myself to suffer under the greatest imputations which evil-minded men might suggest, rather than exculpate myself, and thereby run the hazard of closing the slightest avenue by which a brother slave might clear himself of the chains and fetters of slavery.

I have never approved of the very public manner in which some of our western friends have conducted what they call the *underground railroad,* but which, I think, by their open declarations, has been made most emphatically the *upperground railroad.* I honor those good men and women for their noble daring, and applaud them for willingly subjecting themselves to bloody persecution, by openly avowing their participation in the escape of slaves. I, however, can see very little good resulting from such a course, either to themselves or the slaves escaping; while, upon the other hand, I see and feel assured that those open declarations are a positive evil to the slaves remaining, who are seeking to escape. They do nothing towards enlightening the slave, whilst they do much towards enlightening the master. They stimulate him to greater watchfulness, and enhance his power to capture his slave. We owe something to the slaves south of the line as well as to those north of it; and in aiding the latter on their way to freedom, we should be careful to do nothing which would be likely to hinder the former from escaping from slavery. I would keep the merciless slaveholder profoundly ignorant of the means of flight adopted by the slave. I would leave him to imagine himself surrounded by myriads of invisible tormentors, ever ready to snatch from his infernal grasp his trembling prey. Let him be left to feel his way in the dark; let darkness commensurate with his crime hover over him; and let him feel that at every step he takes, in pursuit of the flying bondman, he is running the frightful risk of having his hot brains dashed out by an invisible agency. Let us render the tyrant no aid; let us not hold the light by which he can trace the footprints of our flying brother. But enough of this. I will now proceed to the statement of those facts, connected with my escape, for which I am alone responsible, and for which no one can be made to suffer but myself.

In the early part of the year 1838, I became quite restless. I could see no reason why I should, at the end of each week, pour the reward of my toil into the purse of my master. When I carried to him my weekly wages, he would, after counting the money, look me in the face with a robber-like fierceness, and ask, "Is this all?" He was satisfied with nothing less than the last cent. He would, however, when I made him six dollars, sometimes give me six cents, to encourage me. It had the opposite effect. I regarded it as a sort of admission of my right to the whole. The fact that he gave me any part of my wages was proof, to my mind, that he believed me entitled to the whole of them. I always felt worse for having received any thing; for I feared that the giving me a few cents would ease his conscience, and make him feel himself to be a pretty honorable sort of robber. My discontent grew upon me. I was ever on the look-out for means of escape; and, finding no direct means, I determined to try to hire my time, with a view of getting money with which to make my escape. In the spring of 1838, when Master Thomas came to Baltimore to purchase his spring goods, I got an opportunity, and applied to him to allow me to hire my time. He unhesitatingly refused my request, and told me this was another stratagem by which to escape. He told me I could go nowhere but that he could get me; and that, in the event of my running away, he should spare no pains in his efforts to catch me. He exhorted me to content myself, and be obedient. He told me, if I would be happy, I must lay out no plans for the future. He said, if I behaved myself properly, he would take care of me. Indeed, he advised me to complete thoughtlessness of the future, and taught me to depend solely upon him for happiness. He seemed to see fully the pressing necessity of setting aside my intellectual nature, in order to contentment in slavery. But in spite of him, and even in spite of myself, I continued to think, and to think about the injustice of my enslavement, and the means of escape.

About two months after this, I applied to Master Hugh for the privilege of hiring my time. He was not acquainted with the fact that I had applied to Master Thomas, and had been refused. He too, at first, seemed disposed to refuse; but, after some reflection, he granted me the privilege, and proposed the following terms: I was to be allowed all my time, make all contracts with those for whom I worked, and find my own employment; and, in return for this liberty, I was to pay him three dollars at the end of each week, find myself in calking tools, and in board and clothing. My board was two dollars and a half per week. This, with the wear and tear of clothing and calking tools, made my regular expenses about six dollars per week. This amount I was compelled to make up, or relinquish the privilege of hiring my time. Rain or shine, work or no work, at the end of each week the money must be forthcoming, or I must give up my privilege. This arrangement, it will be perceived, was decidedly in my master's favor. It relieved him of all need of looking after me. His money was sure. He received all the benefits of slaveholding without its evils; while I endured all the evils of a slave, and suffered all the care and anxiety of a freeman. I found it a hard bargain. But, hard as it was, I thought it better than the old mode of getting along. It was a step towards freedom to be allowed to bear the responsibilities of a freeman, and I was determined to hold on upon it. I bent myself to the work of making money. I was ready to work at night as well as day, and by the most untiring perseverance and industry, I made enough to meet my expenses, and lay up a little money every week. I went on thus from May till August. Master Hugh then refused to allow me to hire my time longer. The ground for his refusal was a failure on my part, one Saturday night, to pay him for my week's time. This failure was occasioned by my attending a camp meeting about ten miles from Baltimore. During the week, I had entered into an engagement with a number of young friends to start from Baltimore to the camp ground early Saturday evening; and being detained by my employer, I was unable to go down to Master Hugh's without disappointing the company. I knew that Master Hugh was in no special need of the money that night. I therefore decided to go to camp meeting, and upon my return to pay him the three dollars. I staid at the camp meeting one day longer than I intended when I left. But as soon as I returned, I called upon him to pay him what he considered his due. I found him very angry; he could scarce restrain his wrath. He said he had a great mind to give me a severe whipping. He wished to know how I dared go out of the city without asking his permission. I told him I hired my time, and while I paid him the price which he asked for it, I did not know that I was bound to ask him when and where I should go. This reply troubled him; and, after reflecting a few moments, he turned to me, and said I should hire my time no longer; the next thing he should know of, I would be running away. Upon the same plea, he told me to bring my tools and clothing home forthwith. I did so; but instead of seeking work, as I had been accustomed to do previously to hiring my time, I spent the whole week without the performance of a single stroke of work. I did this in retaliation. Saturday night, he called upon me as usual for my week's wages. I told him I had no wages; I had done no work that week. Here we were upon the point of coming to blows. He raved, and swore his determination to get hold of me. I did not allow myself a single word; but was resolved, if he laid the weight of his hand upon me, it should be blow for blow. He did not strike me, but told me that he would find me in constant employment in future. I thought the matter over during the next day, Sunday, and finally resolved upon the third day of September, as the day upon which I would make a second attempt to secure my freedom. I now had three weeks during which to prepare for my journey. Early on Monday morning, before Master Hugh had time to make any engagement for me, I went out and got employment of Mr. Butler, at his ship-yard near the drawbridge, upon what is called the City Block, thus making it unnecessary for him to seek employment for me. At the end of the week, I brought him between eight and nine dollars. He seemed very well pleased, and asked me why I did not do the same the week before. He little knew what my plans were. My object in working steadily was to remove any suspicion he might entertain of my intent to run away; and in this I succeeded admirably. I suppose he thought I was never better satisfied with my condition than at the very time during which I was planning my escape. The second week passed, and again I carried him my full wages; and so well pleased was he, that he gave me twenty-five cents, (quite a large sum for a slaveholder to give a slave,) and bade me to make good use of it. I told him I would.

Things went on without very smoothly indeed, but within there was trouble. It is impossible for me to describe my feelings as the time of my contemplated start drew near. I had a number of warm-hearted friends in Baltimore,—friends that I loved almost as I did my life,—and the thought of being separated from them forever was painful beyond expression. It is my opinion that thousands would escape from slavery, who now remain, but for the strong cords of affection that bind them to their friends. The thought of leaving my friends was decidedly the most painful thought with which I had to contend. The love of them was my tender point, and shook my decision more than all things else. Besides the pain of separation, the dread and apprehension of a failure exceeded what I had experienced at my first attempt. The appalling defeat I then sustained returned to torment me. I felt assured that, if I failed in this attempt, my case would be a hopeless one—it would seal my fate as a slave forever. I could not hope to get off with any thing less than the severest punishment, and being placed beyond the means of escape. It required no very vivid imagination to depict the most frightful scenes through which I should have to pass, in case I failed. The wretchedness of slavery, and the blessedness of freedom, were perpetually before me. It was life and death to me. But I remained firm, and, according to my resolution, on the third day of September, 1838, I left my chains, and succeeded in reaching New York without the slightest interruption of any kind. How I did so,—what means I adopted,—in what direction I travelled, and by what mode of conveyance,—I must leave unexplained, for the reasons before mentioned.

I have been frequently asked how I felt when I found myself in a free State. I have never been able to answer the question with any satisfaction to myself. It was a moment of the highest excitement I ever experienced. I suppose I felt as one may imagine the unarmed mariner to feel when he is rescued by a friendly man-of-war from the pursuit of a pirate. In writing to a dear friend, immediately after my arrival at New York, I said I felt like one who had escaped a den of hungry lions. This state of mind, however, very soon subsided; and I was again seized with a feeling of great insecurity and loneliness. I was yet liable to be taken back, and subjected to all the tortures of slavery. This in itself was enough to damp the ardor of my enthusiasm. But the loneliness overcame me. There I was in the midst of thousands, and yet a perfect stranger; without home and without friends, in the midst of thousands of my own brethren—children of a common Father, and yet I dared not unfold to any one of them my sad condition. I was afraid to speak to any one for fear of speaking to the wrong one, and thereby falling into the hands of money-loving kidnappers, whose business it was to lie in wait for the panting fugitive, as the ferocious beasts of the forest lie in wait for their prey. The motto which I adopted when I started from slavery was this—"Trust no man!" I saw in every white man an enemy, and in almost every colored man cause for distrust. It was a most painful situation; and, to understand it, one must needs experience it, or imagine himself in similar circumstances. Let him be a fugitive slave in a strange land—a land given up to be the hunting-ground for slaveholders—whose inhabitants are legalized kidnappers—where he is every moment subjected to the terrible liability of being seized upon by his fellow-men, as the hideous crocodile seizes upon his prey!—I say, let him place himself in my situation—without home or friends—without money or credit—wanting shelter, and no one to give it—wanting bread, and no money to buy it,—and at the same time let him feel that he is pursued by merciless men-hunters, and in total darkness as to what to do, where to go, or where to stay,—perfectly helpless both as to the means of defence and means of escape,—in the midst of plenty, yet suffering the terrible gnawings of hunger,—in the midst of houses, yet having no home,—among fellow-men, yet feeling as if in the midst of wild beasts, whose greediness to swallow up the trembling and half-famished fugitive is only equalled by that with which the monsters of the deep swallow up the helpless fish upon which they subsist,—I say, let him be placed in this most trying situation,—the situation in which I was placed,—then, and not till then, will he fully appreciate the hardships of, and know how to sympathize with, the toil-worn and whip-scarred fugitive slave.

Thank Heaven, I remained but a short time in this distressed situation. I was relieved from it by the humane hand of Mr. DAVID RUGGLES, whose vigilance, kindness, and perseverance, I shall never forget. I am glad of an opportunity to express, as far as words can, the love and gratitude I bear him. Mr. Ruggles is now afflicted with blindness, and is himself in need of the same kind offices which he was once so forward in the performance of toward others. I had been in New York but a few days, when Mr. Ruggles sought me out, and very kindly took me to his boarding-house at the corner of Church and Lespenard Streets. Mr. Ruggles was then very deeply engaged in the memorable *Darg* case, as well as attending to a number of other fugitive slaves, devising ways and means for their successful escape; and, though watched and hemmed in on almost every side, he seemed to be more than a match for his enemies.

Very soon after I went to Mr. Ruggles, he wished to know of me where I wanted to go; as he deemed it unsafe for me to remain in New York. I told him I was a calker, and should like to go where I could get work. I thought of going to Canada; but he decided against it, and in favor of my going to New Bedford, thinking I should be able to get work there at my trade. At this time, Anna,* my intended wife, came on; for I wrote to her immediately after my arrival at New York, (notwithstanding my homeless, houseless, and helpless condition,) informing her of my successful flight, and wishing her to come on forthwith. In a few days after her arrival, Mr. Ruggles called in the Rev. J. W. C. Pennington, who, in the presence of Mr. Ruggles, Mrs. Michaels, and two or three others, performed the marriage ceremony, and gave us a certificate, of which the following is an exact copy:—

> "THIS may certify, that I joined together in holy matrimony Frederick Johnson[†] and Anna Murray, as man and wife, in the presence of Mr. David Ruggles and Mrs. Michaels.
>
> "JAMES W. C. PENNINGTON.
>
> "*New York, Sept.* 15, 1838."

Upon receiving this certificate, and a five-dollar bill from Mr. Ruggles, I shouldered one part of our baggage, and Anna took up the other, and we set out forthwith to take passage on board of the steamboat John W. Richmond for Newport, on our way to New Bedford. Mr. Ruggles gave me letter to a Mr. Shaw in Newport, and told me, in case my money did not serve me to New Bedford, to stop in Newport and obtain further assistance; but upon our arrival at Newport, we were so anxious to get to a place of safety, that, notwithstanding we lacked the necessary money to pay our fare, we decided to take seats in the stage, and promise to pay when we got to New Bedford. We were encouraged to do this by two excellent gentlemen, residents of

* She was free.
† I had changed my name from Frederick *Bailey* to that of *Johnson*.

New Bedford, whose names I afterward ascertained to be Joseph Ricketson and Willam C. Taber. They seemed at once to understand our circumstances, and gave us such assurance of their friendliness as put us fully at ease in their presence. It was good indeed to meet with such friends, at such a time. Upon reaching New Bedford, we were directed to the house of Mr. Nathan Johnson, by whom we were kindly received, and hospitably provided for. Both Mr. and Mrs. Johnson took a deep and lively interest in our welfare. They proved themselves quite worthy of the name of abolitionists. When the stage-driver found us unable to pay our fare, he held on upon our baggage as security for the debt. I had but to mention the fact to Mr. Johnson, and he forthwith advanced the money.

We now began to feel a degree of safety, and to prepare ourselves for the duties and responsibilities of a life of freedom. On the morning after our arrival at New Bedford, while at the breakfast-table, the question arose as to what name I should be called by. The name given me by my mother was, "Frederick Augustus Washington Bailey." I, however, had dispensed with the two middle names long before I left Maryland so that I was generally known by the name of "Frederick Bailey." I started from Baltimore bearing the name of "Stanley." When I got to New York, I again changed my name to "Frederick Johnson," and thought that would be the last change. But when I got to New Bedford, I found it necessary again to change my name. The reason of this necessity was, that there were so many Johnsons in New Bedford, it was already quite difficult to distinguish between them. I gave Mr. Johnson the privilege of choosing me a name, but told him he must not take from me the name of "Frederick." I must hold on to that, to preserve a sense of my identity. Mr. Johnson had just been reading the "Lady of the Lake," and at once suggested that my name be "Douglass." From that time until now I have been called "Frederick Douglass;" and as I am more widely known by that name than by any of the others, I shall continue to use it as my own.

I was quite disappointed at the general appearance of things in New Bedford. The impression which I had received respecting the character and condition of the people of the north, I found to be singularly erroneous. I had very strangely supposed, while in slavery, that few of the comforts, and scarcely any of the luxuries, of life were enjoyed at the north, compared with what were enjoyed by the slaveholders of the south. I probably came to this conclusion from the fact that northern people owned no slaves. I supposed that they were about upon a level with the non-slaveholding population of the south. I knew *they* were exceedingly poor, and I had been accustomed to regard their poverty as the necessary consequence of their being non-slaveholders. I had somehow imbibed the opinion that, in the absence of slaves, there could be no wealth, and very little refinement. And upon coming to the north, I expected to meet with a rough, hard-handed, and uncultivated population, living in the most Spartan-like simplicity, knowing nothing of the ease, luxury, pomp, and grandeur of southern slaveholders. Such being my conjectures, any one acquainted with the appearance of New Bedford may very readily infer how palpably I must have seen my mistake.

In the afternoon of the day when I reached New Bedford, I visited the wharves, to take a view of the shipping. Here I found myself surrounded with the strongest proofs of wealth. Lying at the wharves, and riding in the stream, I saw many ships of the finest model, in the best order, and of the largest size. Upon the right and left, I was walled in by granite warehouses of the widest dimensions, stowed to their utmost capacity with the necessaries and comforts of life. Added to this, almost every body seemed to be at work, but noiselessly so, compared with what I had been accustomed to in Baltimore. There were no loud songs heard from those engaged in loading and unloading ships. I heard no deep oaths or horrid curses on the laborer. I saw no whipping of men; but all seemed to go smoothly on. Every man appeared to understand his work, and went at it with a sober, yet cheerful earnestness, which betokened the deep interest which he felt in what he was doing, as well as a sense of his own dignity as a man. To me this looked exceedingly strange. From the wharves I strolled around and over the town, gazing with wonder and admiration at the splendid churches, beautiful dwellings, and finely-cultivated gardens; evincing an amount of wealth, comfort, taste, and refinement, such as I had never seen in any part of slaveholding Maryland.

Every thing looked clean, new, and beautiful. I saw few or no dilapidated houses, with poverty-stricken inmates; no half-naked children and barefooted women, such as I had been accustomed to see in Hillsborough, Easton, St. Michael's, and Baltimore. The people looked more able, stronger, healthier, and happier, than those of Maryland. I was for once made glad by a view of extreme wealth, without being saddened by seeing extreme poverty. But the most astonishing as well as the most interesting thing to me was the condition of the colored people, a great many of whom, like myself, had escaped thither as a refuge from the hunters of men. I found many, who had not been seven years out of their chains, living in finer houses, and evidently enjoying more of the comforts of life, than the average of slaveholders in Maryland. I will venture to assert that my friend Mr. Nathan Johnson (of whom I can say with a grateful heart, "I was hungry, and he gave me meat; I was thirsty, and he gave me drink; I was a stranger, and he took me in") lived in a neater house; dined at a better table; took, paid for, and read, more newspapers; better understood the moral, religious, and political character of the nation,—than nine tenths of the slaveholders in Talbot county, Maryland. Yet Mr. Johnson was a working man. His hands were hardened by toil, and not his alone, but those also of Mrs. Johnson. I found the colored people much more spirited than I had supposed they would be. I found among them a determination to protect each other from the blood-thirsty kidnapper, at all hazards. Soon after my arrival, I was told of a circumstance which illustrated their spirit. A colored man and a fugitive slave were on unfriendly terms. The former was heard to threaten the latter with informing his master of his whereabouts. Straightway a meeting was called among the colored people, under the stereotyped notice, "Business of importance!" The betrayer was invited to attend. The people came at the appointed hour, and organized the meeting by appointing a very religious old gentleman as president, who, I believe, made a prayer, after which he addressed the meeting as follows: *"Friends, we have got him here, and I would recommend that you young men just take him outside the door, and kill him!"* With this, a number of them bolted at him; but they were intercepted by some more timid than themselves, and the betrayer escaped their vengeance, and has not been seen in New Bedford since. I believe there have been no more such threats, and should there be hereafter, I doubt not that death would be the consequence.

I found employment, the third day after my arrival, in stowing a sloop with a load of oil. It was new, dirty, and hard work for me; but I went at it with a glad heart and a willing hand. I was now my own master. It was a happy moment, the rapture of which can be understood only by those who have been slaves. It was the first work, the reward of which was to be entirely my own. There was no Master Hugh standing ready, the moment I earned the money, to rob me of it. I worked that day with a pleasure I had never before experienced. I was at work for myself and my newly-married wife. It was to me the starting-point of a new existence. When I got through with that job, I went in pursuit of a job of calking; but such was the strength of prejudice against color, among the white calkers, that they refused to work with me, and of course I could get no employment.* Finding my trade of no immediate benefit, I threw off my calking habiliments, and prepared

* I am told that colored persons can now get employment at calking in New Bedford—a result of anti-slavery effort.

myself to do any kind of work I could get to do. Mr. Johnson kindly let me
have his wood-horse and saw, and I very soon found myself a plenty of
work. There was no work too hard—none too dirty. I was ready to saw
wood, shovel coal, carry the hod, sweep the chimney, or roll oil casks,—all
of which I did for nearly three years in New Bedford, before I became
known to the anti-slavery world.

In about four months after I went to New Bedford, there came a
young man to me, and inquired if I did not wish to take the "Liberator." I
told him I did; but, just having made my escape from slavery, I remarked
that I was unable to pay for it then. I, however, finally became a sub-
scriber to it. The paper came, and I read it from week to week with such
feelings as it would be quite idle for me to attempt to describe. The paper
became my meat and my drink. My soul was set all on fire. Its sympathy
for my brethren in bonds—its scathing denunciations of slaveholders—
its faithful exposures of slavery—and its powerful attacks upon the up-
holders of the institution—sent a thrill of joy through my soul, such as I
had never felt before!

I had not long been a reader of the "Liberator," before I got a pretty
correct idea of the principles, measures, and spirit of the anti-slavery reform. I took right hold of the cause. I could do but little; but what I could, I
did with a joyful heart, and never felt happier than when in an anti-slavery
meeting. I seldom had much to say at the meetings, because what I wanted
to say was said so much better by others. But, while attending an anti-
slavery convention at Nantucket, on the 11th of August, 1841, I felt
strongly moved to speak, and was at the same time much urged to do so by
Mr. William C. Coffin, a gentleman who had heard me speak in the colored
people's meeting at New Bedford. It was a severe cross, and I took it up
reluctantly. The truth was, I felt myself a slave, and the idea of speaking to
white people weighed me down. I spoke but a few moments, when I felt a
degree of freedom, and said what I desired with considerable ease. From
that time until now, I have been engaged in pleading the cause of my
brethren—with what success, and with what devotion, I leave those acquainted with my labors to decide.

A P P E N D I X.

I FIND, on reading over the foregoing Narrative that I have, in several
instances, spoken in such a tone and manner, respecting religion, as may

possibly lead those unacquainted with my religious views to suppose me an opponent of all religion. To remove the liability to such misapprehension, I deem it proper to append the following brief explanation. What I have said respecting and against religion, I mean strictly to apply to the *slaveholding religion* of this land, and with no reference whatever to Christianity proper; for, between the Christianity of this land, and the Christianity of Christ, I recognize the widest possible difference—so wide, that to receive the one as good, pure, and holy, is of necessity to reject the other as bad, corrupt, and wicked. To be the friend of the one, is of necessity to be the enemy of the other. I love the pure, peaceable, and impartial Christianity of Christ: I therefore hate the corrupt, slaveholding, women-whipping, cradle-plundering, partial and hypocritical Christianity of this land. Indeed, I can see no reason, but the most deceitful one, for calling the religion of this land Christianity. I look upon it as the climax of all misnomers, the boldest of all frauds, and the grossest of all libels. Never was there a clearer case of "stealing the livery of the court of heaven to serve the devil in." I am filled with unutterable loathing when I contemplate the religious pomp and show, together with the horrible inconsistencies, which every where surround me. We have men-stealers for ministers, women-whippers for missionaries, and cradle-plunderers for church members. The man who wields the blood-clotted cowskin during the week fills the pulpit on Sunday, and claims to be a minister of the meek and lowly Jesus. The man who robs me of my earnings at the end of each week meets me as a class-leader on Sunday morning, to show me the way of life, and the path of salvation. He who sells my sister, for purposes of prostitution, stands forth as the pious advocate of purity. He who proclaims it a religious duty to read the Bible denies me the right of learning to read the name of the God who made me. He who is the religious advocate of marriage robs whole millions of its sacred influence, and leaves them to the ravages of wholesale pollution. The warm defender of the sacredness of the family relation is the same that scatters whole families,—sundering husbands and wives, parents and children, sisters and brothers,—leaving the hut vacant, and the hearth desolate. We see the thief preaching against theft, and the adulterer against adultery. We have men sold to build churches, women sold to support the gospel, and babes sold to purchase Bibles for the *poor heathen! all for the glory of God and the good of souls!* The slave auctioneer's bell and the church-going bell chime in with each other, and the bitter cries of the heart-broken slave are drowned in the religious shouts of his pious master. Revivals of religion and revivals in the slave-trade go hand in hand together. The slave prison and the church stand near each other. The clanking of fetters and the rattling of chains in the prison, and the pious psalm and solemn prayer in the church, may be heard at the same time. The dealers in the bodies and souls of men erect their stand in the presence of the pulpit, and they mutually help each other. The dealer gives his blood-stained gold to support the pulpit, and the pulpit, in return, covers his infernal business with the garb of Christianity. Here we have religion and robbery the allies of each other; slavery and piety linked and interlinked; preachers of the gospel united with slaveholders! A horrible sight, to see devils dressed in angels' robes, and hell presenting the semblance of paradise.

> "Just God! and these are they,
>   Who minister at thine altar, God of right!
> Men who their hands, with prayer and blessing, lay
>   On Israel's ark of light.
>
> "What! preach, and kidnap men?
>   Give thanks, and rob thy own afflicted poor?
> Talk of thy glorious liberty, and then
>   Bolt hard the captive's door?
>
> "What! servants of thy own
>   Merciful Son, who came to seek and save
> The homeless and the outcast, fettering down
>   The tasked and plundered slave!
>
> "Pilate and Herod friends!
>   Chief priests and rulers, as of old, combine!
> Just God and holy! is that church which lends
>   Strength to the spoiler thine?"—*Whittier.*

The Christianity of America is a Christianity, of whose votaries it may be as truly said, as it was of the ancient scribes and Pharisees, "They bind heavy burdens, and grievous to be borne, and lay them on men's shoulders, but they themselves will not move them with one of their fingers. All their works they do for to be seen of men.—They love the uppermost rooms at feasts, and the chief seats in the synagogues, ... and to be called of men, Rabbi, Rabbi.—But woe unto you, scribes and Pharisees, hypocrites! for ye shut up the kingdom of heaven against men; for ye neither go in yourselves, neither suffer ye them that are entering to go in. Ye devour widows' houses, and for a pretence make long prayers; therefore ye shall receive the greater damnation. Ye compass sea and land to make one proselyte, and when he is made, ye make him twofold more the child of hell than your selves.—Woe unto you, scribes and Pharisees, hypocrites! for ye pay tithe of mint, and anise, and cumin, and have omitted the weightier matters of the law, judgment, mercy, and faith; these ought ye to have done, and not to leave the other undone. Ye blind guides! which strain at a gnat, and swallow a camel. Woe unto you, scribes and Pharisees, hypocrites! for ye make clean the outside of the cup and of the platter; but within, they are full of extortion and excess.—Woe unto you, scribes and Pharisees, hypocrites! for ye are like unto whited sepulchres, which indeed appear beautiful outward, but are within full of dead men's bones and of all uncleanness. Even so ye also outwardly appear righteous unto men, but within ye are full of hypocrisy and iniquity."

Dark and terrible as is this picture, I hold it to be strictly true of the overwhelming mass of professed Christians in America. They strain at a gnat, and swallow a camel. Could any thing be more true of our churches? They would be shocked at the proposition of fellowshipping a *sheep*-stealer; and at the same time they hug to their communion a *man*-stealer, and brand me with being an infidel, if I find fault with them for it. They attend with Pharisaical strictness to the outward forms of religion, and at the same time neglect the weightier matters of the law, judgment, mercy, and faith. They are always ready to sacrifice, but seldom to show mercy. These are they who are represented as professing to love God whom they have not seen, whilst they hate their brother whom they have seen. They love the heathen on the other side of the globe. They can pray for him, pay money to have the Bible put into his hand, and missionaries to instruct him; while they despise and totally neglect the heathen at their own doors.

Such is, very briefly, my view of the religion of this land; and to avoid any misunderstanding, growing out of the use of general terms, I mean, by the religion of this land, that which is revealed in the words, deeds, and actions, of those bodies, north and south, calling themselves Christian churches, and yet in union with slaveholders. It is against religion, as represented by these bodies, that I feel it my duty to testify.

I conclude these remarks by copying the following portrait of the religion of the south, (which is, by communion and fellowship, the religion of the north,) which I soberly affirm is "true to the life," and without caricature or the slightest exaggeration. It is said to have been drawn, several years before the present anti-slavery agitation began, by a northern Methodist preacher, who, while residing at the south, had an opportunity to see slaveholding morals, manners, and piety, with his own eyes. "Shall I not visit for these things? saith the Lord. Shall not my soul be avenged on such a nation as this?"

"A PARODY.
"Come, saints and sinners, hear me tell
How pious priests whip Jack and Nell,
And women buy and children sell,
And preach all sinners down to hell,
    And sing of heavenly union.

"They'll bleat and baa, dona like goats,
Gorge down black sheep, and strain at motes,
Array their backs in fine black coats,
Then seize their negroes by their throats,
    And choke, for heavenly union.

"They'll church you if you sip a dram,
And damn you if you steal a lamb;
Yet rob old Tony, Doll, and Sam,
Of human rights, and bread and ham;
    Kidnapper's heavenly union.

"They'll loudly talk of Christ's reward,
And bind his image with a cord,
And scold, and swing the lash abhorred,
And sell their brother in the Lord
    To handcuffed heavenly union.

"They'll read and sing a sacred song,
And make a prayer both loud and long,
And teach the right and do the wrong,
Hailing the brother, sister throng,
    With words of heavenly union.

"We wonder how such saints can sing,
Or praise the Lord upon the wing,
Who roar, and scold, and whip, and sting,
And to their slaves and mammon cling,
    In guilty conscience union.

"They'll raise tobacco, corn, and rye,
And drive, and thieve, and cheat, and lie,

And lay up treasures in the sky,
By making switch and cowskin fly,
   In hope of heavenly union.

"They'll crack old Tony on the skull,
And preach and roar like Bashan bull,
   Or braying ass, of mischief full,
   Then seize old Jacob by the wool,
      And pull for heavenly union.

"A roaring, ranting, sleek man-thief,
Who lived on mutton, veal, and beef,
   Yet never would afford relief
   To needy, sable sons of grief,
      Was big with heavenly union.

" 'Love not the world,' the preacher said,
And winked his eye, and shook his head;
   He seized on Tom, and Dick, and Ned,
Cut short their meat, and clothes, and bread,
      Yet still loved heavenly union.

"Another preacher whining spoke
Of One whose heart for sinners broke:
   He tied old Nanny to an oak,
   And drew the blood at every stroke,
      And prayed for heavenly union.

"Two others oped their iron jaws,
And waved their children-stealing paws;
   There sat their children in gewgaws;
   By stinting negroes' backs and maws,
      They kept up heavenly union.

"All good from Jack another takes,
And entertains their flirts and rakes,
   Who dress as sleek as glossy snakes,
And cram their mouths with sweetened cakes;
      And this goes down for union."

Sincerely and earnestly hoping that this little book may do something toward throwing light on the American slave system, and hastening the glad day of deliverance to the millions of my brethren in bonds—faithfully relying upon the power of truth, love, and justice, for success in my humble efforts—and solemnly pledging my self anew to the sacred cause,—I subscribe myself,

FREDERICK DOUGLASS.

LYNN, *Mass., April* 28, 1845.

THE END.

Textual Introduction

Gerald Fulkerson

This edition of Frederick Douglass's *Narrative* provides for the first time a definitive critical text. After critical reading and collation of potentially authoritative editions and impressions of the *Narrative* and analysis of external evidence, a copy-text has been carefully selected and emended in an effort to reflect Frederick Douglass's authorial intention. A four-part textual apparatus (Textual Notes, List of Emendations, Historical Collation, and Line-End Hyphenation) that documents the editor's choices and much of the data that informed them has been appended. To simplify both reading and quoting the text, a clear-text approach has been taken that relegates all editorial intervention to the appendix. In keeping with the desire to preserve the work as Douglass envisioned it, the text is unmodernized.

The first step in our work on the *Narrative* was to discover as much as possible about its somewhat complicated publication history. To develop a textual lineage, we searched extensively for texts and historical evidence and subsequently sight collated each potentially authoritative edition against the copy-text four times. In Douglass's lifetime the *Narrative* was published in four English-language editions as well being translated into Dutch and French.[1] The foreign-language editions are irrelevant to our effort to produce a critical text and may safely be set aside. Of the four English-language editions, the first was published in Boston and the other three in Great Britain, where Douglass sold copies of the *Narrative* for living expenses during his 1845–47 sojourn.

The first edition (B), published in Boston by the Massachusetts Anti-Slavery Society, entails seven essentially identical impressions printed between 1845 and 1853.[2] William Lloyd Garrison probably edited it, with Douglass maintaining authorial control. B's main text of 125 pages (including an eight-page polemic against religious hypocrisy on the slavery issue that Douglass offered as an "Appendix") is fronted by a "Preface" of ten pages written by Garrison and a "Letter from Wendell Phillips, Esq.," which runs nearly four pages. The second edition, which was self-published with full authorial control and printed in Dublin by Irish abolitionist Richard D. Webb, consists of two printings, the second of which

---

1. *Levensverhaal van Frederik Douglass, een' gewezen' slaaf (door hem zelven geschreven); Uit het Engelsch* (Rotterdam: H. A. Kramers, 1846); *Vie de Frédéric Douglass, esclave americain, écrite par lui-même, traduite de l'anglais par S.-K. Parkes* (Paris: Pagnerre, 1848).

2. The title pages of the impressions, with the exception of the publication year, are identical. The information on the title page of the first impression is as follows: Narrative / of the / Life / of / Frederick Douglass, / an / American Slave. / Written by Himself. / Boston / Published at the Anti-Slavery Office, / No. 25 Cornhill / 1845.

underwent significant revision. Published in late 1845 shortly after Douglass arrived in Dublin, the original printing (D1)[3] contained various alterations that include the addition of a preface written by Douglass, extensive changes in spelling and punctuation, new end matter (an endorsement of the work of the American Anti-Slavery Society headed "To the Friends of the Slave" and "Critical Notices" culled from American papers), and approximately sixty mostly minor substantive changes. The second printing (D2),[4] which Webb printed in February 1846, underwent additional revision: more spelling and punctuation changes appeared; two paragraphs were added to the preface Douglass had written for the first printing; new end matter was attached (the "Critical Notices" section was enlarged, and a published letter "refuting" some aspects of the *Narrative* by American A. C. C. Thompson was included with a response by Douglass); and about thirty changes in wording, most of them insignificant, were made. A third edition became necessary when Douglass hired a different printer, abolitionist and Chartist Joseph Barker, of Wortley, near Leeds, England, to replenish his supply of copies of the *Narrative*.[5] The first (E1) of two printings in this edition (the only one overseen by Barker) was published in the fall of 1846.[6] The extent of Douglass's oversight of Barker's work is problematical, but in view of his lecturing schedule the scrutiny probably was

3. The title page of the first impression of the Dublin edition differs somewhat from the title page of the Boston edition. It arrays the title a bit differently and contains eight lines from a poem by John Greenleaf Whittier: Narrative of the Life / of / Frederick Douglass, / an / American Slave. / Written by Himself. / What, ho!—our countrymen in chains! / The whip on *women's* shrinking flesh! / Our soil still reddening with the stains, / Caught from her scourging, warm and fresh! / What! mothers from their children riven! / What! God's own image bought and sold! / *Americans* to market driven, / And barter'd, as the brute, for gold!—*Whittier* / Dublin: / Webb and Chapman, GT. Brunswick-Street. / 1845.

4. The title page of the second impression of the Dublin edition differs from the title page of the first impression (see previous note) in two conventional ways: (1) after the lines from Whittier, the words "Second Dublin Edition" appear, and (2) the year of publication is printed as "1846."

5. Douglass wrote Barker a letter dated 22 September (no indication of year, but undoubtedly 1846) in which he informed him that he had "just entered into an agreement" with an engraver to have 2,500 copies of his portrait printed, 2,000 of which he would send to Barker within two weeks for use in "the forthcoming edition of my Narrative," (General Correspondence File, reel 8, frames 589–90, FD Papers, DLC). This is the only known correspondence between Douglass and Barker during the weeks before Barker's printing of the *Narrative*. Douglass's letter clearly implies a prior arrangement with Barker and gives the two impressions of the English edition (E1 and E2) an aura of potential authority. Unfortunately, there appears to be no evidence to help us estimate the amount and type of involvement Douglass may have had in the editing of E1.

6. The title page of E1 is identical to the title pages of the two Dublin impressions with regard to the arraying of title and author information and the lines from Whittier (see notes 3 and 4). Following the Whittier lines, the E1 title page contains the following lines: Third English Edition. / Wortley, near Leeds: Printed by Joseph Barker / 1846.

It should be noted that this edition was labeled by Barker the third English edition. Perhaps the best explanation is that Barker counted the two Dublin impressions as "English editions," making his the third. We have found no evidence of English editions published prior to E1.

not close. Barker set the new edition from D2 but incorporated spelling, punctuation, and minor substantive alterations. The most obvious change appears in the end matter, which was expanded by thirty-two pages to include a text of a speech that Douglass had delivered in Finsbury Chapel in London on 22 May 1846. The second printing of the third edition (E2) appeared in 1847,[7] probably after Douglass had embarked for the United States in April. A London printing firm, identified on the title page as R. Yorke Clarke and Co., printed the text without alteration from the plates that Barker had used. A fourth edition (L) was published in London in 1852 by the firm of "Somers & Isaac."[8] This edition, which was set from E without correction of its obvious compositorial errors, is devoid of authority.

This overview makes it clear that only the Boston and Dublin editions possess established authority. Our attention in this introduction will be directed mainly toward the two authoritative editions, but the substantive variants in all four of the English-language editions are reported in the historical collation apparatus.

When Douglass's home in Rochester, New York, burned in 1872, his manuscripts of the *Narrative* as well as any printer's copies that he may have retained were lost. Lacking prepublication forms of the text, therefore, we have chosen the first edition (B) of the *Narrative* as the copy-text. B is the appropriate copy-text because it undoubtedly retains more of the accidentals of Douglass's lost manuscript than do the other texts over which he exercised authorial control. That B retains more of Douglass's accidentals than either D1, D2, or E may be concluded on the general principle that each succeeding editorial processing of the work would inevitably insinuate an additional set of compositorial errors and unauthorized editorial alterations into the text. The *Narrative* text, as an American work passing through the hands of British editors and compositors, was particularly vulnerable to progressive corruption of its spelling and punctuation.

The case for B is strengthened by the fact that many of the changes in both accidentals and substantives in D1 and D2, and in accidentals in E (which adds no significant substantive variants to those found in D2, on which it is based), were adaptations to a literary and cultural milieu other than the one within which Douglass originally wrote. Although alterations in the authoritative British editions have been carefully considered, we have rejected those that seem incompatible with Douglass's fundamental goal of effectively presenting the story of his

7. The title page of E2 is identical to the E1 title page (see previous note) through the "Third English Edition." line. The subsequent lines are as follows: London: / R. Yorke Clarke and Co., / Successors to Harvey and Darton, / 55, Gracechurch Street. / MDCCCXLVII.

8. The title page of the last edition of the *Narrative,* the London edition (L), is arrayed like all of the other British editions through the Whittier lines (see note 3). The next lines are as follows: Sixth Edition / London: / Somers & Isaac, 67, Houndsditch / MDCCCLII.

This edition is identified on its title page as the sixth edition. The printer probably counted the American edition, the two impressions of the Dublin edition, and the two impressions of the English edition as five editions and so numbered his the sixth.

slavery experience to American readers, who constituted his original and primary audience. Both our selection of B as copy-text and our decision-making about potential emendations have been significantly controlled by the position that Douglass's "authorial intent" should be interpreted to refer to his strategic approach to the American, as opposed to the British, public.

Like most autobiographers, Douglass served a complex of purposes and needs in the telling of his story. He claims to have written the *Narrative,* however, as a rhetorical response to a situation that threatened his antislavery career. His career was at first energized and then threatened, ironically, by northerners' response to the quickness of mind, command of language, and poise that characterized his public speaking. By mid-1844, that platform virtuosity had begun to seem to an increasing number of nonabolitionists to be inconsistent with his claim to be a self-educated fugitive slave. Stalwart Philadelphia abolitionist J. Miller McKim, for instance, included a note of alarm in a letter to Garrison after hearing Douglass speak in his home city on 17 August 1844. McKim noted that "many persons in the audience seemed unable to credit the statements which he gave of himself, and could not believe that he was actually a slave. How a man, only six years out of bondage, and who had never gone to school a day in his life, could speak with such eloquence—with such precision of language and power of thought—they were utterly at a loss to devise."[9] When he wrote his second autobiography, *My Bondage and My Freedom,* in 1855, Douglass recalled that by violating the unflattering stereotype of fugitive slaves subscribed to by many northerners and by being reluctant to provide details about his twenty years in slavery, he had put himself "in a pretty fair way to be denounced as an imposter."[10]

In the fall of 1842 Douglass moved his pregnant wife, Anna, and his three children from New Bedford, Massachusetts, where he had lived since his escape from Baltimore in 1838, to Lynn, a town just north of Boston. Living in the environs of Boston, the capital of Garrisonian abolitionism, facilitated Douglass's association with Garrison and Wendell Phillips, his mentors, and provided assurance that his family would be watched after during his frequent absences from home. The most urgent motive for the move, however, probably was the sense that he needed an even safer haven as he wrote an autobiography whose publication could put at risk his freedom and his family's safety. Despite the risks involved, he could no longer avoid revealing the details of his experience in slavery, including the name that he had discarded shortly after reaching the North and the identities of his various masters.

Through the fall, winter, and early spring of 1844–45, Douglass limited his lecturing mainly to eastern Massachusetts in order to make sufficient time for his writing project. He apparently finished writing the body of the manuscript in mid-

9. J. Miller McKim to William Lloyd Garrison, 18 August 1844, in *Lib.,* 30 August 1844.
10. Frederick Douglass, *My Bondage and My Freedom* (New York, 1855), 362.

April. He dated completion of the "Appendix" as 28 April,[11] but a comment by Wendell Phillips in the "Letter" that he contributed to the *Narrative*'s front matter suggests that Douglass had finished the body of the manuscript at least two weeks earlier. In the letter, which he dated 22 April, Phillips emphasized that he had managed to remain ignorant of dangerous information about Douglass's past "till the other day when you read me your memoirs."[12] The mid-April estimate also is supported by the 1 May date on the ten-page "Preface" that Garrison contributed;[13] he must have had possession of a copy of the manuscript long enough to have assimilated it thoroughly before writing the preface. By 1 May, Garrison was probably well along in the process of editing the manuscript for publication.

In mid-May Garrison announced in the *Liberator* that the "long desired Narrative is now presented to the public, in a neat volume occupying 125 pages. . . . The edition is going off rapidly." Garrison included a few excerpts in his announcement and promised more in future issues in the hope that they would "serve to excite a lively desire in all quarters to possess a copy of this extraordinary volume. It is for sale at 25 Cornhill. Price 50 cents. Accompanying it is a finely executed and admirable likeness of the author."[14]

Garrison's appreciation for the "neatness" of the volume and the quality of Douglass's portrait probably reflects his personal involvement in the publication process. Although the nature and extent of Garrison's participation cannot be determined from the sparse documentary evidence bearing on the publication of B, it stands to reason that as the acknowledged leader of the Massachusetts Anti-Slavery Society (the publisher of record), as a journal editor and expert printer, and as Douglass's discoverer and mentor, Garrison would almost certainly have taken it upon himself to see to it that the volume was carefully edited and printed. Garrison implies in his preface, however, that he (or whoever functioned as editor) took a minimalist approach to altering the manuscript. He declared that Douglass had "very properly chosen to write his own Narrative, in his own style, and according to the best of his ability, rather than to employ someone else. It is, therefore," affirmed Garrison, "entirely his own production."[15] Garrison referred specifically to Douglass's independence in developing the manuscript, but he would not have emphasized that it was "entirely" Douglass's own work if he or a colleague were making, or expected to make, substantive editorial alterations of any significance.

The initial impression of B did in fact "go off rapidly," as Garrison had said, and in late June a second printing, a "cheap" or paperbound version selling for

11. Frederick Douglass, *Narrative of the Life of Frederick Douglass, an American Slave* (Boston, 1845), 125.

12. Wendell Phillips, "Letter from Wendell Phillips, Esq.," ibid., xv.

13. William Lloyd Garrison, "Preface," ibid., xii.

14. *Lib.*, 23 May 1845.

15. Garrison, "Preface" to the *Narrative*, viii.

twenty-five cents, was issued.[16] According to Douglass, about 4,500 copies of the *Narrative* had been sold by the time he sailed for Great Britain on 16 August.[17] By mid-September a third printing, bound again in paper, was "for sale at the Anti Slavery office."[18] As 1845 ended, a fourth printing, paperbound, was coming to market.[19] Hardbound printings were issued in 1846, 1847, and 1849, and another paperbound printing appeared in 1853.

Copies of B representing the initial printing (May 1845) and the 1846, 1847, 1849, and 1853 impressions were machine collated in an effort to discover alterations in either accidentals or substantives. The collation indicates that no plate changes occurred. The variants, which consist of the loss of letters and punctuation marks, occur at the beginning or ending of lines and are concentrated at the corners of the pages. Variation of this sort is attributable to significant deterioration of the plates.[20]

In mid-August 1845, approximately three months after the successful launching of B, Douglass, now known to be the former Frederick Augustus Washington Bailey, took precaution against being captured and returned to Maryland by sailing for Great Britain in the company of James N. Buffum, a fellow Lynn abolitionist, and the Hutchinsons, a family of antislavery singers. Only three days after disembarking in Liverpool on 27 August, Douglass and Buffum sailed across the Irish Sea to Dublin, where they were to be house guests of Richard D. Webb, a prominent abolitionist printer and journal editor who had arranged with Douglass to print the *Narrative*.[21] Because most of Douglass's income in Britain was to be derived from selling the *Narrative* at his speaking engagements, revising the book for British consumption and getting it printed were the most urgent items on his agenda. He lectured in Dublin and its environs before D1 was printed, but he could not launch his tour of Ireland, Scotland, and England until copies of the new British edition were in hand.[22]

Webb and Douglass negotiated an agreement whereby Webb would print two thousand copies for a set price plus shipping costs. Webb invested none of his own money in the new edition and so had no financial interest in the number of copies sold. Functioning merely as printer of D1 rather than as its publisher (despite the "Dublin: Webb and Chapman, Gt. Brunswick-Street" imprint on the title page), Webb assumed little responsibility for marketing and distribution. Rather than

16. *Lib.*, 20 June 1845.

17. Douglass, *Narrative of the Life of Frederick Douglass, an American Slave* (Dublin, 1845), iii.

18. *Lib.*, 19 September 1845.

19. Ibid., 2 January 1846.

20. The machine collation was conducted by Professor Noel Polk, University of Southern Mississippi.

21. Douglass to Garrison, 1 September 1845, in *Lib.*, 26 September 1845.

22. Douglass to Garrison, 16 September 1845, in ibid., 10 October 1845; Douglass to Richard D. Webb, 20 January 1846, Anti-Slavery Collection, MB.

binding all two thousand copies at once, he agreed to bind and ship copies to Douglass as needed, and he sent copies to a few British abolitionists who volunteered to sell the book in their home communities.[23]

Webb printed D1 in late September, less than a month after Douglass had become his house guest.[24] He obviously set it from B, deviating from its lineation and pagination only as necessary to absorb the longer substantive alterations. Changes were made in the front and end matter and in the form and content of the main text. Garrison's "Preface" was retitled "Preface to the American Edition" so that Douglass could appropriate "Preface" as the heading for his new two-page introduction, which he inserted ahead of Garrison's piece; the diatribe against American churches for supporting slavery that had been headed "Appendix" in B was now more accurately labeled "Postscript"; a call "To the Friends of the Slave" to support the American Anti-Slavery Society, particularly by sending likely items to Boston for sale in the society's annual bazaar, was placed after the Postscript; and five eulogistic "Critical Notices" from American papers concluded the volume. The new edition contained nearly 350 changes in spelling and punctuation. A distinctively British look was given to D1 by the fifty changes from American to British spelling forms that affected about seventeen word families. "Inquiries" became "enquiries"; "labor" became "labour"; "trousers" became "trowsers"; "color" became "colour"; and "connection" became "connexion." Syntax and rhythm were significantly affected by a myriad of punctuational alterations, especially the deletion of nearly 150 commas and the insertion of 50 others.

Nearly all of the approximately sixty language changes involved only one to three words and were relatively inconsequential. Three substantive changes, however, appear to be aimed at reducing the likelihood that British readers would take offense at Douglass's pointed rebukes of religious hypocrisy. For instance, in B he had written of being "filled with unutterable loathing" when contemplating "the religious pomp and show, together with the horrible circumstances, which every where surround me," but for D1 (and retained in D2 and E) he revised the last phrase to read: "which coexist in the Slave States."[25] The revision seems designed to locate the disgusting hypocrisy unambiguously in the American South or at least on the other side of the Atlantic. In a second passage in B he climaxed a description of the symbiotic relationship between slave dealers and southern preachers by exclaiming, "Here we have religion and robbery the allies of each other—devils dressed in angels' robes, and hell presenting the semblence of paradise." Although in the context "here" represents a metaphysical rather than a geographical nexus, and despite the fact that if it were geographical it could only refer to the southern

23. Douglass to Webb, 7, 22 December 1845, 2 March, 20 April 1846, all in the Anti-Slavery Collection, MB.

24. Douglass to Garrison, 29 September 1845, in *Lib.,* 24 October 1845.

25. *Narrative* (Boston, 1845), 119; *Narrative* (Dublin, 1845), 119.

region of Douglass's native country, he sought to revise away any possible ambiguity. Instead of "Here we have religion and robbery the allies of each other—" British readers of D1 (and of D2 and E) found "There we behold religion and robbery the allies of each other—."[26] The third alteration in this vein consisted of the excision of the last three pages from B's Appendix. In the excised material Douglass presented a fourteen-stanza poem entitled simply "A Parody" that he attributed to a northern Methodist preacher of an earlier generation who had sought to capture the true essence of southern religion and culture as he had experienced it. The first stanza suggests the flavor of the entire poem: "Come, saints and sinners, hear me tell / How pious priests whip Jack and Nell, / And women buy and children sell, / And preach all sinners down to hell, / And sing of heavenly union." Offense might be taken less to the poem itself than to the implications of Douglass's remark that the "religion of the south" (which the poem depicted "without caricature or the slightest exaggeration") was, "by communion and fellowship, the religion of the north." This line of reasoning could easily be extended to suggest that the morally contaminated religion of the United States was, by communion and fellowship, the religion of Ireland, Scotland, and England.[27]

Douglass seems to have reluctantly made these alterations in D1 after prodding from Webb, who began to apply the pressure after Douglass's criticism of American churches in his early speeches in Dublin created an uproar among the Methodists and Friends.[28] When the Friends locked Douglass out of their building, Webb, himself a former Quaker, defended him in a public letter (cosigned by his brother Thomas) in which he charged some among the Friends with being unable to bear "any thing in the slightest degree insinuating that [they] have not done their duty in the Anti-Slavery cause." Webb explicitly supported Douglass's criticism of British and American churches,[29] but he apparently urged Douglass in private to use less acerbic language in discussing the issue. Webb, in what he euphemistically referred to as "one or two cautionary hints as to his demeanour," probably suggested that Douglass's sarcastic attacks were gratuitous in Dublin and offensive to the sensibilities of Irish Christians.[30]

Living under the same roof during the monthlong development of D1 gave Douglass and Webb an unusual opportunity to collaborate, but we know little of it except for their mutual dislike. Webb consistently praised Douglass in the letters he

26. *Narrative* (Boston, 1845), 120; *Narrative* (Dublin, 1845), 120.

27. *Narrative* (Boston, 1845), 122–25.

28. *Dublin Evening Packet,* 11 September 1845, in *Lib.,* 17 October, 1845; Webb to Garrison, 2 October 1845, in ibid., 24 October 1845; John B. Estlin to Webb, 5 November 1845, in Clare Taylor, *British and American Abolitionists: An Episode in Transatlantic Understanding* (Edinburgh, 1974), 240–41.

29. Richard D. Webb and James Webb, "To the Members of the Society of Friends in Dublin," 17 September 1845, in *Lib.,* 24 October 1845.

30. Ibid. Also see John B. Estlin to Webb, 5, 13 November 1845, in ibid., 240–42.

wrote to Garrison for publication in the *Liberator,* but in private correspondence Webb characterized Douglass as insufferably vain, self-serving, and hypersensitive to criticism, albeit unusually effective on the platform.[31] The letters that Douglass wrote to Webb after leaving Dublin in early October have, in turn, an air of irritation about them. Douglass's letters, both in tone and in content, provide important insights into his collaboration with Webb on D2 that are also generally applicable to their work on D1. (Unfortunately, we are bereft of the letters written by Webb to Douglass.)

Douglass's correspondence to Webb reveals that while he weighed and sometimes accepted Webb's advice, he managed the project and made the final decisions. Douglass intensely disliked the first portrait prepared for D2 despite Webb's contrary opinion and insisted with considerable feeling on having a second one made.[32] He approved Webb's proposal that slightly shorter pages be used in D2, but he made his approval contingent: if the change threatened to affect the printing schedule adversely, Webb was to "get it out in the old form," which he did. In the same letter, written from Perth, Scotland, on 20 January 1846, Douglass chided Webb for not sending the three hundred copies of D1 that he had ordered the previous week, reminding him that he was "dependent on it for all my support in this country." Piqued at occasionally having to do without copies to sell at his meetings, Douglass prescribed a solution: "When the next edition is published, I wish you to have it bound up at once, so that I may not have to wait, as I have had to do for the last edition."[33] Not altogether satisfied with the quality of the paper Webb had used for the first impression, Douglass instructed him to use paper at least as good and if possible better for D2. When Webb questioned the inclusion of testimonial letters written by two Belfast clergymen, Douglass asserted his authority, insisting curtly that the letters be inserted in D2, and, if possible, in the thousand remaining unbound copies of D1. He even charged Webb with demonstrating "the spirit of bigotry and sectarianism, in his opposition to the letters."[34]

The most important line in the Douglass-to-Webb correspondence occurs in a letter written in Glasgow in mid-January 1846, about a month before Webb would print D2. Douglass began the letter with a tantalizingly brief passage that apparently confirmed his willingness to hear Webb's advice regarding the text of the *Narrative* as well as suggestions regarding the portrait, paper, testimonial letters, and the like. After acknowledging receipt of "the Books" and "your letter of the 10th. ultimo," Douglass informed Webb that "I have adopted your advice as to how

    31. Webb to Maria Weston Chapman, 16 November 1845, Webb to Edmund Quincy, 2 February 1846, Webb to Maria Weston Chapman, 26 February, 16 May 1846, all in Taylor, *British and American Abolitionists,* 183, 249–50, 253–54, 259–60.
    32. Douglass to Webb, [n.d., probably mid-January] 1846, Anti-Slavery Collection, MB.
    33. Douglass to Webb, 20 January 1846, Anti-Slavery Collection, MB.
    34. Douglass to Webb, 24 December 1845, Douglass to Webb, [n.d., probably mid-January] 1846, Anti-Slavery Collection, MB.

I might correct and amend the narrative."[35] Lacking Webb's letter, we can only infer from internal evidence what he advised, but it is noteworthy that Douglass labeled the proposed changes as "corrections" and "amendments." To Douglass in this context "correcting" the *Narrative* probably meant ridding the text of mistakes in either form or content, and "amending" likely referred to making additional changes that promised to enhance the effectiveness of the book in the British environment.

Douglass and Webb made more than fifty changes in punctuation and spelling, most of them probably in their "corrections" category. The changes in accidentals are largely routine, but one set of spelling alterations is intriguing: in four instances D2 changed D1's "colour" back to B's "color," and in each context Douglass used the word to refer to race. In each of the three other spelling changes in D2 in which the issue was American versus British form, the predictable direction of change is American to British. We will not attempt to explicate a rationale for the "colour"-to-"color" anomaly, but three inferences seem warranted: (1) the four changes, which violate an established pattern of alteration, were deliberate corrections; (2) Douglass, rather than Webb or an Irish compositor, made the changes; and (3) Douglass apparently scrutinized and controlled all aspects of the publication of D1 and D2 (as he must have also of B).

On the "amending" side, Douglass added two paragraphs to the preface that he had written for D1 and retitled it "Preface to the Second Dublin Edition." In the second of the paragraphs, Douglass urged readers to attend to a new "Appendix" (the original appendix was now more appropriately headed "Postscript," as it also had been in D1), which reprinted, along with Douglass's response, a published attack on the reliability of the *Narrative* by an American named A. C. C. Thompson. Douglass also doubled the number of eulogistic reviews of the *Narrative* in the "Critical Notices" section of the end matter, adding six British reviews to the five from American publications that had appeared in D1, including the two letters from Belfast ministers that Webb had discouraged. Douglass also revised the text of the *Narrative,* making upward of thirty substantive changes. Only four of these changes involve more than three words, ranging in length from the addition of an eight-word phrase to the reworking of a passage of several sentences. Two of the longer alterations might have resulted from Webb's advice: one limits alleged lawlessness to "the bounds of the slave states,"[36] and the other appears to recast a sexual reference to make it more palatable to British taste.[37]

In the latter half of February 1846, after the sometimes contentious give-and-take reflected in Douglass's letters, Webb printed D2 in a run of two thousand

35. Douglass to Webb, [n.d., probably mid-January] 1846, Anti-Slavery Collection, MB.
36. *Narrative* (Boston, 1845), 96.
37. Ibid., 62–63.

copies.[38] After Douglass received his first batch of the new printing he managed a mild compliment, writing to Webb, "I have received the books—and am pleased with them."[39]

D1 and D2 possess obvious authority, but evidence supporting E1 and E2 is scanty and support for L probably does not exist. D's substantive variants, therefore, have been adopted where no compelling reason for rejection was discovered. Some of the adopted variants are indifferent, whereas others correct compositorial errors and other kinds of mistakes and flaws, improve readability, and increase the precision, accuracy, or clarity of the diction. A significant minority of the variants in D1 and D2, however, have been rejected for a variety of reasons: (1) some adapt the text to the British audience and away from the primary American context; (2) some are distinctly inferior to the copy-text readings; and (3) some that would otherwise have been adopted were essentially refused by Douglass in the process of writing *My Bondage and My Freedom,* his second autobiography, in 1855.

Although *Bondage and Freedom* (published only two years after the last printing of B) is not a mere expansion of the *Narrative,* it contains many passages drawn from it, some unaltered or nearly so and others revised to some extent. Because the two autobiographies are, indeed, separate though related works, we have not emended B simply to incorporate alterations that appear in correlative passages. Rather, we compared substantive alterations in D1 and D2 with correlative passages in *Bondage and Freedom* in order to analyze the decisions Douglass made when once again presenting his story to American readers. Where Douglass chose to substitute a Dublin-edition variant for a reading in B in a correlative passage in *Bondage and Freedom,* he definitively confirmed, in our view, his preference for the variant. Where he chose to include the reading in B or to freshly revise the B reading, the Dublin-edition variant is considered to have been rejected by Douglass himself.

William Lloyd Garrison noted in his "Preface" to the *Narrative* that Douglass had "chosen to write his own Narrative, in his own style, and according to the best of his ability, rather than to employ some one else." Our hope is that this edition restores the *Narrative* to a state that approximates as closely as possible what Douglass envisioned for it.

38. Webb to Maria Weston Chapman, 26 February 1846, in Taylor, *British and American Abolitionists,* 253–54.
39. Douglass to Webb, 29 March 1846, Anti-Slavery Collection, MB.

Textual Notes

These notes explicate our treatment of problems in the copy-text and of variants in the authoritative texts. In a few instances, the notes explain emendations that address problems in the copy-text not corrected in later editions; in most instances the notes explain why variants (especially substantives, but in some cases also accidentals) appearing in authoritative texts were either accepted into this edition or rejected in favor of copy-text readings. Each note begins with the page and line number of this edition followed by the adopted reading (either the retained reading of the copy-text or the adopted variant), both enclosed in a square bracket. The explanatory note follows the square bracket.

Some emendations are not explained in these notes either because they are simple, self-evident improvements or because they are brief and adopted largely or entirely on the authority of the edition or impression in which they first appear.

The symbols used to indicate the various collated texts are the same ones used in the Textual Introduction and are as follows: (1) the copy-text, first published in Boston in 1845, is identified as B; (2) the first impression of the second edition, published in Dublin in 1845, is identified as D1; (3) the second impression of the Dublin edition, published in 1846, is identified as D2; (4) the first impression of the third edition, published in Wortley near Leeds, England, in 1846, is identified as E1; (5) the second impression of the third edition, published in London in 1847, is identified as E2; and (6) the only impression of the fourth edition, published in London in 1852, is identified as L.

Each textual note dealing with a variant that appears in one or more authoritative texts indicates in which edition or impression the variant first occurs. The first occurrence is especially important because the decision to adopt or refuse a variant always takes into account the authority of the text in which it appears. If the note identifies only one text in which the variant appears without clarifying that it appears only in that text, it may be assumed that the variant appears in all subsequent editions and impressions. If the variant does not appear in all subsequent editions and impressions, the note indicates those in which it occurs. For substantive variants, this information is also available in the Historical Collation.

13.6 tell] The preposition "of" after "tell" in the copy-text (B) is awkward and inaccurate. Douglass was referring only to the slaves' inability to give their dates of birth, not to other information that slaves might relate about their birthdays. Because Douglass made changes in D2 at Richard D. Webb's suggestion, this alteration is almost certainly authoritative.

14.3 journeys] D2's singular noun is not recommended by the sense of the context. Douglass referred to four or five twelve-mile trips that his mother made at night in order to see him.

14.8 recollect] D2's deletion of the preposition "of" after "recollect" removes a superfluous as well as an awkward reading.

18.39 Mr. Severe] Douglass's misspelling of personal names has not been corrected in this edition unless the correction appears in D1 or D2. His spelling of the names of persons he knew or heard of while living in Maryland, especially, should be retained as a significant element of his memory of his slavery experience at the time he wrote the *Narrative*.

An excellent case in point is his recollection of the name of one of the overseers on the Lloyd plantation. By the time Douglass wrote *My Bondage and My Freedom*, his second autobiography, in 1855, he had learned that the name he had remembered as Mr. "Severe" ten years earlier was actually spelled "Sevier" (91–96). With this knowledge he was compelled to exclude his comment in the *Narrative* that "Mr. Severe was rightly named: he was a cruel man." Correcting the *Narrative* spelling obviously would pull most of the punch of his play on words.

19.13 Providence] This capitalization is based not on an alteration in a later edition or impression but on the principle of consistency. In three other passages in B in which "providence" is used in an identical sense (31.4, 31.15, and 47.4), it is capitalized in the last two. The "providence" in B 31.4, however, is capitalized in all subsequent editions and in the correlative passage in *Bondage and Freedom* (139). The weight of the evidence, therefore, is toward Douglass's intent to capitalize, and all four are capitalized in the established text.

20.14 O!"] D1's removal of the period outside the quotation marks in B corrects what is probably a compositor's error.

20.32 conception] Although all subsequent editions and impressions substitute the plural form, the singular is consistent with the context: Douglass was recalling his first insight into the nature of slavery. In the following sentence he refers back to "that conception"—not "those conceptions."

21.24 virtue] Webb may have suggested this alteration to Douglass on either moral or logical grounds or both: that resisting the temptation to steal fruit should not be potentially included in the category "vice" or that the phrase in B is inconsistent with the mutual exclusivity of virtue and vice. D1 deletes the reference to vice.

22.3 Old] Douglass uses the terms "old" and "young" in the passages referring to the two Barneys more as names than as adjectives. The capitalization of "old" and "young" in this context in D1, therefore, is warranted. Douglass also chose to capitalize "Old" in referring to "Old Barney" in *Bondage and Freedom* (112–114).

22.4 Young] See the preceding note. This variant occurs in D1, D2, and E1.

21.11 Old and Young] See the note for line 22.3.

22.23 Old] See the note for line 22.3.

22.28 Old] See the note for line 22.3.

22.34 Old] See the note for line 22.3.

23.11 whom the slave belonged to,] Douglass almost certainly intended to revise B's phrase, "where the slave belonged," to make it parallel with a phrase in the previous paragraph (23.6), where Colonel Lloyd asks a black man whom he meets on a road: " 'Well, boy, whom do you belong to?' " Douglass inserted "to" after "belonged" in D1, but either he or the compositor failed to substitute "whom" for "where."

23.32 did] We have retained the past tense despite the switch to present tense in D1 and D2 for two reasons. First, past tense works as well or better than present tense. Second, Douglass uses the past tense in a closely parallel passage in *Bondage and Freedom* (117).

25.27 but few] D1 reads "but a few." In the correlative passage in *Bondage and Freedom* (122), however, Douglass chose the wording of the copy-text.

26.28 Hicks] B's "Hick," undoubtedly the result of a compositorial error, is rendered as "Hicks" in all subsequent editions and impressions. B's compositor twice rendered the name correctly at 26.39.

26.36 Hicks'] On the ground that the name intended by Douglass is "Hicks" rather than "Hick" (see previous note), it follows that B's possessive form "Hick's" involves a compositorially misplaced apostrophe. The error was corrected in D1 and D2 but recurred in E1, E2, and L.

27.15 Mr. Beal Bondly] D1's deletion of "Mr." is almost certainly a compositor's oversight. Douglass and Webb would have acted with extreme inconsistency to have deleted one "Mr." among many. When initially referring to a white person, Douglass's habit was to use "Mr." or "Mrs." and first (if he knew it) and last name. Several examples occur in the immediate context of this alteration.

28.16 probably seven or] Douglass revised B's reading ("between seven and eight years old") in D2, but his intended revision apparently was not fully implemented: his substitution of "or" for "and" demanded also the deletion of "between," which D2 retains. Either Douglass inadvertently failed to mark the deletion of "between" or the compositor overlooked the deletion.

28.23 scurf,] D2's "scruff" appears to arise from preference for a term that is used by speakers of British English to refer to a thin coating, crust, or film. "Scurf," however, is more precise in this context, where Douglass is commenting on washing to remove "dead skin" from his feet and knees (28.26).

29.19 comfort] The slight awkwardness of the plural coupled with the authority of D2, where the change to the singular noun first appears, supports the adoption of D2's reading.

29.37 Loudon] B's "Louden" could have resulted from Douglass's misspelling of the word in manuscript or from a compositor's misreading. The mistake was corrected in D2 and not repeated in *Bondage and Freedom* (137).

29.39 Fell's] The absence of the apostrophe in B apparently is a compositor's mistake that was corrected in D1. The apostrophe is included in the second appearance of the word in B (93.20) and in both occurrences in *Bondage and Freedom* (137, 308).

30.18 Providence] See the note for 19.13.

30.30 within] All editions and impressions after B substitute "in," but the correlative passage in *Bondage and Freedom* (140) reverts to the B reading.

31.16 gradually] This variant first occurs in the authoritative D2. Douglass apparently substituted "gradually" for "soon" in order to emphasize, as he does at length in *Bondage and Freedom* (139–54), that Sophia Auld's soft heart hardened slowly and incrementally as she sought to be responsive to the wishes of her husband.

31.18 eventually] See the note above.

30.20–21 Thus is slavery the enemy of both the slave and the slaveholder.] Appearing first in D2, this drawing out of the moral of his discussion of the gradual change in Sophia Auld is undoubtedly authorial.

36.14 wished] It is problematic whether B's "wishing" or D2's "wished" is the preferable reading, but the authority of D2 is the determining factor.

37.34 italics] The capitalization of "italics" in B is probably a compositor's mistake that D1 corrects. The parallel passage in *Bondage and Freedom* (171), contains the lowercase "i."

38.7 son, Richard,] Consistency within the immediate context requires either that "Richard" be set off with commas or that "Captain Anthony" (38.8), "Andrew" (38.8–9), and "Lucretia" (38.9) not be. The absence of commas on either side of Richard is probably a compositor's error that was corrected in D1.

38.27 all were] The transposition of subject and verb in D2 is both preferable and authoritative.

39.28 fate] D's omission of a direct object in this sentence, probably a compositor's oversight, was not corrected in subsequent editions. Both "fate" and our placement of it seem called for by the context because Douglass seems to have been varying the cliché "a fate worse than death."

39.34 had] The D1 reading is simpler and cleaner and supported by the use of the same tense in a closely parallel passage in *Bondage and Freedom* (180).

41.29 his] The phrase "betwixt himself and brother" seems to call for a third-person possessive pronoun before "brother," the lack of which is probably owing to a compositor's oversight. The addition of "his" was first made in D2 and retained in subsequent editions and impressions.

48.31–48.38 St. Michaels . . . of] The extensive alteration of these lines, appearing first in D2, may be intended to condense and tighten a wordy passage. It seems more likely that Douglass was responding to the urgings of Webb to delete sexual references that the British public would deem unnecessary or coarse. The edited passage omits the description of Caroline as well as the exclamation that

Covey "hired a married man of Mr. Samuel Harrison, to live with him one year; and him he used to fasten up with her every night!"

When he wrote a parallel passage in *Bondage and Freedom* (218), Douglass included a close paraphrase of B's reading, including the exclamation. We reject the D2 reading despite its probable authority because it appears to be an adaptation to British readers that he discarded when he wrote his second autobiography.

49.18 beam] In *Bondage and Freedom* (219–21), Douglass quoted a three-page passage from the *Narrative* that includes the line under consideration. He used B as the source of the quotation and retained "beam" even though "gleam" is substituted in D1 and all other editions and impressions.

49.26 many] D1's "much" is inexplicable except as a compositor's error. D2 reverted to "many," and the correction is retained in all other editions and impressions.

50.11 get] Douglass retained "get" in the *Narrative* passage quoted in *Bondage and Freedom* that is referenced in the note for line 49.18. Each edition and impression after B substitutes "go."

55.18 industrious ones] D2 deletes "ones," but Douglass retained the noun in the correlative sentence in *Bondage and Freedom* (251).

55.22 ball playing] D1's transposition of words in B's "playing ball" is ratified by the correlative sentence in *Bondage and Freedom* (252).

58.25 county,] The alteration of "county" to "country" in D1 is likely a compositor's error. Douglass might credibly write from personal knowledge of the reputation of slaveholders "in the whole county," but not in the "whole country."

58.26 privilege of] The awkwardness of this sentence is due in part to its syntax and in part to the apparent omission of a noun and a preposition before "getting." The omission, probably a compositor's error, remained uncorrected in later impressions and editions.

58.31 who] D2 appropriately substitutes the personal pronoun "who" for the impersonal "that."

59.36 is] The change to past tense in D1 was not retained by Douglass when he included the passage intact (as a footnote) in *Bondage and Freedom* (264).

62.29 subjected] D1 substitutes "subject," but in *Bondage and Freedom* (286) Douglass retained the stronger notion of being interrupted and scrutinized as opposed merely to opening themselves to the possibility or probability of scrutiny.

62.32 words:—] D1 deletes "to wit" no doubt because it is redundant. Douglass left the phrase off when he reworded the parallel passage in *Bondage and Freedom* (286).

63.14 and in] The addition of "and" in D1 was also used by Douglass in the parallel passage in *Bondage and Freedom* (289).

64.4 at] The substitution of "in the barn" for "at the barn" in D1 was ignored by Douglass when he wrote the parallel passage in *Bondage and Freedom* (291).

64.27 can't] D2 avoids a double negative by substituting "can" for "can't." Douglass, however, apparently intended to use the double negative to give authentic flavor to an exclamation attributed to fellow slave Henry Harris because he retained it in the parallel passage in *Bondage and Freedom* (293).

64.28 damned!] Almost certainly the five substitutions of "d——d" in D2 for the spelling out of the expletive (67.25; 68.24; 69.21; 69.22) were the result of the urging of Webb and exemplify the attempt to adapt the text to British taste.

65.20 ever] The change from "ever" to "even" in D1 is probably compositorial: it involves a single letter and undermines the sense of the sentence. A denial that they "even" intended to run away makes sense as a defence against the charge that they had actually sought to escape, but the accusation lodged against them was only that they had conspired to flee.

66.9 if] B's "though" is an awkward choice of prepositions that Douglass corrected in D2.

66.16 supposed] The change to the present tense in D1 is not justified by the context. It seems clear that Douglass was describing his state of mind in jail as a slave, not offering his contemporary analysis of events.

68.29 ship-yard, within the bounds of the Slave States.] Whether this phrase was inserted in D2 as an adaptation to the concerns of British readers or not, it was fully authorized and Americanized by Douglass's paraphrase of it in the parallel passage in *Bondage and Freedom* (315). He even added a temporal qualification ("at that time") and tightened the geographical restriction ("in any other part of Maryland").

69.7 was] D1 pairs "A large company of men" with the appropriate singular verb form.

71.5–8 very public manner . . . *upperground railroad.*] The variant introduced in D1 simplifies sentence structure and improves readability. We must assume, however, that Douglass preferred what he had written in 1845, for he lifted the parallel passage in *Bondage and Freedom* (323) bodily from B.

71.9 willingly] D1's deletion of "willingly" removes a mild redundancy, but in the parallel passage in *Bondage and Freedom* (323–24), Douglass chose to retain B's reading.

81.18–19 every where surround me. We] The variant "co-exist in the Slave States. They," which appears in D1, appears to be a clear instance of adaptation to British sensibilities. Writing in Massachusetts, Douglass asserts in B that religious hypocrisy pervades his surroundings; but revising in Ireland, he probably was pressured by Webb to exclude the North (where many churches had close ties to British counterparts) from the charge.

82.6–9 Here . . . see] "Here we have" in B is altered in D1 to "There we behold." D2 retains "There we behold" and embellishes the passage with two additional phrases deploring the union of slavery and religion.

We reject D1's "There we behold" as an adaptation to British concerns and incorporate D2's embellishment, which is undoubtedly from the pen of Douglass and has no taint of adaptation to a secondary audience.

83.1 twofold] D2's "tenfold" is a puzzling substitution because in B Douglass accurately quotes most of Matt. 23:15 (King James Version), including the reference to the Pharisees making their converts twofold more a child of hell than themselves.

83.11 outwardly appear] D1's transposition of these words, which is retained in D2, E1, and E2, is puzzling for the reason given in the previous note. Douglass quotes Matt. 23:28 (King James Version) accurately in B, so the transposition is inferior and without apparent reason.

83.21 faith.] This is yet a third example (see the two notes immediately preceding) of Douglass quoting or paraphrasing the King James Version of the Bible accurately in B only to undermine the accuracy in D1 or D2. In this example, he accurately paraphrases Matt. 23:23, in which Jesus is quoted as specifying the weightier matters of the law to be judgment, mercy, and faith. Inexplicably, D1 substitutes "truth" for "faith."

83.33 feel] B's "have felt" was changed to "felt" in D1 and then to the adopted present tense in D2, which is later than D1 and more explicitly authoritative.

83.34–86.5 I . . . END.] The British editions delete these final pages of B, probably out of the desire of both Webb and Douglass to avoid offending British church people. The Textual Introduction elaborates further on the probable reason for the deletion of this material.

List of Emendations

The List of Emendations records each of the variant readings incorporated into the copy-text. Each entry in the list begins with the page and line number of this edition. An asterisk preceding the page and line number indicates that an explanatory note relating to that entry can be found in the Textual Notes. The adopted reading follows the page and line number and is set off by a square bracket. After the square bracket, an edition/impression symbol indicates the text in which the adopted variant first appears. Several entries lack an edition/impression symbol because the adopted reading does not appear in any of the relevant texts. For a key to the edition/impression symbols, see the comments that introduce the Textual Notes.

*13.6 tell] D2; tell of
*14.8 recollect] D2; recollect of
19.6 what] D2; that
19.8 blasphemy] D1; of blasphemy
*19.13 Providence] providence
*20.14 O!"∧] D1; O!."
*21.24 virtue] D1; virtue or the vice
*22.3 Old] D1; old
*22.4 Young] D1; young
*22.11 Old and Young] D1; old and young
*22.23 Old] D1; old
*22.28 Old] D1; old
*22.34 Old] D1; old
*23.11 whom the slave belonged to,] where the slave belonged,
*26.28 Hicks] D1; Hick
*26.36 Hicks'] D1; Hick's
*28.16 probably seven or] between seven and
*29.19 comfort] D2; comforts
*29.37 Loudon] D2; Louden
*29.39 Fell's] D1; Fells
*30.18 Providence] D1; providence
31.10 towards] D1; toward

*31.16 gradually] D2; soon
*31.18 eventually] D2; soon
*31.20–21 demon. Thus is slavery the enemy of both the slave and the slaveholder.] D2; demon.
32.39 look at] D2; look upon
34.4 lamb-like] D1; ~∧~
34.31 the] D1; our
34.31 on] D1; upon
34.32 the] D2; that
*36.14 wished] D2; wishing
*37.34 italics] D1; Italics
*38.7 son, Richard,] D1; ~∧ ~∧
*38.27 all were] D2; were all
*39.34 had] D1; had had
40.32 Virginia's] D2; Virginia
*41.29 his brother] D2; brother
42.25 than] D2; than a
46.31 gate] D1; woods gate
47.24 word] D1; words
50.37 some] D1; an
51.21 to do] to
55.18 sober, staid,] D1; staid, sober,
*55.22 ball playing] D1; playing ball
57.23 shelter, under∧] D1; ~∧ ~,

*58.31 who] D2; that
60.15 the Sabbath school] D1;
   Sabbath school
*62.32 words:—] D1; ~, to wit:—
62.37 County] D1; county
*63.14 and in] D1; and
63.29 the manure] D1; manure
64.11 by my name,] D1; by name
*66.9 if] D2; though
*68.29 shipyard, within the bounds
   of the Slave States.] D2;
   shipyard.
68.39 sufferings] D1; suffering
*69.7 was] D1; were
69.19 towards] D1; toward
72.27 week,] D1; ~;
73.11 go] D1; get
73.13–14 to pay] D1; pay
73.22 the] D1; that the

74.10 good] D1; a good
74.29 to] D1; with
74.32—in what direction] D2; what
   direction
75.9 unfold] D1; to unfold
77.29 any] D2; either
79.31 and my] D1; and
80.19 measures,] D1; ~ʌ
80.34 on] D2; since
81.2 to such] D1; of such
81.5 no reference whatever] D1; no
   possible reference
*82.7–9 other; slavery and piety . . .
   see] D2; other—
82.26 thine?"—*Whittier.*] D1;
   thine?"
83.22 These] D1; They
83.33 represented] D1; presented
*83.33 feel] D2; have felt

Line-End Hyphenation in the Copy-Text

The list below contains all the possible compound words hyphenated at end-of-line in the *Narrative* copy-text. The form in which each possible compound is presented indicates the editor's decision regarding the form (hyphenated or unhyphenated) that the compound should take when it occurs within a line. The editor's decisions were based on Douglass's usage in the *Narrative* and in other writings.

1.10	harvest-time	49.27	misunderstanding	88.31	without
2.2	twenty-eight	49.31	however	90.6	over-powered
5.20	slaveholder	52.27	slaveholder	96.30	ship-yard
9.19	overseership	55.2	sometimes	97.22	mid-day
18.29	overseer	57.6	farm-renter	98.9	bloody-minded
19.9	slaveholders	58.20	however	100.13	slaveholders
27.14	oyster-shells	60.8	without	101.13	themselves
28.18	grandmother	63.31	sometimes	108.24	fellow-men
28.23	elsewhere	65.16	meanwhile	111.9	gentlemen
30.7	slaughter-house	68.10	bare-headed	111.10	afterward
33.31	understood	73.8	however	111.21	stage-driver
35.32	cowskin	77.9	slave-driver	112.31	non-slaveholding
37.25	newspaper	77.14	slaveholders	113.9	slaveholders
43.4	ship-yard	82.29	somewhat	116.21	anti-slavery
43.14	larboard	82.32	interlinked	116.27	however
44.7	meeting-house	85.18	overtaken	119.5	cradle-plunderers
45.8	twenty-four	87.22	ourselves	119.10	class-leader
46.15	fellow-slaves	87.27	undertaking	121.15	yourselves
48.1	grandchildren	88.12	overwhelmed	122.30	without

Line-End Hyphenation in the Yale Edition

In quoting from the Yale edition, the only line-end hyphens that should be retained are the following.

16.38	horror-stricken	44.23	class leaders	69.20	bloody-minded
33.13	half-starved	47.5	pocket-knife	75.17	hunting-ground
36.33	fellow-slaves	55.6	negro-breaker	78.1	non-slaveholders
37.24	ship-yard	58.29	love-feast	80.23	anti-slavery
40.15	mud-chimney	61.4	life-giving	81.20	blood-clotted
42.24	corn-meal	62.19	father-in-law	83.17	*man*-stealer

Historical Collation

All substantive variants from this edition appearing in potentially authoritative editions and impressions of the *Narrative* are listed here. Although all variants, including accidentals as well as substantives, have been collated, this list contains only the substantive variants, which are more significant for our purpose. Because all editions of the *Narrative* subsequent to the copy-text were printed in Great Britain, they contain many punctuation, capitalization, and spelling changes intended to adapt the text to British readers. It would be superfluous to include those alterations here.

Each entry begins with the page/line number and reading of the Yale edition set off by a square bracket. After the square bracket, each edition/impression containing the reading of this edition is cited and set off by a semicolon. Rejected variants and the citation of each edition/impression in which they appear complete the entries.

For an explanation of the symbols representing the editions/impressions, see the introduction to the Textual Notes.

13.6 tell] D2, E1, E2, L; tell of B, D1
14.3 journeys] B; journey D1, D2, E1, E2, L
41.8 recollect] D2, E1, E2, L; recollect of B, D1
19.6 what] D2, E1, E2, L; that B, D1
19.8 blasphemy] D1, D2, E1, E2, L; of blasphemy B
20.30 those] B, D1, D2; these E1, E2, L
20.32 conception] B; conceptions D1, D2, E1, E2, L
21.24 virtue] D1, D2, E1, E2, L; virtue of the vice B
23.11 belonged,] B; belonged to, D1, D2, E1, E2, L
23.32 did] B, E1, E2, L; do D1, D2
25.27 but few] B; but a few D1, D2, E1, E2, L
26.28 Hicks,] D1, D2, E1, E2, L; Hick, B
27.15 Mr. Beal] B; Beal D1, D2, E1, E2, L
28.16 and] B, D1; or D2, E1, E2, L
28.23 scurf,] B, D1; scruff, D2, E1, E2, L
28.25 to,] B, D1, D2; to do so, E1, E2, L
28.26 me] B, D1, D2; me that E1, E2, L
29.19 comfort] D2, E1, E2, L; comforts B, D1
30.30 within] B; in D1, D2, E1, E2, L

31.10 towards] D1, D2, E1, E2, L; toward B

31.16 gradually] D2, E1, E2, L; soon B, D1

31.18 eventually] D2, E1, E2, L; soon B, D1

31.20–21 demon. Thus is slavery the enemy of both the slave and the slave-holder.] D2, E1, E2, L; demon. B, D1

32.22 I had] B, D1, D2; I E1, E2, L

32.39 look at] D2; look upon B, D1; looked at E1, E2, L

34.22 by which I] B, D1, D2, E1, E2; by which L

34.30–31 in the] D1, D2, E1, E2, L; in our B

34.31 on] D1, D2, E1, E2, L; upon B

34.32 the] D2, E1, E2, L; that B, D1

36.14 wished] D2, E1, E2, L; wishing B, D1

36.38 Irishman] B, D1, D2; Irishmen E1, E2, L

37.21 for] B, D1, D2; for the E1, E2, L

38.27 all were] D2, E1, E2, L; were all B, D1

39.34 had] D1, D2, E1, E2, L; had had B

40.32 Virginia's] D2, E1, E2, L; Virginia B, D1

41.29 his brother] D2, E1, E2, L; brother B, D1

42.17 development] B, D1, D2; developement E1, E2, L

42.25 than] D2, E1, E2, L; than a B, D1

43.25 with] B; in D1, D2, E1, E2, L

46.3 Master] B, D1, D2; Mr. E1, E2, L

46.31 gate] D1, D2, E1, E2, L; woods gate B

47.24 word,] D1, D2, E1, E2, L; words, B

48.31–48.38 St. Michaels. . . . of] B, D1; St. Michaels. To complete the wickedness of this transaction, Covey hired of Mr. Samuel Harrison a married slave, who was torn from his own wife, and compelled to live as the husband of this wretched woman. Eventually she gave birth to twins, and such was the joy of Covey and D2, E1, E2, L

49.18 beam] B; gleam D1, D2, E1, E2, L

49.26 many] B, D2, E1, E2, L; much D1

50.11 get] B; go D1, D2, E1, E2, L

50.13 being] B, D1, E1, E2, L; been D2

50.25 a man] B, D1, E1, E2, L; man D2

50.37 some] D1, D2, E1, E2, L; an B

52.34 that] B, D1, D2; that as E1, E2, L

55.18 sober, staid,] D1, D2, E1, E2, L; staid, sober B

55.18 industrious ones] B, D1; industrious D2, E1, E2, L

55.22 ball playing,] D1, D2; ball-playing E1, E2, L; playing ball B

57.5 first] B; 1 D1, D2, E1, E2, L

58.25 county,] B; country, D1, D2, E1, E2, L

58.31 who] D2, E1, E2, L; that B, D1

59.19 to see] B, D1, D2; see E1, E2, L

59.36 is] B; was D1, D2, E1, E2, L

60.15 the Sabbath school] D1, D2; the Sabbath-school E1, E2, L; Sabbath school B

62.29 subjected] B; subject D1, D2, E1, E2, L

62.32 words:–] D1, D2, E1, E2, L; words, to wit:— B

63.14 and in] D1, D2, E1, E2, L; in B

63.28 to] B, D1, D2; to experience E1, E2, L

63.29 spreading the manure] D1, D2, E1, E2; spreading manure B

64.4 at] B; in D1, D2, E1, E2, L

64.7 Master] B, D1, D2; Mr. E1, E2, L

64.11 by my name,] D1, D2, E1, E2; by my mame L; by name B

64.27 can't] B, D1; can D2, E1, E2, L

65.20 ever] B; even D1, D2, E1, E2, L

66.9 if] D2, E1, E2, L; though B, D1

66.16 supposed] B; suppose D1, D2, E1, E2, L

68.29 ship-yard, within the bounds of the Slave States.] D2, E1, E2, L; ship-yard B, D1

68.39 sufferings] D1, D2, E1, E2, L; suffering B

69.7 was] D1, D2, E1, E2, L; were B

69.16 sympathized] B; sympathised D1, D2, E1, E2, L

69.19 toward a colored] B; towards a coloured D1; towards a colored D2, E1, E2, L

70.28 guarding a] B, D1, D2, E2, L; guarding E1

71.5–8 very public manner . . . *upperground railroad.*] B; publicity which some of the western abolitionists have given to their system of assisting fugitives in their flight to Canada. They call it the *underground railroad;* but by their open declarations it has ceased to be a secret to any body. D1, D2; publicity which some of the western abolitionists have given to their system of assisting fugitives in their flight to Canada. They call it *the underground railroad;* but by their open declarations it has ceased to be a secret to any body. E1, E2, L

71.9 willingly subjecting] B; subjecting D1, D2, E1, E2, L

73.10 early] B, D1, D2; early on the E1, E2, L

73.11 go] D1, D2, E1, E2, L; get B

73.13–14 to pay] D1, D2, E1, E2, L; pay B

73.22 the] D1, D2, E1, E2, L; that the B

74.10 good] D1, D2, E1, E2, L; a good B

74.29 to] D1, D2, E1, E2, L; with B

74.32 —in what direction] D2, E1, E2, L; —what direction B, D1

75.9 unfold] D1, D2, E1, E2, L; to unfold B

76.2 toward] B, D1, D2; towards E1, E2, L

76.26 this] B, D1, D2; the E1, E2, L

77.29 any] D2, E1, E2, L; either B, D1

79.31 and my] D1, D2, E1, E2, L; and B

80.title APPENDIX.} B, L; POSTSCRIPT D1, D2, E1, E2

80.title–86.5 APPENDIX . . . END] B, D1, D2, E1, E2; *omit* L

80.34 on] D2, E1, E2; since B, D1

81.2 to] D1, D2, E1, D2; of B

81.5 no reference whatever] D1, D2, E1, E2; no possible reference B

81.18 every where surround me. We] B; coexist in the Slave States. They D1, D2, E1, E2

82.6 Here we have] B; There we behold D1, D2, E1, E2

82.7–9 other; slavery and piety linked and interlinked; preachers of the gospel united with slaveholders! A horrible sight, to see devils] D2, E1, E2; other— devils] B, D1

82.26 thine?"—*Whittier.*] D1, D2, E1, E2; thine?" B

83.1 twofold] B, D1; tenfold D2, E1, E2

83.11 outwardly appear] B; appear outwardly D1, D2, E1, E2

83.21 faith.] B; truth. D1, D2, E1, E2

83.22 These] D1, D2, E1, E2; They B

83.33 represented] D1, D2, E1, E2; presented B

83.33 feel] D2, E1, E2; felt D1; have felt B

83.34–86.5 I . . . END.] B; *omit* D1, D2, E1, E2

Historical Annotation

The two line counts supplied below for the annotation of passages in the text refer to first the Yale edition and then to the 1845 Boston edition. Line counts include chapter headings.

3.2/iii.2   I] The son of impoverished Nova Scotian immigrants to Massachusetts, William Lloyd Garrison (1805–79) learned the printer's trade as a youth and went on to become one of the nation's most influential reform journalists. In 1831, he brought out the first issue of the Boston *Liberator,* which endorsed immediate emancipation. Later Garrison became an advocate for temperance, women's rights, and many other causes. His uncompromising radical positions helped cause the schism in the abolitionist movement in 1840. Thereafter he served as president of the American Anti-Slavery Society and led the "Garrisonian" wing of abolitionism until the Civil War. John L. Thomas, *The Liberator: William Lloyd Garrison* (Boston, 1963); James Brewer Stewart, *William Lloyd Garrison and the Challenge of Emancipation* (Arlington Heights, Ill., 1992); *Dictionary of American Biography,* 20 vols. (New York, 1928–36), 7 : 168–72.

3.2–3/iii.2–3   an anti-slavery convention in Nantucket] On 10–12 August 1841, Douglass attended a special summer convention on the island of Nantucket called by the Massachusetts Anti-Slavery Society. Garrison also attended this gathering and strongly applauded Douglass's novice performance as an abolitionist orator. *Lib.,* 20 August 1841; McFeely, *Frederick Douglass,* 86–90.

3.10/iii.13   a resident of New Bedford] Douglass lived in New Bedford, Massachusetts, after his escape from slavery, staying in the city from 1838 until 1842. McFeely, *Frederick Douglass,* 74–92.

3.23–24/iv.1–2   "gave . . . MAN,"] *Hamlet,* act 3, sc. 4, line 62.

3.35–36/iv.18–19   "created. . . angels"] A close paraphrase of Ps. 8 : 5; Heb. 2 : 7.

4.8/iv.31   A beloved friend from New Bedford] In Chapter 11, Douglass identifies this individual as William C. Coffin. Coffin (1816–?) was a resident of New Bedford who in 1845 was an accountant for the local Mechanics Bank. An ardent abolitionist, Coffin was a good friend of William Lloyd Garrison and served as recording secretary of the Bristol County Anti-Slavery Society from the 1830s. Coffin, a Quaker, also advocated the doctrine of nonresistance and was jailed briefly in 1845 in New Bedford for refusing to swear an oath to the authority of a local judge. *Lib.,* 3 September 1841, 18 April, 23 May 1845; Henry H. Crapo, *New Bedford Directory [for 1845]* (New Bedford, 1845), 794; D. Hamilton Hurd, comp., *History of Bristol County, Massachusetts, with Biographical Sketches of*

Many of Its Pioneers and Prominent Men (Philadelphia, 1883), 105; Walter M. Merrill and Louis Ruchames, eds., *The Letters of William Lloyd Garrison*, 6 vols. (Cambridge, Mass., 1971–81), 2 : 712 (hereafter cited as *Garrison Letters*); *Narrative* (Boston, 1845), 117.20.

4.16/v.5–6   PATRICK HENRY] Patrick Henry (1736–99), a Virginia patriot, lawyer, and Revolutionary statesman, attended the First Continental Congress at Philadelphia and was governor of Virginia from 1776 to 1779. *DAB*, 7 : 554–59.

4.19–20/v.10–11   the peril which surrounded this self-emancipated young man] The vulnerability of fugitive slaves in Massachusetts had been highlighted by the capture of George Lattimer in Boston in October 1842. After abolitionists failed to find legal means to block his return to the South, Lattimer's freedom was purchased for four hundred dollars by northern sympathizers. Henry Wilson, *History of the Rise and Fall of the Slave Power in America*, 3 vols. (Boston, 1872–77), 1 : 477–87; Donald M. Jacobs, "A History of the Boston Negro from the Revolution to the Civil War" (Ph.D. diss., Boston University, 1968), 209–21.

4.25–26/v.19   the old Bay State] Massachusetts derived its nickname "Old Bay State" from its original name, the Massachusetts Bay Colony. Mitford M. Mathews, *A Dictionary of Americanisms on Historical Principles*, 2 vols. (New York, 1965), 2 : 1155.

4.26/v.19–20   "YES!" shouted the whole mass] Nantucket abolitionist Anna Gardner confirms that the convention members shouted their pledge to protect Douglass from reenslavement. McFeely, *Frederick Douglass*, 87–89, 394n.

4.27/v.21   Mason and Dixon's line] Disputes between Pennsylvania on the north and Maryland and Virginia on the south were resolved when English surveyors Charles Mason and Jeremiah Dixon determined and marked the precise borders between these colonies in 1763–67. Hubertis M. Cummins, *The Mason and Dixon Line: Story for a Bicentenary, 1763–1963* (n.p., 1962).

5.1/vi.1   Massachusetts Anti-Slavery Society] In late fall 1831, William Lloyd Garrison convened a series of meetings to advance support in the Boston area for the principles of immediate emancipation. Out of these meetings emerged the New England Anti-Slavery Society in early 1832. As abolitionist strength grew in the region, state-level societies were formed and the group renamed itself the Massachusetts Anti-Slavery Society in 1835. Dwight Lowell Dumond, *Antislavery: The Crusade for Freedom in America* (Ann Arbor, Mich., 1961), 172–73.

5.1/vi.2   JOHN A. COLLINS] Vermont native John Anderson Collins (1810–c. 1879) attended Middlebury College and Andover Theological Seminary before becoming a lecturer for the Massachusetts Anti-Slavery Society in the late 1830s. He broke his ties with the Garrisonian wing of the abolitionist movement in 1843 in order to devote himself to advancing the utopian philosophy of Robert Owen. Collins resided briefly on a communal farm near Skaneateles, New York, and ultimately settled in California. Carleton Mabee, *Black Freedom: The Nonviolent*

Abolitionists from 1830 Through the Civil War (London, 1970), 76, 80–82, 88, 112–25, 212, 264, 394n; *DAB,* 4 : 307–08.

5.8–9/vi.12   American . . . Anti-Slavery Society] Inspired by the success of the British emancipation movement, a group of sixty-two American abolitionists, representing Quakers, free blacks, New York evangelicals, and such New England radicals as William Lloyd Garrison, met in Philadelphia in December 1833 and founded the American Anti-Slavery Society. Garrison drafted most of the society's original Declaration of Sentiments, which endorsed a blend of immediatist principles and moral suasion tactics. By the time Douglass became a lecturer for the American Anti-Slavery Society in the early 1840s, the organization had suffered a serious schism when many abolitionists had quit in protest to Garrison's stands on women's rights, religious orthodoxy, and an independent antislavery political party. Merton L. Dillon, *The Abolitionists: The Growth of a Dissenting Minority* (DeKalb, Ill., 1974), 52–53, 113–26; James Brewer Stewart, *Holy Warriors: The Abolitionists and American Slavery* (New York, 1976), 50–51, 89–96.

5.18/vi.25–26   "grow . . . God,"] Garrison slightly adapts 2 Pet. 3 : 18.

5.25/vi.34–35   CHARLES LENOX REMOND] Born to free black parents in Salem Massachusetts, Charles Lenox Remond (1810–73) was an early member of the New England Anti-Slavery Society. A talented abolitionist lecturer, Remond toured the British Isles in 1840–41. He and Douglass frequently traveled together as speaking agents of the Massachusetts Anti-Slavery Society. A loyal Garrisonian, Remond denounced Douglass's embrace of political abolitionism in the 1850s. Les Wallace, "Charles Lenox Remond: The Lost Prince of Abolitionism," *Negro History Bulletin,* 40 : 696–701 (May–June 1977); *DAB,* 15 : 499–500.

6.1–2/vii.19   DANIEL O'CONNELL] Irish lawyer and parliamentarian, Daniel O'Connell (1775–1847) was a leader of the movements to repeal the Act of Union between England and Ireland and to remove civil disabilities on Roman Catholics. An abolitionist from the 1820s, O'Connell loyally supported William Lloyd Garrison and his followers' cause despite the backlash it caused for American support for the Irish repeal movement. Douglas C. Raich, "Daniel O'Connell and American Anti-Slavery," *Irish Historical Studies,* 20 : 3–25 (March 1976); Gilbert Osofsky, "Abolitionists, Irish Immigrants, and the Dilemmas of Romantic Nationalism," *American Historical Review,* 80 : 889–912 (October 1975); *DNB,* 14 : 816–34.

6.4–5/vii.22–23   speech . . . in the Conciliation Hall, Dublin] Garrison refers to a controversial speech that Daniel O'Connell delivered in Dublin's Conciliation Hall, the headquarters for the Loyal National Repeal Association. Founded in April 1840, that organization sought the repeal of the legislation of 1800 that abolished the separate Irish parliament and merged the governments of Ireland and Great Britain. O'Connell's speech denounced slavery, as Garrison reported, but it also pledged Irish support for British efforts to block American expansion. The speech produced dissension in Irish nationalist circles and hostile attacks from the

United States. Angus Macintyre, *The Liberator: Daniel O'Connell and the Irish Party, 1830–1847* (New York, 1965), 80, 162–63; Raich, "Daniel O'Connell," 19.

6.29/viii.20–21   arm . . . save] A paraphrase of Isa. 50 : 2: "Is my hand shortened at all, that it cannot redeem?"

6.30–31/viii.22–23   "in slaves and the souls of men."] Rev. 18 : 13.

6.34/viii.28   SLAVERY AS IT IS.] An allusion to Theodore Weld's *American Slavery As It Is: Testimony of a Thousand Witnesses* (New York, 1839).

7.18–22/ix.22–29   the description . . . spirit of freedom] Garrison alludes to a passage that appears in Chapter 10. *Narrative* (Boston, 1845), 64.4–65.26.

7.23–24/ix.30–31   a whole Alexandrian library of thought] Founded in the third century B.C. by Egyptian ruler Ptolemy I, the library at Alexandria was reputed to hold half a million literary works. Damaged in fighting when the Romans under Julius Caesar besieged Alexandria in 47 B.C., the library continued to function until the late third century A.D. Walter M. Ellis, *Ptolemy of Egypt* (London, 1994), 55–56.

8.24–25/xi.13–14   two instances of murderous cruelty] An allusion to Douglass's accounts of the murders of slave Bill Demby by overseer Austin Gore and of a second slave by Maryland farmer John Beale Bordley in Chapter 4. *Narrative* (Boston, 1845), 22.25–24.8, 25.19–26.4.

8.30–31/xi.22–23   The Baltimore American, of March 17, 1845] This news item from the Baltimore *American & Commercial Daily Advertiser* of 17 April, not March, 1845 appeared in Garrison's Boston *Liberator* of 9 May 1845, the same issue that contained a copy of the "Preface" he wrote for Douglass's *Narrative*.

8.33/xi.26   Charles county, Maryland] The site of the earliest European settlements in present-day Maryland, Charles County lies in the southern portion of the state along the Potomac River. Leon E. Seltzer, ed., *The Columbia Lippincott Gazetteer of the World,* rev. ed. (New York, 1962), 374.

8.34/xi.27   a young man, named Matthews] Probably William B. Matthews, a seventeen-year-old youth from Charles County, Maryland, at the time of the incident. 1850 U.S. Census, Maryland, Charles County, 578; Baltimore *Sun,* 18 April 1845.

8.35/xi.28–29   whose father . . . at Washington] William B. Matthews's father was John Matthews (c. 1783?), a wealthy slaveowner and landholder in Charles County, Maryland. The Matthews family owned property in the Middletown district of the county. 1850 U.S. Census, Maryland, Charles County, 578; Baltimore *Sun,* 18 April 1845.

9.5–6/xii.5   incompetent to testify against a white man] Garrison possibly relies on the compilation of slave codes by Theodore Weld that concluded that statutes, as well as public opinion, precluded testimony from slaves and free blacks when a white person was accused. [Weld,] *American Slavery,* 148–49.

9.14–15/xii.17   a cloud of witnesses] Heb. 12 : 1.

9.25–26/xii.31–32   " . . . NO UNION WITH SLAVEHOLDERS!"] In 1844, the

American Anti-Slavery Society adopted a resolution, penned by Garrison, branding the U.S. Constitution a proslavery document and calling for a dissolution of the Union. The motto Garrison quotes later appeared on the masthead of his Boston *Liberator*. Walter H. Merrill, *Against Wind and Tide: A Biography of William Lloyd Garrison* (Cambridge, Mass., 1963), 204–14, 255, 269–75; Thomas, *Liberator,* 328–59, 374.

10.2/xiii.2   WENDELL PHILLIPS] Boston-born and Harvard-educated Wendell Phillips (1811–84) ranked second only to Garrison in influence in the American Anti-Slavery Society in the 1840s and 1850s. A highly gifted orator, Phillips was in demand as a lecturer even in nonabolitionist circles. Besides abolition, Phillips championed woman suffrage, prohibition, penal reform, Indian rights, and legislative protection for workers. James Brewer Stewart, *Wendell Phillips: Liberty's Hero* (Baton Rouge, 1986); Irving H. Bartlett, *Wendell Phillips: Brahmin Radical* (Boston, 1961); *DAB,* 14 : 546–47.

10.5/xiii.5–6   "The Man and the Lion,"] Phillips loosely adapts a fable by Aesop, alternatively known as "The Lion and the Statue." Thomas Newbigging, *The Fables and Fabulists: Ancient and Modern* (1895; Freeport, N.Y., 1972), 9.

10.16/xiii.20   the West India experiment] The Abolition Act passed by Parliament on 28 August 1833 began the gradual emancipation of slavery in Great Britain's West Indian colonies. The following year, the legislation freed all slaves under six but held the remainder to work for the former masters as apprentices for a period ending 1 August 1838. The owners received twenty million pounds in compensation for the emancipated slaves. William A. Green, *British Slave Emancipation: The Sugar Colonies and the Great Experiment* (Oxford, 1976), 129–75.

10.26/xiv.5–6   the "white sails" of the Chesapeake] Phillips probably alludes to the same passage in Chapter 10 that Garrison earlier had.

10.36/xiv.19   Valley of the Shadow of Death] Ps. 23 : 4.

11.25–26/xv.19   the halter about their necks] Possibly an allusion to the statement that early U.S. historian Jared Sparks in 1840 claimed that Benjamin Franklin had made to John Hancock at the time of the signing of the Declaration of Independence: "Yes, we must indeed all hang together, or most assuredly we shall all hang separately." Carl Van Doren, *Benjamin Franklin* (Garden City, N.Y., 1941), 551–52.

12.8/xvi.12–13   *"hide* the outcast,"] A slight misquotation of Isa. 16 : 3.

13.5/1.2   in Tuckahoe, near Hillsborough] Talbot County, on Maryland's Eastern Shore, had been an important tobacco-growing region since colonial times. In 1788 the state legislature designated Easton, until then known as Talbot Town, as the administrative center for state operations for all nine Eastern Shore counties. Hillsborough (or Hillsboro) is situated northeast of Easton on Tuckahoe Creek, a tributary of the Choptank River that forms part of the eastern boundary of Talbot County. Dickson J. Preston, *Talbot County: A History* (Centreville, Md., 1983), 140, 191, 256; Paul Wilstach, *Tidewater Maryland* (Indianapolis, 1931), 104–05.

13.6–7/1.4   knowledge of my age] As nearly as can be determined, Douglass was born in February 1818. Ledger books kept by his master Aaron Anthony contain a table, "My Black People," with the notation "Frederick Augustus son of Harriott Feby 1818." Further evidence for the year 1818 is presented in Preston, *Young Frederick Douglass,* 31–34, 218–19nn1–5; Aaron Anthony Ledger B, 1812–26, folder 95, 165, Dodge Collection, MdAA.

13.16/2.3–4   my master] Aaron Anthony (1767–1826), Frederick Douglass's first owner and possibly his father, was born at Tuckahoe Neck in present-day Caroline County, Maryland. Anthony's father was a poor and illiterate farmer who died when Aaron was only two. Despite his impoverished origins, Anthony acquired a rudimentary education and a small amount of property. He became the captain in 1795 of the *Sally Lloyd,* the family schooner of Edward Lloyd IV, the wealthiest planter in Talbot County. In 1797 he increased his wealth through his marriage to Ann Catherine Skinner, the daughter of an old and prominent Eastern Shore family, who brought with her the slave family into which Douglass was later born. Soon thereafter, Anthony became chief overseer and general manager of the Lloyd family's thirteen farms, one of the largest estates in the United States. He remained in this position for the remainder of his life, all the while accumulating land and slaves of his own. By the time of his death in 1826, Anthony had become a moderately wealthy planter, accumulating three farms totaling 597 ½ acres, thirty slaves worth $3,065, and personal property. His estate was valued at $8,042. Anthony Family Bible, Oxford Museum, Oxford, Md.; Harriet L. Anthony, annotated copy of *My Bondage and My Freedom,* folder 93, 58, Dodge Collection, MdAA; Inventory of estate of Aaron Anthony, 13 January 1827, Talbot County Inventories, box 13, 5–9, MdTCH; Hulbert Footner, *Rivers of the Eastern Shore: Seventeen Maryland Rivers* (New York, 1944), 285, 299–304; Charles B. Clark, ed., *The Eastern Shore of Maryland and Virginia,* 3 vols. (New York, 1950), 1 : 491–92; Preston, *Young Frederick Douglass,* 22–30; idem, "Aaron Anthony" (unpublished paper, Easton, Md., 1977), MdTCH.

13.21/2.6   Harriet Bailey] Harriet Bailey (1792–1825) was the second child of a free black man, Isaac Bailey, and his enslaved wife, Betsey. She was owned by her mother's master, Aaron Anthony. From 1808 until her death, she was hired out by Anthony to local farmers as a field hand. In February 1818, while serving Perry Steward, a tenant farmer on Anthony's Holme Hill Farm in Tuckahoe Creek, she gave birth to Frederick Augustus Bailey, her fourth of six or seven children. In late 1825 or early 1826, she died on the Holme Hill Farm in Tuckahoe Creek after a long illness. Aaron Anthony, Ledger B, 1812–26, folder 95, 165, Dodge Collection, MdAA; Preston, *Young Frederick Douglass,* 8, 9, 17, 21, 34–35, 62–64, 205, 206, 219n9.

13.21/2.7   Isaac] Born some time before 1775, Isaac Bailey was a free black man and the husband of Betsey Bailey, a slave owned by Aaron Anthony. Isaac and Betsey lived together on Anthony's Tuckahoe Creek farm. A sawyer, Bailey was frequently employed by both Anthony and Edward Lloyd V to provide lumber for their plantations. On occasion, he hired one of Anthony's slaves to assist him in his work. He also sometimes earned wages as a plowman and harvest laborer on Anthony's farms. Bailey appears in the 1820 Talbot County census as a free black presiding over a large household with four adult women and nine children. The 1840 census lists him as living with one adult woman and a young boy. Bailey died during the 1840s. Ledger B, 1812–26, folder 95, Ledger C, 1809–27, folder 96, Anthony Family Papers, Dodge Collection, MdAA; 1820 U.S. Census, Maryland, Talbot County, 336; 1840 U.S. Census, Maryland, Talbot County, 9; Preston, *Young Frederick Douglass,* 17–20.

13.22/2.7   Betsy Bailey] Betsey Bailey (1774–1849), the maternal grand-mother of Frederick Douglass, grew up a slave on the Skinner plantation in Talbot County, Maryland. In 1797 she became the property of Aaron Anthony, who acquired her and several other slaves through his marriage to Ann Skinner. Anthony moved her to his farm on Tuckahoe Creek in Talbot County. She married Isaac Bailey, a free black who earned his living as a sawyer, and lived with him in her cabin. There she bore nine daughters and three sons. She was also a midwife, a service for which Anthony paid her. Upon Anthony's death in 1826, Bailey was inherited by Andrew Skinner Anthony, Aaron's son; when Andrew died in 1833, she became the slave of John Planner Anthony. Despite this succession of masters and the death of her husband, she remained in her cabin on the Tuckahoe Creek farm, living alone, nearly destitute, and going blind. In 1840, Thomas Auld, John Anthony's uncle, learned of Bailey's condition and sent for her, caring for her in his Talbot County home until her death. Aaron Anthony Slave Distribution, 22 October 1827, Talbot County Distributions, V.JP#D, 58–59, MdTCH; Inventory of Negroes owned by Aaron Anthony, 19 December 1826, folder 71, Aaron Anthony Slave Distribution, 27 September 1827, folder 77, "My Black People[s] Ages," Aaron Anthony Ledger A, folder 94, Aaron Anthony Ledger B, 1812–26, folder 77, 159, 165–68, Harriet Anthony's annotated copy of *Bondage and Freedom,* folder 93, 180, all in the Anthony Family Papers, Dodge Collection, MdAA; Douglass to Thomas Auld, 3 September 1848, 3 September 1849, in *NS,* 8 September 1848, 7 September 1849, reprinted in *Lib.,* 22 September 1848, 14 September 1849; Preston, *Young Frederick Douglass,* 8, 16–20, 167.

14.2/2.32   Mr. Stewart] From 1817 to 1821, Perry Ward Steward (?–1821), a tenant farmer, rented Holme Hill Farm from Aaron Anthony and hired the slave Harriet Bailey as a domestic servant. A Perry W. Stewart was listed in the 1820 Census as the head of a large household of eleven members. Aaron Anthony Ledger A, 1790–1818, file #94, 18, 19, 22, Dodge Collection, MdAA; 1820 U.S. Census, Maryland, Talbot County, 336; Preston, *Young Frederick Douglass,* 35, 219n7.

14.14/3.17   Lee's Mill] Levi Lee owned a mill near Holme Hill Farm and the Tuckahoe River in 1820. In that year, he headed a large household of eight family members and six slaves. 1820 U.S. Census, Maryland, Talbot County, 48; Preston, *Young Frederick Douglass,* 36.

15.14/5.8   God cursed Ham] Douglass refers to the account in the book of Genesis in which Noah curses Canaan, the son of Ham, for an offense that Ham had committed against his father, Noah. Through an obscure history the meaning of the curse "a servant of servants shall he be unto his brethren" had evolved in Christian Europe as a justification for the enslavement of Africans, the "sons of Ham." Proslavery advocates in the American South used this argument extensively in the renewed debates of the 1840s. Gen. 9 : 25; David Brion Davis, *The Problem of Slavery in the Age of Revolution, 1770–1823* (Ithaca, N.Y., 1975), 539–41, 555–56; Larry E. Tise, *Proslavery: A History of the Defense of Slavery in America, 1701–1840* (Athens, Ga., 1987), 106, 118, 189; George M. Fredrickson, *The Black Image in the White Mind: The Debate on Afro-American Character and Destiny, 1817–1914* (New York, 1971), 60–61.

15.25/5.24   Mr. Plummer] This individual is probably either James Plummer or Philemon Plummer. Both men were longtime residents of Talbot County and, at various times during Douglass's youth, worked for Aaron Anthony as overseers on his Tuckahoe farms. Philemon Plummer is listed in Anthony's accounting records for 1819. Aaron Anthony Day Books, folder 97, 30, Dodge Collection, MdAA; Preston, *Young Frederick Douglass,* 71, 222n7.

15.34–35/6.4–5   an own aunt of mine] Hester Bailey (1810–?) was one of twelve children born to Isaac and Betsey Bailey and owned by Aaron Anthony of Talbot County. The last trace of Hester and the lone child she bore was recorded in 1827, when she was awarded to Thomas Auld after the death of Aaron Anthony. Aaron Anthony Slave Distribution, 22 October 1827, Talbot County Distributions, V.JP#D, 58–59; Preston, *Young Frederick Douglass,* 18, 27, 206, 221n2.

16.15–16/7.1   Colonel Lloyd] Edward Lloyd V (1779–1834) of Wye House was the scion of Talbot County's first family. One of the state's largest landowners and slaveowners, he was also Maryland's most successful wheat grower and cattle raiser of his era. As a charter member of the Maryland Agricultural Society, a founder of at least two banks, and a speculator in coal lands, he became the wealthiest of a long line of Lloyds that reached back to colonial Maryland. In terms of slaves alone, his huge holdings increased from 420 in 1810 to 545 in 1830. An eager student of politics as an adolescent and a frequent auditor of political debate at the Annapolis State House, Edward V became a Republican delegate to the state legislature as soon as he reached the age of majority in 1800. The following year, he was active in securing passage of a bill removing all restrictions to white male suffrage. From 1806 to 1808 he was a U.S. congressman, voting in 1807 against a bill to end the African slave trade. For the next two years he was governor of Maryland, and from 1811 to 1816 he returned to the state legislature. In 1819 he was elected to the U.S. Senate, from which he resigned in 1826 to return to the Maryland senate, where he was president until 1831. Edward V married Sally Scott

Murray on 30 November 1797 and had six children with her. 1810 U.S. Census, Maryland, Talbot County, 342; Oswald Tilghman, *History of Talbot County, Maryland, 1661–1861,* 2 vols. (Baltimore, 1915), 1 : 184–210; Footner, *Rivers of the Eastern Shore,* 283–90; Preston, *Young Frederick Douglass,* 26, 30, 48–54, 57–58, 74, 82; *Biographical Directory of the American Congress, 1774–1989: Bicentennial Edition* (Washington, D.C., 1989), 1381.

16.16/7.2   Ned Roberts] Ned Roberts (1810–?) was a slave owned by Edward Lloyd V. It was 1825 when Aaron Anthony discovered that his slave Hester Bailey was continuing to see Ned Roberts. Return Book, 1 January 1824, Land Papers—Maintenance of Property, Land Volume 39, reel 10, Lloyd Family Papers, MdHi.

17.8/8.11   two sons, Andrew] Andrew Skinner Anthony (1797–1833) was the eldest son of Aaron and Ann Catherine Skinner Anthony and the nephew of Edward Lloyd V. His father apprenticed him as a young man to James Neall, a cabinetmaker, in Easton, Maryland. After completing his apprenticeship, Anthony migrated to Indiana, where he married Ann Wingate of Martin County in 1823. He and his bride returned to Talbot County shortly thereafter. In 1826 Andrew's father died and he inherited a third of his estate, including eight slaves. Although he increased his estate and owned twenty slaves, Andrew suffered from alcoholism and operated a whiskey shop in his final years. John Manross to Douglass, 14 January 1856, General Correspondence File, reel 1, frames 654–56, FD Papers, DLC; Harriet Anthony's annotated copy of *Bondage and Freedom,* folder 93, 176 Dodge Collection, MdAA; 1830 U.S. Census, Maryland, Talbot County, 51; Preston, *Young Frederick Douglass,* 26, 29, 218n17, 224n10.

17.8/8.12   Richard] Richard Lee Anthony (1800–28), the second eldest of three children born to Aaron and Ann Anthony, was trained as a blacksmith for five years before inheriting land, money, and slaves after his father's death in November 1826. Douglass incorrectly asserted that Richard died before his father. Harriet L. Anthony's annotated copy of *Bondage and Freedom,* folder 93, 173–74, Dodge Collection, MdAA; Aaron Anthony Slave Distribution, 22 October 1827, Talbot County Distributions, V.JP#D, 58–59, MdTCH; Preston, *Young Frederick Douglass,* 27, 28, 29, 52, 91, 218n17.

17.8–9/8.12   one daughter, Lucretia] Lucretia Planner Anthony Auld (1804–27) was the third child and only daughter of Aaron and Ann Anthony. In 1823 she married Thomas Auld, a boarder in her father's household and an employee of Edward Lloyd. Lucretia subsequently moved to Hillsborough, Maryland, where she and her husband opened a store. Following the deaths of her father and brother Richard Lee, Lucretia and her older brother Andrew inherited their father's estate. Her portion included the young slave Frederick Douglass. She died in 1827 and was survived by one child, Arianna Amanda Auld. Auld Family Bible (courtesy of Carl G. Auld); McFeely, *Frederick Douglass,* 27; Preston, *Young Frederick Douglass,* 28, 30, 62, 87–88, 223n6; Preston, *Talbot County,* 191; Emerson B. Roberts, "A Visitation of Western Talbot," *MdHM,* 41 : 244–45 (September 1946).

17.9/8.13   Captain Thomas Auld] Born in St. Michaels, Maryland, Thomas Auld (1795–1880) was the eldest son of Hugh and Zipporah Auld. Trained as a shipbuilder, Auld supervised the construction of the Lloyd sloop, the *Sally Lloyd,* and subsequently became its captain. In 1823, he met and married Lucretia Anthony while a boarder in the Anthony home. Shortly thereafter, in 1827, Auld became a storekeeper in Hillsborough, Maryland, and inherited Douglass along with ten other slaves from the estate of Aaron Anthony. He later kept store in St. Michaels where he also served as postmaster, before retiring to a nearby farm. The 1850 census listed him as a "farmer" with $8,500 worth of real estate. References to Thomas Auld in Douglass's *Narrative* and public speeches are generally uncomplimentary although Douglass disclaimed any personal hostility toward his former owner. A reconciliation occurred in the post-Reconstruction period when Douglass visited the dying Auld in St. Michaels. *NASS,* 25 November 1845; *NS,* 8 September 1848, 7 September 1849; Baltimore *Sun,* 19 June 1877; Aaron Anthony Slave Distribution, 22 October 1827, Talbot County Distributions, V.JP#D, 58–59, MdTCH; 1850 U.S. Census, Maryland, Talbot County, 1169 (schedule of free inhabitants); Benjamin Quarles, *Frederick Douglass* (Washington, D.C., 1948), 342–43; Tilghman, *Talbot County,* 1 : 395; Preston, "Aaron Anthony," 5; Roberts, "Visitation of Western Talbot," 235–45.

17.10/8.14   the home plantation of Colonel Edward Lloyd] Settled by Edward Lloyd I in 1658, Wye House, the home plantation of the Lloyds, was situated on a peninsula formed by the Wye River on the north and the Miles River on the south. By 1790, Edward Lloyd IV, father of Edward Lloyd V, owned 11,884 acres in the region. The mansion house to which Douglass refers was built in 1784 and overlooks Lloyd's Cove on the Wye River. Aaron Anthony and his family lived in the "Captain's House," a brick outbuilding near the mansion. Douglass lived at Anthony's home at Wye House from August 1824 to March 1826. Footner, *Rivers of the Eastern Shore,* 269–93; H[enry] Chandlee Forman, *Old Buildings, Gardens, and Furniture in Tidewater Maryland* (Cambridge, Md., 1967), 51–80; Preston, *Young Frederick Douglass,* 37–40, 199.

17.21–22/9.4–5   This sloop was named Sally Lloyd] In 1819 Edward Lloyd V ordered the construction of a new sloop to replace the aging schooner *Elizabeth & Ann,* which carried his crops to markets in Baltimore and Annapolis and brought back supplies to his scattered Talbot County farms. Thomas Auld had supervised the construction, in Joseph Kemp's St. Michaels shipyard, of the replacement vessel, named the *Sally Lloyd* in honor of the colonel's eldest daughter, Sally Scott Lloyd. Auld remained in Lloyd's employment as the master of the *Sally Lloyd,* which was manned by a slave crew. The latter gained celebrity status among the Lloyd slaves because of their contact with the world outside the rural plantations and their ability to purchase small items in the cities for resale to other slaves. Various account books and cash books, Land Papers—Maintenance of Property, Land Volume 39, reel 10, Lloyd Family Papers, MdHi.

17.22/9.5   one of the colonel's daughters] Sally Scott Lloyd Lowndes, the second daughter of Edward Lloyd V, was the namesake of her mother Sally Scott Murray Lloyd. She married Charles Lowndes, a U.S. Navy officer, on 24 May 1824. Colonel Lloyd purchased an estate called the Anchorage on the Miles River as a gift for the couple. Their son Lloyd Lowndes served as governor of Maryland from 1896 to 1900. Rossiter Johnson, ed., *The Twentieth Century Biographical Dictionary of Notable Americans,* 10 vols. (Boston, 1904), 7:n.p.; Tilghman, *Talbot County,* 1 : 207; Preston, *Young Frederick Douglass,* 47, 222n4.

17.24–25/9.8–9   Peter, Isaac, Rich, and Jake] Two of the slaves who served as the crew of the *Sally Lloyd* appear in the business records of Edward Lloyd V: Peter (1799–?) and Rich (1817–?). Various account books and cash books, Land Papers—Maintenance of Property, Land Volume 39, reel 10, Lloyd Family Papers, MdHi.

17.28/9.13–14   three to four hundred slaves] Douglass exaggerates the number of slaves owned by Edward Lloyd V. In 1824, the year Douglass arrived on the Lloyd's main plantation, there were 181 slaves at Wye House, including the fifteen owned by Aaron Anthony who also lived there. The Lloyds owned slaves on adjoining farms as well, though their number is not available. Edward Lloyd IV owned 305 slaves in 1790, and his grandson, Edward Lloyd VI, owned an estimated 700 slaves, including those on his Mississippi Valley plantations. Return Book, 1 January 1824, Land Papers—Maintenance of Property, Land Volume 39, reel 10, Lloyd Family Papers, MdHi; Footner, *Rivers of the Eastern Shore,* 280–81; Tilghman, *Talbot County,* 1 : 225; Preston, *Young Frederick Douglass,* 48, 220n13.

17.31/9.17   Wye Town] Wye Town is located at the confluence of the Miles River and the Wye River in Talbot County, next to the main Lloyd plantation Wye House. At the urging of the Lloyds, the Maryland General Assembly had established the site of a town here in 1683 which was later abandoned. Wye Town Farm, part of the land owned here by the Lloyds, encompassed 260 acres. Henry Chandlee Forman, *Tidewater Maryland Architecture and Gardens* (New York, 1956), 49–54.

17.31/9.17   New Design] New Design Farm was one of several smaller plantations owned by Edward Lloyd V in Talbot County. At least through the 1820s, Lloyd used it primarily for growing wheat. Various account books and cash books, Land Papers—Maintenance of Property, Land Volume 39, reel 10, Lloyd Family Papers, MdHi.

17.32/9.19   Noah Willis] In 1819 Aaron Anthony's records indicate that he employed a Noah Willes. A Noah Willis is listed in the 1820 census as an overseer in Talbot County. He was between 26 and 45 years old. Willis is listed again in the 1830 census but without any job designation. He was married by then, having eight children under 15 in his household, and owned four slaves. Willis held over 400 acres of land by the late 1820s. Aaron Anthony Papers, Ledger A, 1790–1818, file

94, 19; 1820 U.S. Census, Maryland, Talbot County, 7; 1830 U.S. Census, Maryland, Talbot County, 14; Whitman H. Ridgway, *Community Leadership in Maryland, 1790–1840: A Comparative Analysis of Power in Society* (Chapel Hill, 1979), 339.

17.33/9.20   Mr. Townsend] Between 1809 and 1812, George Townsend worked for Aaron Anthony, probably as an overseer. In 1820, he was between twenty-six and forty years of age, and managed a farm which had 23 slaves. 1820 U.S. Census, Maryland, Talbot County, 6; Aaron Anthony Ledger C, 1809–27, folder 96, 3, 35, 69, 114, 119, 128, 171, 177, 286, 315, Dodge Collection, MdAA.

18.3/9.30   Austin Woolfolk] Austin Woolfolk of Augusta, Georgia, became a slave trader serving the Southwest, which rapidly expanded following the Battle of New Orleans in 1815. He settled in Baltimore in 1819 to avail himself both of the large surplus slave population in the state and the excellent shipping facilities which the port afforded. During the 1820s he lived on Pratt Street to the west of the city's commercial center. Woolfolk's business prospered as he sent agents throughout Maryland ready to pay high prices in cash for young black males. He annually transported from 230 to 460 slaves to markets in New Orleans, many of them having been purchased from planters on the Eastern Shore. In the 1830s, however, Woolfolk's business declined due to increased competition from larger firms, a decrease in the number of slaves for sale owing to manumissions and owner emigrations, and the heightened opposition of Marylanders to the interstate slave trade. Preston, *Young Frederick Douglass,* 50, 58, 76–80, 96, 102; William Calderhead, "The Role of the Professional Slave Trader in a Slave Economy: Austin Woolfolk, A Case Study," *Civil War History,* 23 : 195–211 (September 1977).

18.10–11/10.8   negro cloth] Coarse, durable, inexpensive cloth manufactured for sale to slaveowners for their servants.

18.34/11.8–9   Mr. Severe] During the years 1809–12 and possibly thereafter, William Sevier worked for Aaron Anthony, probably as an overseer on his farms. In 1820, he was between twenty-six and forty years old. At that time Sevier occupied a small red frame house on the east side of Wye House's Long Green, and was Edward Lloyd V's overseer for the more than 150 slaves at the main plantation. Aaron Anthony Ledger A, 1790–1818, folder 94, 19, Ledger C, 1809–27, folder 96, 1, 3, 13, 87, 119, 124, 177, 286, 291; 1820 U.S. Census, Maryland, Talbot County, 7; Preston, *Young Frederick Douglass,* 70–71, 222n5 and n6.

19.14/12.3   Mr. Hopkins] James Hopkins briefly took the place of William Sevier as overseer of the Wye House plantation. Preston, *Young Frederick Douglass,* 73.

19.25–26/12.20   the *Great House Farm*] A reference to the principal plantation of Edward Lloyd V, the Wye House plantation. Douglass visited there in June 1881 and several younger members of the Lloyd family escorted him around the grounds. Preston, *Young Frederick Douglass,* 192–96.

21.2/14.29–30   "there . . . heart."] Douglass quotes line 8 from *The Time*

Piece by William Cowper. J.C. Bailey, ed., *The Poems of William Cowper* (London, 1905), 267.

21.17–18/15.19–20   the chief gardener, (Mr. M'Durmond.)] In 1824 Aaron Anthony hired William McDermott to work for Edward Lloyd V. McDermott lived and ate at Anthony's house at least through spring 1825. Aaron Anthony Ledger A, 1790–1818, folder 94, 42, 43, Dodge Collection, MdAA.

22.3–4/16.24   Old Barney and Young Barney] Old Barney was Barnett Sampson (c. 1768–?). He was owned by Edward Lloyd V and was the father of Young Barney, Barnett Bentley (c. 1810–?). He was listed as fifty-five years old in January 1824. Return Book, 1 January 1824, Land Papers—Maintenance of Property, Land Volume 39, reel 10, Lloyd Family Papers, MdHi.

22.31/17.31   Edward] Born in the Annapolis home of his maternal grandparents, Edward Lloyd VI (1798–1861) was the oldest child and principal heir of his father's great wealth. Educated at the Wye House plantation by tutors, the younger Lloyd received charge of a nearby plantation where his father built him the beautiful Wye Heights mansion upon his marriage in 1824 to Alicia McBlair, daughter of a Baltimore merchant. She died prematurely in 1838 after bearing five children. After inheriting the bulk of his father's landholdings, Lloyd successfully shifted from tobacco to grain farming and weathered the agricultural depression that struck most of the Eastern Shore in the 1840s and 1850s. Lloyd also purchased cotton growing land in Mississippi in 1837 and later added more in Arkansas and Louisiana. He transferred some of his swelling slave population to those new plantations. Although reputedly a stern disciplinarian, he did try to avoid separating families during these relocations and when sales occurred. A life-long Democrat, Lloyd served as a delegate to the Maryland constitutional convention of 1850 and as a state senator (1851–52). 1850 U.S. Census, Maryland, Talbot County, 6–10 (slave schedule); Tilghman, *Talbot County,* 1 : 210–21; Preston, *Young Frederick Douglass,* 42–43, 44–45, 70, 192; J. Donnell Tilghman, "Wye House," *MdHM,* 48 : 89–108 (June 1953).

22.31/17.31   Murray] James Murray Lloyd (1803–47) was the middle son of Edward Lloyd V and Sally Murray Scott. When he married, his father built a mansion for him called Presqu'ile which quickly became a Talbot County showplace. In 1840, he was one of the region's richest farmers, owning 113 slaves. 1840 U.S. Census, Maryland, Talbot County, 60; Stella Pickett Hardy, *Colonial Families of the Southern States of America* (New York, 1911), 387; Preston, *Young Frederick Douglass,* 47, 49–50, 69, 70; Tilghman, *Talbot County,* 1 : 207, 222.

22.31/17.31   Daniel] Daniel Lloyd (1811–75) was the sixth-born child and youngest son of Edward Lloyd V. Daniel became a farmer and his wealth increased steadily, expanding the number of slaves he owned from 18 to 36 between 1840 and 1850. By the latter year, he possessed real estate valued at $25,000. After the death of his father, Lloyd resided at the nearby Wye Heights Plantation, earlier built for Edward Lloyd VI and his wife. Daniel's son, Henry, was Maryland's governor in the 1880s. 1840 U.S. Census, Maryland, Talbot County, 59; 1850 U.S. Census, Maryland, Talbot County, 11a (free schedule), 14 (slave schedule); Preston, *Young Frederick Douglass,* 54–55, 61, 81, 221n21; Tilghman, *Talbot County,* 1 : 207, 212.

22.32/17.32   Mr. Winder] Edward Stoughton Winder, son of Levin Winder, the sixteenth governor of Maryland, and Mary Sloss, married Elizabeth Tayloe Lloyd, the eldest daughter of Edward Lloyd V, in 1820. Their son, Charles Sidney Winder, became a Confederate brigadier general. Edward most likely died before 1850 as that year's census lists Elizabeth, rather than him, as the family head. 1850 U.S. Census, Maryland, Talbot County, 52; Tilghman, *Talbot County,* 1 : 207; Preston, *Young Frederick Douglass,* 221–22; Hardy, *Colonial Families,* 387; *National Cyclopaedia of American Biography* (New York, 1898), 5 : 514.

22.32/17.32   Mr. Nicholson] Joseph Nicholson was the son of Rebecca Lloyd, Edward V's sister, and her husband, Joseph Hopper Nicholson (1770–1817), a Democratic-Republican congressman from Baltimore from 1799 through 1806 and thereafter a prominent Maryland jurist. The younger Nicholson was the nephew of Edward Lloyd V, not the son-in-law, as Douglass identifies him. Preston, *Young Frederick Douglass,* 70, 222n4; Hardy, *Colonial Families,* 500–11; *DAB,* 13 : 505–06; *BDAC,* 1570.

22.32/17.32–18.1   Mr. Lowndes] Born in Kent County, Maryland, Charles Lowndes (1798–1885) entered the navy as a midshipman in 1815. He married Sally Scott Lloyd in the mid-1820s and by 1840 was a prosperous Talbot County farmer with thirty-five slaves. By the start of the Civil War, he had risen to the rank of captain in the U.S. Navy. Suspected of Confederate sympathies, he was placed on the retired list in 1862 and later promoted to commodore and placed on a war prize commission. 1840 U.S. Census, Maryland, Talbot County, 70; Preston, *Young Frederick Douglass,* 47, 222; Johnson, *Twentieth Century Biographical Dictionary,* 7 : n.p.; Christopher Johnston, "Lowndes Family," *MdHM,* 2 : 279 (September 1907); *Appleton's Cyclopaedia of American Biography,* 6 vols. (New York, 1888–89), 4 : 44.

22.34/18.3–4   William Wilkes] William Wilks (c. 1791–?) was a slave of Edward Lloyd V. Sometime in the first half of the 1830s he purchased his freedom and moved to Baltimore. In that city, Wilks worked as a general laborer and resided on Lexington Street, east of Park Street. Return Book, 1 January 1824, Land Papers—Maintenance of Property, Land Volume 39, reel 10, Lloyd Family Papers, MdHi; *Matchett's Baltimore Director[y] . . . 1835–6* (Baltimore, 1835), 275; *Matchett's Baltimore Director[y] . . . 1837–8* (Baltimore, 1837), 472.

22.39/18.9   the riches of Job] Douglass refers to the biblical story of Job, where his wealth is enumerated and he is described as "the greatest of all in the east." Job 1 : 1–3.

23.26–27/19.13–14   a still tongue makes a wise head] This saying probably had its roots in an old English epigram, "Hauyng a styll toung he had a besy head." *The Proverbs and Epigrams of John Heywood* (1562; New York, 1967), 214.

24.5/20.6–7   Jacob Jepson] Jacob Gibson (1759–1818), a slaveowner locally feared for his volatile temper, resided at Marengo, a plantation bordering the Lloyd property. Douglass mistakenly refers to him as "Jacob Jepson." Appointed an associate judge for Talbot County in 1802, Gibson won election to the legislature in 1806. Residents remembered him because of his numerous vitriolic broadsides and newspaper essays as well as his physical assaults on his enemies. The 1810 U.S. census listed him as the owner of thirty-four slaves, whom Gibson reputedly ruled over as a stern taskmaster. Gibson's plantation belonged to his son Fayette at the time to which Douglass refers. 1810 U.S. Census, Maryland, Talbot County, 342; Tilghman, *Talbot County,* 1 : 231–56; Preston, *Young Frederick Douglass,* 60, 221n28.

24.18–19/20.25   Mr. Austin Gore] Austin Gore (1794–1871), also referred to as Orson Gore in the Lloyd family account and cash books, was the overseer of Edward Lloyd V's Davis's Farm plantation where in 1822 a young slave named Bill Demby died. A friend of Gore's later challenged Douglass's assertion that Gore coolly murdered Demby, insisting that he was "a respectable citizen living near St. Michaels, and . . . a worthy member of the Methodist Episcopal Church; . . . all who know him, think him anything but a murderer." Lloyd apparently tolerated Gore's brutal actions because he later promoted him to be overseer of the much larger Wye House plantation. The 1830 U.S. census listed Gore as the head of a household which contained three boys and two girls under 10, his wife, and an elderly woman. Only a child at the time of Demby's death, Douglass must have constructed his narrative of the incident from plantation legends. A. C. C. Thompson, "To the Public—Falsehood Refuted," reprinted in the *NASS,* 25 November 1845 and in *Lib.,* 12 December 1845; Various account books and cash books, Land Papers—Maintenance of Property, Land Volume 39, reel 10, Lloyd Family Papers, MdHi; 1830 U.S. Census, Maryland, Talbot County, 14.

25.27/22.29   by the name of Demby] Bill Demby (c. 1802–22) lived with twenty-two other slaves, including his family, on Davis's Farm, one of several Talbot County plantations owned by Edward Lloyd V. Plantation records indicate that Demby, a prime field hand, died sometime during the year 1822. Return Book, 1 January 1822, 1 January 1823, Land Papers—Maintenance of Property, Land Volume 39, reel 10, Lloyd Family Papers, MdHi; Preston, *Young Frederick Douglass,* 72–73, 213n10.

26.22/24.12   Mr. Thomas Lanman] Thomas H. W. Lambdin (c. 1807–?) had labored at a number of trades by 1850: ship carpenter, schoolteacher, town bailiff for St. Michaels (1848), and miller (1850). In 1850 he was married and had five young children. He owned real estate valued at $1,000.00 in that year. In a rebuttal to Douglass's negative characterization, a Maryland friend described Lambdin as "too good-natured and harmless to injure any person but himself." A. C. C.

Thompson, "To the Public—Falsehood Refuted," reprinted in *NASS,* 25 November 1845 and in *Lib.,* 12 December 1845; Tilghman, *Talbot County,* 2 : 395.

26.28/24.21   Mr. Giles Hicks] A Giles Hicks resided in Caroline County, Maryland in 1820. 1820 U.S. Census, Maryland, Talbot County, 92.

26.29/24.22   my wife's] Anna Murray Douglass (c. 1813–82), Frederick Douglass's first wife, was born free in Denton, Caroline County, Maryland. She was the eighth child of Bambarra Murray and his wife Mary, slaves who had been manumitted shortly before Anna's birth. At seventeen she moved to Baltimore, where she worked as a domestic. She met Douglass at meetings of the East Baltimore Mental Improvement Society, helped finance his escape, and, according to plan, joined him in New York City, where they were married on 15 September 1838. During Douglass's tour of the British Isles in 1845–47 she remained in Lynn, Massachusetts, where she supported herself by binding shoes. There she gained a reputation for frugality and skillful household management—qualities that would contribute greatly to her family's financial prosperity over the years. A member of the Lynn Ladies' Anti-Slavery Society and a regular participant in the annual antislavery bazaars in Boston, she continued her antislavery activities after moving to Rochester in 1847. Unlettered, reserved, and, according to her husband, never completely at ease in white company, she seldom appeared at public functions with Douglass. She was nevertheless affectionately remembered by her husband's associates as a "warm" and "hospitable" hostess at their home. On 9 July 1882, Anna Douglass suffered an attack of paralysis in Washington, D.C. She died there on 4 August. In January 1884 Douglass married Helen Pitts, a white woman. *Lib.,* 18 November, 2 December 1853; Philadelphia *Christian Recorder,* 20 July 1882; Washington *Post,* 5 August 1882; Rosetta Douglass Sprague, *Anna Murray Douglass: My Mother as I Recall Her* (1900; Washington, D.C., 1923); Jane Marsh Parker, "Reminiscences of Frederick Douglass," *Outlook* 51 : 552–53 (6 April 1895); Preston, *Young Frederick Douglass,* 149, 151, 154, 159; Quarles, *Frederick Douglass,* 9–10, 100–01, 106, 109–10, 297–98.

27.15/25.25   Mr. Beal Bondly] John Beale Bordley (1800–82) was the son of Matthias Bordley (1757–1828) and the grandson of John Beale Bordley (1727–1804), a noted agriculturalist and Revolutionary War era patriot from Maryland. Often called simply Beale Bordley, John Beale Bordley was born on his father's Wye Island estate, across the river from the Lloyd plantation, and remained there until his mid-twenties when he moved to Philadelphia to study law with Pennsylvania Chief Justice John Bannister Gibson. Quickly tiring of the law, Bordley came to develop a very successful career as a portrait painter of prominent figures in Baltimore, Philadelphia, and elsewhere. A number of his paintings are held by the Maryland Historical Society. Francis Sims McGrath, "A Letter to Eileen," *MdHM,* 24 : 306 (December 1929); Eugenia Calvert Holland and Louisa MacGill Gray, comps., "Miniatures in the Collection of the Maryland Historical Society," *MdHM,* 51 : 342, 346, 353 (December 1956); Anna Wells Rutledge, "Portraits

Painted Before 1900 in the Collection of the Maryland Historical Society . . . ,"
MdHM, 41 : 35, 36, 43 (March 1946); Baltimore *American and Commercial
Advertiser,* 14 March 1882; Francis Sims McGrath, *Pillars of Maryland* (Richmond, 1950), 393.

28.3/26.26   tow linen] Rough, unbleached cloth manufactured from tow, the
shortest fibers taken from flax or hemp.

28.19/27.24   Mr. Hugh Auld] Born in Talbot County, Maryland, Hugh Auld
(1799–1861) moved as a young man to Baltimore. There he worked as a ship's
carpenter, master shipbuilder, shipyard foreman, and occasionally served as a
magistrate. Prior to moving to Baltimore, Hugh married Sophia Keithley. Between
1826 and 1833 and again between 1836 and 1838, the young Frederick Douglass
lived and worked in their household, lent to them by his owner, Hugh's brother
Thomas. In 1845, Hugh, incensed by Douglass's depiction of his family in the
Narrative, bought Douglass, then on a lecture tour of Britain, from his brother
Thomas. According to the *Pennsylvania Freeman,* Auld was determined to reenslave Douglass and "place him in the cotton fields of the South" if the fugitive ever
returned to the United States. In 1846, two British abolitionists, Anna and Ellen
Richardson, offered to buy Douglass from Auld; in exchange for $711.66 (£150
sterling) raised among British reformers, Auld signed the manumission papers that
made Douglass a free man. *PaF,* 26 February 1846; *Lib.,* 6 March 1846; Walter
Lourie to Ellis Gray Loring, 15 December 1846, reel 1, frame 644, Benjamin F.
Auld to Douglass, 11, 27 September 1891, reel 6, frames 240–41, 257–58, Douglass to Benjamin F. Auld, 16 September 1891, reel 6, frames 246–47, J. C. Schaffer
to Helen Pitts Douglass, 21 October 1896, reel 8, frames 92–93, General Correspondence File, FD Papers, DLC; Talbot County Records, V.60, 35–36, MdTCH,
Easton, Md. (a copy is found on reel 1, frames 637–39, FD Papers, DLC); Hugh
Auld Family Genealogical Chart, prepared by Carl G. Auld, Ellicott City, Md., 5
June 1976; Preston, *Young Frederick Douglass,* 81, 84–85, 92, 143, 173–75.

28.23/27.29   scurf] Scales of epidermis continually being detached from the
skin.

28.38–39/28.19–20   I had two sisters] Sarah Bailey (1814–?) was Frederick
Douglass's oldest sister and the second of seven children born to Harriet Bailey.
Aaron Anthony owned Sarah but after his death in 1826, she became the chattel of
his son, Andrew Skinner Anthony. In 1832, Andrew sold Bailey, her son Henry,
and four other slaves to Perry Cohee of Lawrence County in south Mississippi.
Douglass and Sarah remained separated until 1883, when she, then living in
Louisville, Kentucky, and calling herself Mrs. Sarah Pettit, wrote to Douglass and
reestablished their relationship. Sarah O. Pettit to Douglass, 26 September 1883,
General Correspondence File, reel 3, frame 778–80, FD Papers, DLC; Aaron
Anthony Slave Distribution, 22 October 1827, Talbot County Distributions,
V.JP#D, 58–59, MdTCH; Sale of Slaves, Andrew S. Anthony to Perry Cohee, 14
July 1832, Talbot County Records, V. 50, 192–93, MdTCH.

28.38–39/28.19–20   I had two sisters] The third oldest of six children born to
Harriet Bailey and the sister of Frederick Douglass, Eliza Bailey (1816–c. 1876)
was a slave owned by Aaron Anthony. When Anthony died in 1826, Eliza became
the property of Thomas Auld, Anthony's son-in-law. Eliza married Peter Mitchell,
a free black who worked as a field hand in Talbot County, with whom she had nine
children. In 1836, Mitchell bought Eliza and their then two children from Thomas
Auld for one hundred dollars. After settling on an acre of land which they rented
from Samuel and John Hambleton of Talbot County, they raised their own vegetables and meat and hired themselves out as a domestic and a field hand, respec-
tively. Eliza and her brother Frederick were separated after the latter's escape from
slavery in 1838. On 6 June 1844, Mitchell freed Eliza and the other children
because state laws no longer required removal from Maryland upon manumission.
Eliza and Frederick were reunited in 1865 when Douglass stopped in Baltimore
while on a speaking tour. New York *Independent,* 2 March 1865; Lewis Douglass
to Douglass, 9 June 1865, FD Papers, Moorland-Spingarn Library, DHU; Aaron
Anthony Slave Distribution, 22 October 1827, Talbot County Distributions,
V.JP#D, 58–59, Sale of Slaves, Thomas Auld to Peter Mitchell, 25 January 1836,
Talbot County Records, V.52, 258, Manumission of Eliza Mitchell, 1 July 1844,
Talbot County Records, V.58, 234–35, all in MdTCH; Preston, *Young Frederick
Douglass,* 164–65, 184, 206–07, 229n7.
28.39/28.20   and one brother] Perry Bailey (1813–?), the oldest of seven
children born to Harriet Bailey and Frederick Douglass's brother, was the slave of
Aaron Anthony. When Anthony died in 1826, Perry was inherited by Anthony's
son, Andrew J. Anthony. Andrew died in 1832, leaving Perry, now married to a
slave named Maria, to John P. Anthony, who sold Maria to a slaveowner in Brazos
County, Texas. Perry followed his wife to Texas, where a post-emancipation labor
shortage allowed him to earn "fifteen dollars gold wages a month." In 1867, Perry,
Maria, and their four children traveled to Rochester to reunite with Frederick.
Elated by this reunion, Douglass built a cottage for them on his Rochester estate,
where the family stayed for two years. In 1869, Perry and Maria returned to
Maryland's Eastern Shore where Perry died some time after 1878. Perry Downs to
Douglass, 21 February 1867, Douglass Papers, Moorland-Spingarn Library, DHU;
Douglass to J. J. Spelman, 11 July 1867, reprinted in New York *Independent,* 25
July 1867; Douglass to Theodore Tilton, 2 September 1867, FD Papers, NHi; Anna
Downs to Douglass, 5 October 1869, General Correspondence File, reel 2, frames
497–99, FD Papers, DLC; Aaron Anthony Slave Distribution, 22 October 1827,
Talbot County Distributions, V.JP#D, 58–59, MdTCH; Preston, *Young Frederick
Douglass,* 175–77, 206.
29.11/29.5   Cousin Tom] Tom Bailey (1814–?), the fourth of Milly Bailey's
seven children and Douglass's cousin, was a slave belonging to Aaron Anthony.
When Anthony died in 1826, Bailey became the property of Thomas Auld. Auld
granted Bailey his freedom in 1845. The last record of Bailey's existence is a letter

to Douglass from his son Lewis, who visited Talbot County in 1865. During his visit, Lewis wrote, he met with Bailey, who was still living in St. Michaels. Lewis Douglass to Douglass, 9 June 1865, FD Papers, Moorland-Spingarn Library, DHU; Aaron Anthony Slave Distribution, 22 October 1827, Talbot County Distributions, V.JP#D, 58–59, MdTCH; Preston, *Young Frederick Douglass,* 91, 174, 206, 221n29, 230n25.

29.21/29.18   Miles River] Originally known as the St. Michaels River, the twelve-mile-long Miles River lies entirely within Talbot County. The right-angled river flows southwest for its first eight miles and then flows northwest to meet the Chesapeake Bay at the town of St. Michaels. Footner, *Rivers of the Eastern Shore,* 236, 239–40, 255.

29.21/29.18–19   on a Saturday morning] Douglass departed St. Michaels for Baltimore on a Saturday in March 1826, probably the 18th. Preston, *Young Frederick Douglass,* 82.

29.34–35/30.5   at Smith's Wharf, not far from Bowley's Wharf] Smith's Wharf and Bowley's Wharf were two sturdily-built wharves below Pratt Street in Baltimore's inner harbor, the Basin, west of Fells Point. The city directory at times spelled the latter as "Bowly's Wharf." *Matchett's Baltimore Directory for 1827* (Baltimore, 1827), 18–19 (street register); Sherry H. Olson, *Baltimore: The Building of an American City* (Baltimore, 1980), 60.

29.36–39/30.7–8   the slaughterhouse of Mr. Curtis] The Baltimore city directory of 1824 lists two "victuallers": Thomas Curtain on Eden Street and James Curtain on Bond Street. Three years later the city directory lists Thomas Curtis as a "victualler." *Matchett's Baltimore Directory for 1824,* 74; *Matchett's Baltimore Directory for 1827,* 70.

29.38/30.10   my new home in Alliciana Street] Neither the 1824 nor 1827 Baltimore directories, the only extant directories in this period, list Hugh Auld's residence. The Baltimore City Commission on Historical and Architectural Preservation established that Hugh Auld's house was on the southeast corner of Aliceanna and Durham (formerly Happy Alley) streets in Fells Point. Contemporary sources spelled the street "Alisanna" (1824) or "Alice Anna" (1827). *Matchett's Baltimore Directory, for 1824* (Baltimore, 1824), 343; *Matchett's Baltimore Directory for 1827,* 1 (street register); Fielding Lucas, Jr., *Plan of the City of Baltimore* (Baltimore, 1836); Preston, *Young Frederick Douglass,* 223n1.

29.39/30.11   near Mr. Gardner's ship-yard] William Gardner, a ship carpenter or shipbuilder, resided on Fleet Street, Fells Point, between 1827 and 1836. The shipyard of George and William Gardner was at the "lower end of Fountain Street," on the eastern edge of the Fells Point wharf area. *Matchett's Baltimore Director[y] . . . 1831* (Baltimore, 1831), 141, 5 (street register).

29.39/30.11   on Fells Point] Fells Point, first settled by William Fell in 1726, was a separate enclave east of Baltimore center not annexed to Baltimore until 1773. This hooked piece of land jutting into the outer harbor had been a shipbuilding site since the mid-eighteenth century. After the War of 1812 it was the construction site for the famous Baltimore clipper ships. By the time of Douglass's arrival, Fells Point was a heavily-populated neighborhood whose residents worked in shipbuilding and other maritime pursuits. Shipyards and wharves for unloading cargo lined its waterfront. To reduce the frequency of yellow fever epidemics, a marshy area between Fells Point and the central city was dredged in the 1820s to form the City Dock, also called the City Block, which added to the Fells Point wharf area. A drawbridge at the entrance to the City Dock connected Block Street in Fells Point to the Basin area wharves. J. Thomas Scharf, *History of Baltimore City and County from the Earliest Period to the Present Day* (Philadelphia, 1881), 54, 59–60, 292–94; Olson, *Baltimore,* 52–53, 85.

30.1–2/30.13   their little son Thomas] Thomas Auld (1824–48), the son of Hugh and Sophia Auld and the nephew of Thomas Auld, Aaron Anthony's son-in-law, was the charge of the young slave Douglass. He died in an unsuccessful attempt by the brig *Tweed* to rescue a sinking British vessel. Benjamin F. Auld to Douglass, 11 September 1891, General Correspondence File, reel 6, frame 240, FD Papers, DLC; Preston, *Young Frederick Douglass,* 148, 228n10.

30.4/30.17   Sophia Auld] Sophia Keithley Auld (1797–1880) was born in Talbot County, Maryland, to Richard and Hester Keithley. Her parents were poor, devout Methodists who held to the antislavery teachings of their church. Before marrying Hugh Auld, she worked as a weaver. Soon after their marriage, the couple moved to Baltimore, where Hugh worked as a ship's carpenter, master shipbuilder, and shipyard fireman. Between 1826 and 1833, and again in 1836–38, the young slave Frederick Douglass lived and worked in their household. Both Douglass and Sophia Auld retained enormous affection for one another long after Douglass had established himself in the North. Douglass tried to visit Auld in Baltimore during the Civil War. Years after her death, Auld's son Benjamin told Douglass that "mother would always speak in the kindest terms of you, whenever your name was mentioned." Baltimore *Sun,* 5 July 1880; Benjamin F. Auld to Douglass, 11 September 1891, General Correspondence File, reel 6, frame 240, FD Papers, DLC; Preston, *Young Frederick Douglass,* 87, 165–66, 168.

31.28/33.12–13   If you give nigger an inch, he will take an ell. A paraphrase of the old English proverb, "For whan I gaue you an ynche, ye tooke an ell." An ell is an antiquated English unit of length equal to forty-five inches. Heywood, *Proverbs and Epigrams,* 78.

32.35/35.13   Philpot Street] Philpot Street ran east to west, parallel to the waterfront on Fells Point. The Aulds moved to Philpot Street in 1827 or 1828 soon after Hugh Auld began working at Durgin and Bailey's shipyard. Benjamin F. Auld to Douglass, 27 September 1891, General Correspondence File, reel 6, frames 257–58, FD Papers, DLC; Lucas, *Plan of the City of Baltimore.*

32.35/35.13   Mr. Thomas Hamilton] Thomas Hamilton, a ship carpenter, lived at 22 Philpot Street in Baltimore from at least 1831 through 1838. In 1833 his address was probably incorrectly listed as 18 Philpot Street. *Matchett's Baltimore Director[y] . . . 1831,* 163; *Matchett's Baltimore Director[y] . . . 1833* (Baltimore, 1833), 83; *Matchett's Baltimore Director[y] . . . 1835–6,* 110; *Matchett's Baltimore Director[y] for 1837–8,* 154.

33.9/35.31   *gip*] Gypsy.

34.2/37.13–14   for every mourner that came within her reach] Possibly a loose paraphrase of Prov. 25 : 20–23.

34.38/38.31–32   Durgin and Bailey's ship-yard] John Durgin and Thomas Bailey operated a shipwright business on Philpot Street in Fell's Point in the late 1820s and the 1830s. Douglass later recalled that as a boy he carried Auld's dinner to him while Auld was employed as a carpenter at this shipyard near the Auld home. Bailey continued as a ship carpenter in the same area into the 1830s. Douglass to Benjamin F. Auld, 24 March 1894, SC-163, Mrs. Howard V. Hall Collection of Auld Family Papers, MdAA; *Matchett's Baltimore Director[y] . . . 1829* (Baltimore, 1829), 94; *Matchett's Baltimore Director[y] . . . 1831,* 21; *Matchett's Baltimore Director[y] . . . 1835–36,* 12.

35.8/39.12   "The Columbian Orator"] Boston schoolteacher and book-seller Caleb Bingham (1757–1817) authored the *Columbian Orator* (1797; Boston, 1827), one of the first textbooks on English grammar and rhetoric published in the United States. It contained short extracts from speeches by such famous orators as William Pitt, George Washington, Charles James Fox, and Cicero, as well as plays and poems on the themes of patriotism, education, and freedom. The *Columbian Orator* remained one of the most popular textbooks of its kind in America through the 1820s. Bingham himself contributed an essay on oratorical skills, "General Directions for Speaking," whose rules Douglass followed in his early years as a public speaker. *NCAB,* 8 : 19; *DAB,* 2 : 273–74.

35.9–10/39.14–15   a dialogue between a master and his slave] The anonymous "Dialogue between a Master and Slave" is a conversation between a master and slave in which the slave is caught trying to run away for the second time. Bingham, *Columbian Orator,* 1827 ed., 240–42.

35.19–20/39.27–28   Sheridan's mighty speeches on and in behalf of Catholic Emancipation] Although Richard Sheridan (1751–1816), the Irish orator, playwright, and politician who entered Parliament in 1780, championed Irish and other reform causes, the only speech extracted in the *Columbian Orator* is "Mr. Sheridan's Speech Against Mr. Taylor," which is not on Catholic "emancipation." Douglass is probably referring to another selection in the anthology entitled "Part of Mr. O'Connor's Speech in the Irish House of Commons, in Favor of the Bill for Emancipating the Roman Catholics, 1795." Arthur O'Connor (1763–1852), a liberal Protestant member of the Irish parliament, was a strong supporter of Catholic rights, including "Catholic emancipation" or the right of Catholics to hold office and sit in Parliament. O'Connor resigned his seat after delivering this speech.

Bingham, *Columbian Orator,* 1827 ed., 130–31, 243–48; *Dictionary of National Biography,* 21 vols. (London, 1921–22), 18 : 78–85, 21 : 394–95.

36.29–30/42.1–2   petitions from the north] The sending of petitions to Congress, calling for an end to the slave trade and to slavery in the District of Columbia, dated back to the early years of the federal government. In 1828, a national petition drive had helped force the House of Representatives to vote on abolishing slavery in the District of Columbia. The newly organized movement for immediate emancipation adopted the petition strategy in the 1830s and deluged Congress with antislavery memorials bearing thousands of signatures. Louis Filler, *The Crusade Against Slavery, 1830–1860* (New York, 1960), 3, 99; Russel B. Nye, *Fettered Freedom: Civil Liberties and the Slavery Controversy, 1830–1860* (1949; Ann Arbor, Mich., 1963), 41–51.

36.34–35/42.9   on the wharf of Mr. Waters] George P. Waters was a ship chandler and grocer who operated both of his businesses very near the wharf he owned at the south end of Fell Street in Fell's Point. *Matchett's Baltimore Director[y] . . . 1833,* 189, 15 (street register); *Matchett's Baltimore Director[y] . . . for 1835–6,* 267; Lucas, *Plan of the City of Baltimore.*

37.18/43.9   larboard side] The left side of a ship when looking toward the bow.

37.34/44.1   Webster's Spelling Book] The first version of the spelling book, *A Grammatical Institute of the English Language* (Hartford, Conn., 1783), by Noah Webster (1758–1843), a Connecticut teacher, editor, and Federalist politician, rapidly became the standard spelling and pronunciation guide in the new nation. In 1788 the title became *The American Spelling Book* and in 1829 *The Elementary Spelling Book.* Harry R. Warfel, *Noah Webster: Schoolmaster to America* (New York, 1936); Richard J. Moss, *Noah Webster* (Boston, 1984); *DAB,* 19 : 594–97.

37.39/44.7–8   the Wilk Street meeting-house] The Fifth Methodist Episcopal Church, on the corner of Wilke (Wilks) Street and Apple Alley, was about seven blocks from Auld's house on Philpot Street. *Matchett's Baltimore Director[y] . . . 1831,* 16 (street register); *Matchett's Baltimore Director[y] . . . 1837–8,* 18; Lucas, *Plan of the City of Baltimore.*

38.8/44.18   youngest son, Richard, died] Douglass is mistaken in believing that Richard died before his father. According to the Anthony Family Bible, Richard did not die until 18 May 1828, and had shared in the division of his father's estate. Harriet Anthony's annotated copy of *Bondage and Freedom,* folder 93, 173–74, Aaron Anthony Slave Distribution, 27 September 1827, folder 77, both in Dodge Collection, MdAA; Preston, "Aaron Anthony," 5.

38.9/44.20   Captain Anthony, died] Aaron Anthony died on 14 November 1826, at age 59. According to his great-granddaughter Harriet Lucretia Anthony, he was buried in an unmarked grave in the family graveyard on Holme Hill Farm. Harriet Anthony's annotated copy of *Bondage and Freedom,* folder 93, 173–74, Harriet Anthony mss. notes, 1919, folder 89, 9–11, both in Dodge Collection, MdAA; Preston, *Young Frederick Douglass,* 29–30.

38.19/45.7   Captain Rowe] Captain Joseph H. Rowe lived in Baltimore on Market Street south of Bank Street from at least 1831 through 1836. *Matchett's Baltimore Director[y] . . . 1831,* 320; *Matchett's Baltimore Director[y] . . . 1833,* 159; *Matchett's Baltimore Director[y] . . . 1835–6,* 222.

38.19/45.7–8   the schooner Wild Cat] The schooner *Wild Cat* was a slow, shallow-draft merchant ship designed to carry cargo up and down the tidal creeks of the Chesapeake Bay. Preston, *Young Frederick Douglass,* 88.

38.33/45.27   then came the division] Aaron Anthony's heirs, Richard Anthony, Andrew Anthony, and Thomas Auld, agreed to the division of his slaves on 27 September 1827. Twenty-eight slaves, including Frederick Douglass, comprised the division and were valued at $2,805. Frederick was among the slaves awarded to Thomas Auld, widower of Lucretia Anthony Auld. Aaron Anthony Slave Distribution, 27 September 1827, folder 77, Dodge Collection, MdAA; Aaron Anthony Slave Distribution, 22 October 1827, Talbot County Distributions, V.JP#D, 58–59, MdTCH.

39.26/47.5–6   was sent immediately back to Baltimore] After court-appointed appraisers oversaw the actual assignment of Aaron Anthony's slaves to each of his heirs, Douglass probably returned to Baltimore by November 1827 at the latest. Preston, *Young Frederick Douglass,* 90.

39.31/47.12–13   my mistress, Lucretia, died] Lucretia Anthony Auld died 6 July 1827. Douglass is mistaken in his recollection that he was awarded to Lucretia, as she had died after her father Aaron Anthony but before his estate was settled. County records indicate that Frederick was awarded to her husband Thomas Auld as her heir. Anthony Family Bible, Oxford Museum, Oxford, Md.; Aaron Anthony Slave Distribution, 22 October 1827, Talbot County Distributions, V.JP#D, 58–59, MdTCH; Preston, "Aaron Anthony," 5.

39.32/47.13–14   one child, Amanda] Born in Hillsborough, Maryland, Arianna Amanda Auld Sears (1826–78) was the only child of Thomas and Lucretia Anthony Auld. With her mother's death in 1826 and her father's subsequent remarriage, she fell under the charge of her stepmother Rowena Hambleton Auld. In 1843 she married John L. Sears, a Philadelphia coal merchant, with whom she bore four children. The Sears moved to Philadelphia, but returned to Maryland in the early 1860s, settling in Baltimore. Amanda Auld's childhood acquaintance with Frederick Douglass was reestablished in 1859 when he called upon her while on a speaking engagement in Philadelphia. Douglass and Auld maintained a warm friendship over the years that followed; after her death in 1878, Auld's husband John wrote to Douglass, "God bless you for your kindness to her." Auld Family Bible (courtesy of Carl G. Auld); New York *Herald,* 6 September 1866; Philadelphia *Evening Bulletin,* 6 September 1866; John L. Sears to Douglass, 10 January 1878, Thomas E. Sears to Douglass, 1 February 1878, General Correspondence File, reel 3, frames 215–16, reel 3, frame 225, FD Papers, DLC; Preston, *Young Frederick Douglass,* 30, 106–

07, 168–70; McFeely, *Frederick Douglass,* 297, 306; Roberts, "Visitation of Western Talbot," 245.

39.32–33/47.14–15   after her death, Master Andrew died] Andrew Anthony died in June 1833 but not before he had sold several of Douglass's Bailey relatives to a Mississippi slaveholder. Andrew Anthony Slave Distribution, 28 August 1835, Talbot County Distributions, V.JB#D, 1825–45, 185–86, MdTCH; Preston, *Young Frederick Douglass,* 110, 225.

40.20–21/48.20–21   the slave's poet, Whittier] Born in Haverhill, Massachusetts, Quaker poet and abolitionist John Greenleaf Whittier (1807–72) was a journalist and editor for such journals as *Free Press, American Manufacturer,* Washington (D.C.) *National Era,* and the *Atlantic Monthly.* Among Whittier's volumes of poetry are *Voices of Freedom* (1846), *The Panorama and Other Poems* (1856), and *At Sundown* (1890). Douglass often quoted Whittier's poems in his speeches. Edward Wagenknecht, *John Greenleaf Whittier: A Portrait in Paradox* (New York, 1967); *DAB,* 20 : 174.

40.33/48.33   Woe is me, my stolen daughters] Douglass quotes the first twelve lines from the 1838 poem, "The Farewell of a Virginia Slave Mother to Her Daughter Sold into Southern Bondage," by John G. Whittier. *The Poetical Works of John Greenleaf Whittier,* 4 vols. (Boston, 1892), 3 : 56.

41.13/49.25   Rowena Hamilton] Rowena Hambleton Auld (1812–42) was the eldest daughter of William Hambleton, a wealthy slaveowner in Martingham, Maryland. She became the second wife of Thomas Auld on 21 May 1829. Auld Family Bible (Courtesy of Carl G. Auld); Preston, *Young Frederick Douglass,* 106–07; Roberts, "Visitation of Western Talbot," 245.

41.14/49.26   Mr. William Hamilton] William Hambleton (c. 1783–?), not Hamilton, descended from an old Eastern Shore family and lived at Martingham, a Talbot County plantation. He was the father of Rowena Hambleton Auld and the brother of "Purser" Samuel Hambleton who had won national fame as a hero at the Battle of Lake Erie. In 1850 Hambleton possessed real estate valued at $10,000 and owned ten slaves. 1850 U.S. Census, Maryland, Talbot County, 1016 (schedule of free inhabitants), 32 (slave schedule); Preston, *Young Frederick Douglass,* 108, 109, 130.

41.17/49.30   to live with himself at St. Michael's] Hugh Auld returned Douglass to Thomas Auld in St. Michaels in March 1833 not 1832 as Douglass erroneously believed at the time of writing the *Narrative.* Preston, *Young Frederick Douglass,* 104–05.

41.35/50.21   Captain Edward Dodson] Edward Dodson was captain of a packet ship that conveyed passengers and freight between St. Michaels, Talbot County, and Baltimore during the early nineteenth century. In 1830 he was in his twenties and lived in Talbot County. The members of his household included three children, two white women both in their twenties, and a slightly older free black woman. 1830 U.S. Census, Maryland, Talbot County, 37; Tilghman, *Talbot County,* 2 : 396.

41.37/50.24   on reaching North Point] North Point, on Chesapeake Bay east of
Baltimore, is located at the mouth of the Patapsco River at the tip of Patapsco River
Neck. To reach northern ports from Baltimore, ships traveled around North Point
and headed north on the bay to the Chesapeake and Delaware Canal, which opened
to navigation in 1830. Scharf, *Baltimore City and County,* map preceding p. 13;
George Rogers Taylor, *The Transportation Revolution, 1815–1860* (New York,
1951), 41–42.

42.5–6/51.4   at St. Michael's, in March, 1832] Actually March 1833.

42.25/52.4   my aunt Priscilla] Priscilla Bailey (1816–?), the eleventh of
twelve children born to Isaac and Betsey Bailey, was a slave belonging to Aaron
Anthony. When Anthony died in 1826, his son Richard Lee Anthony inherited her.
Aaron Anthony Slave Distribution, 22 October 1827, Talbot County Distributions,
V.JP#D, 58–59, MdTCH; Preston, *Young Frederick Douglass,* 18, 206.

42.26/52.4   Henny] Henny Bailey (1816–?), a cousin of Frederick Douglass,
was one of seven children born to Milly Bailey, a slave on one of Aaron Anthony's
farms. Henny was apparently ill-fitted for work: Anthony estimated her value at
fifty dollars in 1826, less than half the value he placed on her younger cousin
Frederick. When Anthony died in 1826, his son-in-law Thomas Auld inherited
Bailey and four other slaves. Some time before 1840, Auld granted Bailey her
freedom. The last record of Henny's existence is an entry in the 1840 U.S. Census,
which identifies her as a free black, between the age of thirty-six and fifty-five,
living in St. Michaels District. Inventory of Negroes owned by Aaron Anthony, 19
December 1826, folder 71, Aaron Anthony, Ledger B, 1812–1826, folder 95, 159,
both in Dodge Collection, MdAA; Aaron Anthony Slave Distribution, 22 October
1827, Talbot County Distributions, V.JP#D, 58–59, MdTCH; 1840 U.S. Census,
Maryland, Talbot County, 42; Preston, *Young Frederick Douglass,* 91, 174,
225n14.

43.29–30/53.30–31   my master attended a Methodist camp-meeting] Douglass accompanied his master, Thomas Auld, to some of the services at a Methodist
camp meeting held at Haddaway's Woods on what is presently known as the
Tilghman Peninsula along the Chesapeake. The meeting lasted from 16 to 21
August 1833 and attracted people from as far as Baltimore. Preston, *Young Frederick Douglass,* 111–13.

44.9/54.24–25   Mr. Storks] The Reverend Levi Storks was the circuit preacher
of the Talbot Circuit of the Methodist Episcopal Church in 1832 and 1833. When
the British invaded the Eastern Shore in 1814, Storks served as a private in a local
regiment. In 1820 he was probably an overseer in Talbot County and in 1834, he
married Anne G. Nicholson. 1820 U.S. Census, Maryland, Talbot County, 6;
William M. Marine, *The British Invasion of Maryland, 1812–1815* (Baltimore,
1913), 451; Edith G. Bevan, "Maryland Bookplates," *MdHM,* 39 : 93–94 (March
1944); Thomas H. Sewell, "St. Michaels Methodism" (unpublished paper, 1894),
717, 723, MdAA.

44.9/54.25   Mr. Ewery] In 1832, William Uriey (c. 1810–80) was a circuit preacher for the Methodist Episcopal Church's Talbot Circuit, which included St. Michaels Parish. Sewell, "St. Michaels Methodism," 717.

44.9/54.25   Mr. Humphry] Joshua Humphries (c. 1801–79) entered the Methodist Episcopal ministry in 1829 and soon became a prominent member of that faith in Talbot County. In 1834 he was the presiding elder and circuit preacher for the Talbot Circuit. Humphries continued in charge in the Talbot Circuit in 1835 when he issued an important report on the state of Sunday schools. James M. McCarter and Benjamin F. Jackson, eds., *Historical and Biographical Encyclopedia of Delaware* (Wilmington, Del., 1882), 410; Sewell, "St. Michaels Methodism," 675, 730.

44.9/54.25   Mr. Hickey] William—or possibly Thomas—Hickey was a Methodist preacher who in the 1830s rode a circuit which included St. Michaels Parish. Sewell, "St. Michaels Methodism," 723; Preston, *Young Frederick Douglass,* 114, 226n16.

44.10/54.26   Mr. George Cookman] Born into a wealthy family in Hull, England, George Cookman (1800–41) began working in his father's merchant firm at the age of twenty. Between 1821 and 1823, he visited the United States on business and during this sojourn became convinced of his duty to preach the gospel. Despite his father's protestations, he resolved to settle permanently in America and become a Methodist minister. Soon after migrating in 1825, Cookman became a popular figure in the Methodists' Philadelphia Conference, preaching throughout parts of Pennsylvania, New Jersey, Maryland, and the District of Columbia. His powerful sermons won him the position of chaplain to the U.S. Congress. As revivals were sweeping the Eastern Shore, Cookman became the minister of the St. Michaels Methodist Episcopal church in the summer of 1829 and labored to hold it in the denomination. He remained in that position at least through the early 1830s. By 1830 Cookman was married and had two young sons. He had some antislavery leanings and apparently persuaded Samuel Harrison, one of Talbot County's largest slaveholders, to emancipate all of his adult male slaves in his will. In March 1841, the steamship *President* on which Cookman was sailing for England was lost at sea. 1830 U.S. Census, Maryland, Talbot County, 6; Matthew Simpson, ed., *Cyclopaedia of Methodism,* 5th rev. ed. (Philadelphia, 1882), 255–56; Preston, *Young Frederick Douglass,* 114–15, 226n17; Sewell, "St Michaels Methodism," 665–67, 675–76, 677–78, 680, 707; *ACAB,* 1 : 722.

44.12/54.29   Mr. Samuel Harrison] Samuel Harrison (?–1837) was one of the wealthiest slaveholders in Talbot County: in 1802 he inherited a lucrative import and export business from his father Thomas Harrison. He increased his fortune in the 1810s by lending money and supplies to those engaged in the then booming shipbuilding industry of Talbot County and by 1830 he owned 84 slaves. At the request of his friend and confidante, the Reverend George Cookman, Harrison stipulated in his will that all adult male slaves be manumitted upon his death. 1830

U.S. Census, Maryland, Talbot County, 42; Tilghman, *Talbot County,* 2 : 379, 383, 389–90, 397; Preston, *Young Frederick Douglass,* 115, 226n17.

44.21/55.8   Mr. Wilson] Nathan Wilson (c. 1797–c. 1861), an unmarried Quaker about fifty years old, taught at a local school for whites in the early 1840s near Denton in Caroline County, only a few miles from Talbot County. While Quakerism no longer was the influential religious force on the Eastern Shore that it had been in the eighteenth century, numerous Quakers remained in the region and some continued to argue against slavery and for teaching the slaves to read the Scriptures. This particular teacher could plausibly have been interested in opening a Sabbath school for blacks, as could have any of the other various Quaker Wilsons who populated Talbot and other Eastern Shore counties. Among other local whites interested in black education was Louisa Hambleton from the Eastern Shore's famous first family, who unsuccessfully attempted to open a Sabbath school for St. Michaels' slaves in 1843. Robert Todd, *Methodism of the Peninsula* (Philadelphia, 1886), 249–53; Kenneth Carroll, *Quakerism on the Eastern Shore* (Baltimore, 1970), 219, 245; Sewell, "St. Michaels Methodism," 687.

44.23/55.11   Mr. West] Garretson West (1800–53) was famous among Methodists in St. Michaels, Maryland, for his religious enthusiasm and moral zeal. Although he worked first as an oysterman and later as a teamster, West primarily devoted himself to spurring public prayer, exhorting the faithful at the Methodist classes he led, and—despite his illiteracy—conversing at length with others over the meaning of various biblical passages. In 1829, West was elected to the board of trustees of the Methodist church in St. Michaels and held that position until 1836. He also was appointed that church's sexton in 1830 and again in 1836. At the time of his death, West was married, had at least one child, and had accumulated little wealth. 1850 U.S. Census, Maryland, Talbot County, 80; Tilghman, *Talbot County,* 2 : 400–01; Todd, *Methodism of the Peninsula,* 113–23; Preston, *Young Frederick Douglass,* 116; Sewell, "St. Michaels Methodism," 672–74, 680–81, 701, 707, 727.

44.23/55.12   Mr. Fairbanks] Wrightson Fairbank or Fairbanks (c. 1806–?) was a resident of Talbot County who in 1850 worked as a merchant and headed a household that included his wife, four children, and two female relatives. He owned neither land nor slaves. Fairbanks was an active member of the Methodist Episcopal Church in St. Michaels and ran unsuccessfully for the board of trustees of the parish in September 1835. 1850 U.S. Census, Maryland, Talbot County, 80; Sewell, "St. Michaels Methodism," 725.

44.32–33/55.25   beaten with many stripes] A paraphrase of Luke 12 : 47.

45.25/57.5–6   Edward Covey] Edward Covey (1806?–75), who started out as a poor farm-renter from Talbot County, Maryland, managed to accumulate $23,000 in real estate by 1850. Covey's reputation as a slave breaker enabled him to rent or even to receive the free use of field hands from local slaveowners anxious to have their slaves taught proper discipline. Harriet Lucretia Anthony, the great granddaughter of Aaron Anthony, remembered that "Mr. Covey was really noted for his cruelty and meanness." Inventory of the Estate of Edward Covey, 15 May 1875, Talbot County Inventories, TNC#3, 578, MdTCH; Harriet Anthony's annotated copy of *My Bondage and My Freedom,* folder 93, 203, Dodge Collection, MdAA; 1850 U.S. Census, Maryland, Talbot County, 240 (schedule of free inhabitants); Preston, *Young Frederick Douglass,* 117–31.

46.13/58.15   in-hand . . . off-hand] In a team of harnessed animals, the in-hand one is directly under control of the driver.

50.5/65.4   ague] A fit of shaking or shivering, often accompanying a violent fever.

50.27/66.2   Bill Smith] Bill Smith (1804–?) was a slave owned by Samuel Harrison of Rich Neck Manor and hired out as a servant to Edward Covey in 1834. Smith probably received his freedom in 1837, as Samuel Harrison's will stipulated that all adult male slaves should be freed upon his death. Simpson, *Cyclopaedia of Methodism,* 225; Preston, *Young Frederick Douglass,* 119, 122, 123, 128, 226n17.

50.28/66.4   fanning wheat] Exposing cut grain to the wind to have the chaff blown away.

51.1–2/66.21   treading-yard] Place where plants are beaten down into a smaller size for storage by means of treading.

52.29/69.19   Mrs. Kemp's fields] Elizabeth Doyle Kemp (c. 1787–?) probably owned a farm adjacent to the farm Edward Covey rented from her son, John. Married to the shipbuilder Thomas Kemp in Baltimore in November 1809, Elizabeth moved with him in 1816 to a 236-acre farm, Wades Point, west of the town of St. Michaels in Talbot County. After his death in March 1824, most of his property was divided between his two eldest sons, Thomas and John, but provisions were also made for Elizabeth. In 1830 she was the head of a household which comprised five white males, two white females, six male slaves, and three female slaves. 1830 U.S. Census, Maryland, Talbot County, 38; M. Florence Bourne, "Thomas Kemp, Shipbuilder, and His Home, Wades Point," *MdHM,* 49 : 271–89 (December 1954); Preston, *Young Frederick Douglass,* 118.

52.38/69.32   Sandy Jenkins] Sandy Jenkins was a slave owned by William Groomes of Easton, Maryland, who often hired him out to farmers in Talbot County. Preston, *Young Frederick Douglass,* 125–26, 131, 134–36, 138–39, 227n3.

57.5–6/77.4   Mr. William Freeland] William Freeland, the son of William and Elizabeth Freeland of Talbot County, Maryland, was a farmer and slaveowner near St. Michaels. The 1820 U.S. Census lists William as a young adult between sixteen and twenty-five years of age. Between 1820 and 1830, and perhaps later, he lived in a household headed by his mother. They shared their home with two white boys and six slaves. By 1830 the Freeland's household had diminished: Elizabeth and William now lived with only one young white man and four slaves. 1820 U.S. Census, Maryland, Talbot County, 10; 1830 U.S. Census, Maryland, Talbot County, 35.

57.32/78.9   the Rev. Daniel Weeden] Daniel Weeden (c. 1794–?) was a farmer
and Methodist minister in Talbot County. Although an overseer without any of his
own slaves in 1820, Weeden appears by 1830 to have become an independent
farmer with two slaves and a growing family. By 1850 he owned six slaves. In 1839
Weeden forced a free black man back into slavery by revealing that he had served
time in a Maryland jail. He then purchased the man at a greatly reduced price. By
the early 1840s Weeden was well established as a local minister, having presided
over a number of Talbot County weddings in 1843 and 1844. 1820 U.S. Census,
Maryland, Talbot County, 7; 1830 U.S. Census, Maryland, Talbot County, 32;
1840 U.S. Census, Maryland, Talbot County, 36a; 1850 U.S. Census, Maryland,
Talbot County, 37 (slave schedule); Preston, *Young Frederick Douglass,* 130,
227n8; Charles Montgomery Haddaway III, "Marriages Recorded in Talbot
County Newspapers: 1819–1823, 1841–1843, & 1870," *MdHM,* 81 : 254, 260,
262, 267, 268, 270 (Fall 1986).

57.32–33/78.10   the Rev. Rigby Hopkins] Rigby Hopkins was a Methodist
minister who had long lived and farmed in Talbot County. In 1830 he was between
50 and 60 years old and had within his household two white males, six white
females, and one black female. While in 1820 he owned seventeen slaves, in 1830
he had none, possibly indicating a preference for renting black labor by then. 1820
U.S. Census, Maryland, Talbot County, 19; 1830 U.S. Census, Maryland, Talbot
County, 31; Preston, *Young Frederick Douglass,* 130.

57.33–34/78.11–12   the Reformed Methodist Church] An agitation for
greater lay authority inside the Methodist Episcopal Church resulted in the expul-
sion of a small number of members and some congregations from the Methodist
Episcopal Church in the mid-1820s. Additional sympathizers of this reform movement withdrew and formed the Associate Methodist Church in 1828, soon after
renamed the Methodist Protestant Church. This controversy inspired a large majority of the members of the Sardis Chapel in St. Michaels to affiliate with the new
denomination. The minority led by the Reverend George Cookman and Garretson
West successfully retained the original church building and eventually rebuilt their
congregation's numbers. In the late 1850s, the Methodist Protestant Church underwent a sectional schism over the slavery issue as had its parent Methodist Episcopal Church in the mid-1840s and the Maryland conference sided with the South.
Sewell, "St. Michaels Methodism," 674–99; Ancel H. Bassett, *A Concise History
of the Methodist Protestant Church from Its Origin* (Pittsburgh, 1887), 167–221;
Simpson, *Cyclopaedia of Methodism,* 602–07.

62.11/85.29   " . . . that we knew not of"] *Hamlet,* act 3, sc. 1, lines 81–82.

62.13/85.31–86.1   resolved upon liberty or death] Douglass paraphrases Pa-
trick Henry's speech in a Virginia revolutionary convention, on 23 March 1775.
William Wirt, *Sketches of the Life and Character of Patrick Henry,* 7th ed. (New
York, 1835), 141.

62.17/86.6   Henry Bailey] Henry Bailey (1820–?) was the youngest of twelve children born to Douglass's maternal grandparents, Isaac and Betsey Bailey. Henry was owned by Aaron Anthony of Talbot County; when Anthony died in 1826, Henry became the property of Richard Lee Anthony. When Richard died in 1828, Thomas Auld, Richard's brother-in-law, became Henry's master. Aaron Anthony Slave Distribution, 22 October 1827, Talbot County Distributions, V.JP#D, pp. 58–59, MdTCH; Preston, *Young Frederick Douglass,* 18, 109, 206.

62.22/87.1   Easter holidays] Easter Sunday in 1836 fell on 3 April.

64.21–22/89.24   Tom Graham, the constable] Thomas Graham was the constable for St. Michaels Parish in 1833 and the next-door neighbor of Thomas Auld. In 1830 he was between the age of forty and fifty, married, the father of one son, and the owner of one female slave. He appears to have died between 1846 and 1850 as he was not listed in the census for the latter year. After the publication of the *Narrative,* Graham publicly disputed Douglass's characterization of his treatment by Auld. *Lib.,* 20 February 1846; 1830 U.S. Census, Maryland, Talbot County, 39; 1840 U.S. Census, Maryland, Talbot County, 48a; Preston, *Young Frederick Douglass,* 116, 136–37.

65.28–29/91.23–24   the sheriff, Mr. Joseph Graham] Joseph Graham (c. 1797–?) was the sheriff of Talbot County in 1836. By 1830 he was married and the father of two young daughters. Graham was still alive in 1878 when Douglass returned to visit Talbot County. 1830 U.S. Census, Maryland, Talbot County, 36; Preston, *Young Frederick Douglass,* 139, 190.

66.36/93.24–25   to my old home at Baltimore] Douglass returned to Baltimore in mid-April 1836. While Douglass makes no mention of the Aulds having moved, Benjamin Auld thought that his family had moved from Philpot Street to "Fell Street" around 1834. The Baltimore city directories list Hugh Auld as residing on Philpot Street until 1837, when he is listed as a shipwright on "Falls Street south of Thames." Benjamin F. Auld to Douglass, 27 September 1891, General Correspondence File, reel 6, frames 257–58, FD Papers, DLC; *Matchett's Baltimore Director[y] . . . 1837–8,* 50.

67.14/94.17   cant] To tilt or turn over an object.

67.18/94.22   fall] The loose end of a hoisting tackle.

67.22/94.28   *bowse*] To haul an object by means of a tackle.

67.37–38/95.19–20   at once to put a stop to it] Most free blacks in Baltimore held jobs as laborers, draymen, and servants, though they also held such craft positions as carpenter, blacksmith, barber, and caulker. They dominated the latter two trades through the 1850s. In the mid-1830s Baltimore witnessed increasing mob violence, brought on by worsening economic conditions and the failure of the Bank of Maryland in 1834. Claiming that free blacks were depriving them of jobs, white Baltimore workers unsuccessfully petitioned the Maryland legislature in the 1830s and 1840s to restrict free blacks from working in certain trades. Economic competition between the races continued, and in 1845 Dr. R. S. Steuart of Baltimore claimed that white labor had driven blacks out of many unskilled jobs in the Fells

Point area. "The Condition of the Coloured Population of the City of Baltimore," *Baltimore Literary and Religious Magazine* 4 : 174–75 (April 1838); Ira Berlin, *Slaves Without Masters: The Free Negro in the Antebellum South* (New York, 1974), 217–49; Jeffrey R. Brackett, *The Negro in Maryland: A Study of the Institution of Slavery* (Baltimore, 1889), 210; James M. Wright, *The Free Negro in Maryland, 1634–1860* (New York, 1921), 154–55, 172; Olson, *Baltimore,* 98–101; M. Ray Della, Jr., "The Problems of Negro Labor in the 1850s," *MdHM,* 66 : 25 (Spring 1971).

68.27/96.28   death by Lynch law] The actual individual for whom the term "lynch law" derived its name has been disputed but the expression was in common use by the early nineteenth century as a description for the punishment of individuals without due process of law. David C. Roller and Robert W. Twyman, eds., *The Encyclopedia of Southern History* (Baton Rogue, 1979), 762–64.

69.4–5/97.19   to Esquire Watson's, on Bond Street] William H. Watson (?–1846) was a justice of the peace and prominent attorney, who lived at 76 Bond Street in Baltimore's Fells Point district in the late 1830s. He joined a Baltimore volunteer battalion as a captain during the war with Mexico. Watson quickly rose to the rank of lieutenant colonel but died in the Battle of Monterey in October 1846. *Matchett's Baltimore Director[y] . . . 1837–8,* 321; J. Thomas Scharf, *The Chronicles of Baltimore; Being a Complete History of "Baltimore Town" and Baltimore City from the Earliest Period to the Present Time* (Baltimore, 1874), 516, 517; Morris Radoff, ed., *The Old Line State: A History of Maryland* (Baltimore, 1971), 258.

69.28/98.21   Mr. Walter Price] Walter Price, whose family had long been engaged in shipbuilding, operated a shipyard on Fell Street south of Thames Street along the waterfront in the 1830s. By the latter part of the decade, a number of Baltimore shipbuilders had begun construction of fleet clippers which found their way into the international slave trade. Brazilian and Cuban slave traders prized these ships for their ability to evade the British blockade of Africa's Slave Coast. Benjamin Auld thought that Hugh Auld began working for Walter Price about 1834, after serving a short period as a master builder in partnership with Edward Harrison. Both Auld and Douglass worked for Price during the construction of at least three ships, which he covertly sold in Cuba or Brazil. *Matchett's Baltimore Director[y] . . . 1837–8,* 258; Benjamin F. Auld to Douglass, 27 September 1891, General Correspondence File, reel 6, frames 257–58, FD Papers, DLC; Howard I. Chapelle, *The Search for Speed Under Sail, 1700–1855* (New York, 1967), 297–312; Preston, *Young Frederick Douglass,* 145–47, 228n8.

69.31/98.25–26   to the most experienced calkers] Blacks, both free and slave, dominated the semi-skilled caulking occupation in Baltimore in the 1830s. The largest Baltimore slaveholders in the 1810s and 1820s included master shipbuilders who used slave caulkers in their own shipyards or hired them out to other shipbuilders. Though information on caulkers' wages in the 1830s is elusive, free black caulkers earned $1.50 per day in 1812 and during the height of wartime building had raised their daily wages to $1.67 1/4. Slave caulkers in the same year earned $1.25 to $1.31 1/4 per day. By 1838 free blacks had formed their own organization, the Caulker's Beneficial Association. Controlling the trade through the 1850s, by the end of that decade members of the Association were receiving $1.75 a day, while their apprentices were paid $1.50. The black caulkers owed their power to an alliance with the white shipwrights' association to control wages and conditions in shipbuilding. Blacks' hold on the trade was shaken when clashes erupted in 1858 between black Association members and white caulkers who were willing to accept lower wages. Blacks faced increasing discrimination in the 1860s, prompting black carpenters and caulkers to organize their own shipyard in 1866. In 1871 Douglass visited the Fells Point shipbuilding area and commented on the success of the black shipyard, noting that the "leading shipbuilders [of] forty years ago, are all gone, and have not even left their firms behind to perpetuate their names." Ironically, in 1836–38 some of the Fells Point shipyards where Douglass worked as a caulker built ships destined for the illegal African slave trade. [Washington, D.C.] *New National Era,* 6 July 1871; "Condition of the Coloured Population," 174; Charles G. Steffen, *The Mechanics of Baltimore: Workers and Politics in the Age of the Revolution, 1763–1812* (Urbana, Ill., 1984), 38–42; Barbara Jeanne Fields, *Slavery and Freedom on the Middle Ground: Maryland During the Nineteenth Century* (New Haven, 1985), 37–38, 40–62; Wright, *Free Negro in Maryland,* 154–55; Preston, *Young Frederick Douglass,* 145–47, 228; Bettye C. Thomas, "A Nineteenth Century Black Operated Ship-yard, 1866–1884: Reflections upon its Inception and Ownership," *JNH,* 59 : 1–3 (January 1974); Della, "Problems of Negro Labor," 14–32.

71.6/101.6   the *underground railroad*] Northern blacks along with some sympathetic white supporters maintained a loose, clandestine system to clothe, feed, and shelter fugitive slaves from the South. In addition, "vigilance committees" operated in many northern communities to expose the presence of slave hunters and, on occasion, to rescue fugitives in the process of rendition to their masters. Larry Gara, *The Liberty Line: The Legend of the Underground Railroad* (Lexington, Ky., 1961), *passim.*

72.8/102.31–32   came to Baltimore to purchase his spring goods] This visit apparently occurred in March 1838. McFeely, *Frederick Douglass,* 64.

73.5/103.1   allow me to hire my time] In the urban South masters commonly hired their slaves out to other employers for specified periods of time. The less common practice of allowing their slaves to seek their own employment and pay their masters a specified sum grew over time, causing public fears that it would undermine the slave system itself. The Maryland legislature periodically passed legislation to control or abolish this practice, with little result. Richard C. Wade, *Slavery in the Cities: The South, 1820–1860* (New York, 1964), 38–54; Robert S. Starobin, *Industrial Slavery in the Old South* (New York, 1970), 128–37; Brackett, *Negro in Maryland,* 104–08, 174.

73.7–8/104.22–23   my attending a camp meeting] Douglass attended a camp meeting on the weekend of 4–5 August 1838. Revivals abounded in the South in the hot month of August, two more occurring near Baltimore the following weekend. Baltimore *Sun,* 8 August 1838; Preston, *Young Frederick Douglass,* 152–53.

73.38/106.2–3   Mr. Butler, at his ship-yard] Samuel Butler, a Baltimore ship carpenter, established a shipyard in 1819 in partnership with Robert Lambdin. Apparently Lambdin moved to St. Michaels, Talbot County, in 1830 while maintaining his financial interest in the yard. Butler remained to manage the operation throughout the 1830s during which time it launched the noted ship *Catherine.* Entries for Samuel Butler, a ship carpenter on Exeter Street, and Robert Lamden, a ship carpenter on City Block, appear in the 1840 city directory. *Matchett's Baltimore Director[y], for 1840–41* (Baltimore, n.p.), 86, 221; Chapelle, *Search for Speed Under Sail,* 302; John Philips Cranwell, ed., "Ship-Building on the Chesapeake: Recollections of Robert Dawson Lambdin," *MdHM,* 36 : 172 (June 1941); Lewis Addison Beck, "The *Seaman* and the *Seaman's Bride,* Baltimore Clipper Ships," *MdHM,* 51 : 305 (December 1956).

74.31/107.16–17   succeeded in reaching New York] Not until 1881 did Douglass publicly reveal the details of his escape from slavery. On 3 September 1838, he boarded a train bound from Baltimore to New York City. Douglass had borrowed the uniform and seaman's protection papers of a free black friend in Baltimore. Fortunately for Douglass the conductor did not check the description in the papers carefully and several white acquaintants on the train failed to recognize him. Douglass, "My Escape from Slavery," *Century Magazine,* 23 : 125–31 (November 1881), reprinted in idem, *Life and Times of Frederick Douglass* (1894; New York, 1941), 218–23.

75.36/109.16   Mr. DAVID RUGGLES] David Ruggles (1810–49), a free black man, was born and educated in Norwich, Connecticut. In 1827 he moved to New York, where he worked as a grocer. In 1834 he opened a printing and book shop that specialized in abolitionist literature. Ruggles became active in the New York antislavery movement, serving as a writer, lecturer, and traveling agent for the reform publication, *Emancipator and Journal of Public Morals.* He also was a conductor on the Underground Railroad, editor of the *Genius of Freedom* and the *Mirror of Liberty,* and secretary to the New York Vigilance Committee. His career in the antislavery movement ended abruptly in 1842 when temporary blindness, an illness that would plague him for the remainder of his life, forced him to curtail his activities and seek medical attention. At the Northampton Association of Education and Industry in Florence, Massachusetts, he underwent hydrotherapy, which temporarily relieved his blindness. Soon thereafter he began a new career as a hydrotherapist in Northampton, Massachusetts, treating such celebrated individuals as Sojourner Truth and William Lloyd Garrison. His reputation as a hydrotherapist gave him a prominence that rivaled his stature as an abolitionist. *NASS,* 20 December 1849; *Lib.,* 21 December 1849; New York *Evangelist,* 27 December

1849; *ASB,* 29 December 1849; *NS,* 1 February 1850; I. Garland Penn, *Afro-American Press and Its Editors* (Springfield, Mass., 1891), 118; Rayford W. Logan and Michael R. Winston, eds., *Dictionary of American Negro Biography* (New York, 1982), 536–38.

76.5/109.26–27   the memorable *Darg* case] The Darg case became a celebrated example of the persecution of abolitionists by established local authorities and proslavery newspapers. In August 1838, Thomas Hughes, a slave, escaped from his owner, John P. Darg of Arkansas, while the two were in New York City. Hughes also stole approximately $8,000 from Darg. He soon sought assistance from Isaac T. Hopper, a leading Quaker abolitionist. Suspicious of Hughes, Hopper housed him for only one night and soon thereafter learned of the stolen money. While Hopper did not want to harbor a felon, he also did not want to return a man to slavery. Seeking counsel from David Ruggles and other abolitionists, Hopper learned that Darg would free Hughes and not charge him if all of his money was returned. The abolitionists immediately commenced recovering the money but local police officials working with Darg were intent upon convicting Hopper, Ruggles, Barney Corse, and others as accomplices to the theft. Only after sixteen months of legal hearings and the brief imprisonment of both Ruggles and Corse did the prosecution abandon its case as hopeless. The outcome for Hughes is not known. New York *Colored American,* 15 September 1838, 26 January 1839; Isaac T. Hopper, *Exposition of the Proceedings of John P. Darg, Henry W. Merritt, and Others, in Relation to the Robbery of Darg, . . .* (New York, 1840); Dorothy B. Porter, "David M. Ruggles, An Apostle of Human Rights," *JNH,* 28 : 23–50 (January 1943).

76.18/110.13   the Rev. J. W. C. Pennington] Born into slavery as Jim Pembroke, James William Charles Pennington (1809–71) was owned by Frisbie Tilghman of Maryland's Eastern Shore until the age of twenty-one, when he fled north to the home of a Pennsylvania Quaker who taught him to read and write. Later Pennington found work in Long Island, attended night school and private tutorials, and taught black children in Newtown, New York, and New Haven, Connecticut. In 1840, after studying theology in New Haven, Pennington entered the Congregational ministry in Hartford, Connecticut, where he ministered to a black congregation. In 1847 he left to serve another black church in New York City. Committed to a variety of reform causes such as temperance, missionary work, and world peace, Pennington's greatest exertions were devoted to the antislavery movement. In 1843 he traveled to England as a delegate-at-large to the World's Anti-Slavery Convention in London and lectured throughout Europe. Fearing recapture after the passage of the Fugitive Slave Law, Pennington again traveled abroad in 1850, remaining there until a Hartford friend, John Hooker, was able to purchase his freedom. In addition to many sermons, addresses, and regular contributions to the *Anglo-African Magazine,* Pennington wrote *A Text Book of the Origins and History, &c., &c. of the Colored People* (1841), and an autobiography.

J. W. C. Pennington, *The Fugitive Blacksmith*, 3d ed. (London, 1850); *DANB*, 488–90; *DAB*, 14 : 441–42.

76.18–19/110.14   Mrs. Michaels] In the late 1830s, Mrs. D. Michaels owned and operated a boardinghouse in New York City at 33–36 Lespanard Street. She was married to Joseph Michaels who made floor mats and dealt in scrap metal, glass, and rags. [New York] *Weekly Advocate,* 14 January 1837; [New York] *Colored American,* 20 October 1838.

76.30/111.1–2   Mr. Shaw in Newport] George C. Shaw lived in Newport, Rhode Island. In 1840, he was the corresponding secretary for the Newport Anti-Slavery Society, a group supporting William Lloyd Garrison's New England Anti-Slavery Society. *Lib.,* 21 February 1840.

77.1/111.11   Joseph Ricketson] Joseph Ricketson (1771–1841) was the owner of a candle factory and oil refinery in New Bedford, Massachusetts. He also helped form the New Bedford Fire Society in 1807, served as a cashier and a director of the New Bedford Commercial Bank and as a trustee of the New Bedford Lyceum and Antheneum. Ricketson was a Quaker and committed to various reform and antislavery endeavors. Although a scrupulously honest and hard-working businessman, Ricketson's last years were spent close to poverty because of several serious business reversals. Henry H. Crapo, *The New Bedford Directory [for 1836]* (New Bedford, 1836), 18; idem, *The New Bedford Directory [for 1841]* (New Bedford, 1841), 30; *Vital Records of New Bedford, Massachusetts, to the Year 1850,* 3 vols. (Boston, 1932), 1 : 386, 3 : 138; Leonard Bolles Ellis, *History of New Bedford and Its Vicinity, 1602–1892* (Syracuse, 1892), 252, 509, 516, 517, 629; *Our County and Its People: Descriptive and Biographical Record of Bristol County, Massachusetts* (Boston, 1899), 351n1, 353, 406; Daniel Ricketson, *The History of New Bedford, Bristol County, Massachusetts* (New Bedford, 1858), 232–34; Hurd, *Bristol County,* 92, 105, 111.

77.2/111.11–12   William C. Taber] A descendant of one of the earliest settlers of New Bedford, Massachusetts, William C. Taber (1797–?) operated a profitable store which sold books, stationery, charts, and engravings. In the 1850s Taber led local businessmen in converting from whale oil for illumination to gas, coal oil, and kerosene and was the first president of the New Bedford Gas-Light Company. He was long active in the city's financial institutions, having served at different times as a director of both the Marine Bank and the New Bedford Institution For Savings. Taber also represented New Bedford at one point in the Massachusetts legislature. An ardent Quaker, Taber held the post of first clerk at the New Bedford Monthly Meeting for nineteen years. He married Hannah Shearman of the same town. Crapo, *New Bedford Directory [for 1836],* 84; idem, *New Bedford Directory [for 1841],* 19; idem, *New Bedford Directory [for 1845],* 14; idem, *The New Bedford Directory [for 1856]* (New Bedford, 1856), 164; Hurd, *Bristol County,* 91–92, 105, 148; Ellis, *New Bedford,* 422, 469, 475, 517, 566, 638, 721; *Our County,* 353–54, 372–73, 416–17, and "Personal References," 343.

77.7/111.19 Mr. and Mrs. Johnson] Owners of a confectionery shop and a thriving catering business, Nathan Johnson (?–1880) and Mary Page Johnson (?– c. 1870) were two of the most prominent blacks in New Bedford, Massachusetts. They had helped and housed black fugitives on many occasions and Nathan had long been an active abolitionist, serving as a manager of the American Anti-Slavery Society at one point. In 1832, Nathan represented New Bedford at the National Negro Convention in Philadelphia and in 1837 he was one of three local African Americans chosen to question all county political candidates as to their view on slavery and the slave trade. Johnson left New Bedford for California in 1849 and did not return until 1871 after his wife, who had remained behind, died. [New York] *Colored American,* 18 November 1837; Henry H. Crapo, *The New Bedford Directory [for 1838]* (New Bedford, 1838), 77; *Vital Records of New Bedford,* 2 : 309, 396; Barbara Clayton and Kathleen Whitley, *Guide to New Bedford* (Chester, Conn., 1979), 134–35; Merrill and Ruchames, *Garrison Letters,* 2 : 712; McFeely, *Frederick Douglass,* 76, 77, 78, 84.

77.26–27/112.15 the "Lady of the Lake,"] Sir Walter Scott (1771–1832) published *The Lady of the Lake* in Edinburgh in 1810. Ellen Douglas and her father, Lord James of Douglas, are the principal characters. *The Poetic Works of Sir Walter Scott,* 12 vols. (Edinburgh, 1880,) 8 : 8, 63, 75–76; Paul Harvey, ed., *The Oxford Companion to English Literature,* 4th ed. (New York, 1967), 458, 735–36.

79.1–2/114.28 ". . . and he took me in"] Douglass paraphrases Matt. 25 : 35.

80.8/116.25 the "Liberator."] Pioneer abolitionist William Lloyd Garrison published the weekly Boston newspaper, the *Liberator,* from 1831 to 1865. The paper advocated women's rights, temperance, pacifism, and a variety of other reforms in addition to immediate emancipation. Thomas, *The Liberator,* 127–28, 436; *DAB,* 7 : 168–72.

80.23–24/117.17 an anti-slavery convention at Nantucket] A reference to the same abolitionist convention at Atheneum Hall in Nantucket, Massachusetts, on 10–12 August 1841, which Garrison described in his Preface to the *Narrative.* Douglass spoke in favor of a resolution condemning northern white racial prejudice on 11 August. Douglass had earlier addressed antislavery meetings in New Bedford, Massachusetts. *Lib.,* 29 March, 9 July, 20 August 1841.

81.16/118.26–119.1 "stealing . . . in."] Robert Pollok, *The Course of Time, A Poem* (Boston, 1843), Book 8, lines 616–18: "He was a man / Who stole the livery of the court of heaven, / To serve the Devil in."

82.26/120.13–28 Strength to the spoiler thine?] With minor punctuation changes, Douglass quotes the first four stanzas of John Greenleaf Whittier's 1835 poem, "Clerical Oppressors." *Poetical Works of John Greenleaf Whittier,* 3 : 38–39.

82.28–83.12/121.1–30 "They bind . . . of hypocrisy and iniquity."] An adaptation of Jesus' denunciation of the scribes and Pharisees in Matt. 23 : 4–28.

84.1–84.3/123.4–6 "Shall I . . . a nation as this?"] Jer. 5 : 9, 29.

85.5/124.15 Bashan bull] A paraphrase of Ps. 22 : 12.

Prefaces and Appendixes to the Later Editions

As described in the Textual Introduction, two editions of the *Narrative* published after the original 1845 Boston edition possess obvious authority (D1: Dublin, 1845, and D2: Dublin, 1846). A third edition (E1: Wortley, near Leeds, England, 1846) possibly reflects Douglass's authorial intentions.

In both Dublin editions, Douglass retitled the *Narrative*'s original "Preface," written by William Lloyd Garrison, as "Preface to the American Edition." In D1, Douglass prepared his own "Preface" and had it printed before Garrison's. For D2, Douglass added two additional paragraphs to his Preface and again had it placed before Garrison's. Both prefaces are reproduced below. The E1 edition reprinted Douglass's Preface in the D2 edition without change and therefore has not been reproduced.

The history of the end matter found in the editions of the *Narrative* is more complicated. Beginning with D1, Douglass gave his original "Appendix" the more accurate label "Postscript." To the D1, D2, and E1 editions Douglass appended an increasing number of documents. These additions were cumulative, and no authorial alterations or deletions occurred from edition to subsequent edition. Following the Postscript, the D1 edition printed "To the Friends of the Slave," a call for support to the American Anti-Slavery Society signed by sympathetic British women. This edition concluded with a section titled "Critical Notices." That last section reproduced excerpts from five positive newspaper reviews of the *Narrative,* originally published in the American press.

The end matter for the D2 edition was significantly longer. The Postscript now was followed by an "Appendix," containing an exchange between Marylander A. C. C. Thompson and Douglass concerning the accuracy of key sections of the *Narrative*. The northern press had widely published both Thompson's original public letter and Douglass's reply in late 1845 and early 1846. Following this Appendix, Douglass reproduced the Critical Notices section but with the addition of several new favorable reviews from British sources. The D2 edition concluded with the unchanged text of the "To the Friends of the Slave" call. The E1 edition's end matter differs from that of D2 in only one respect. Douglass inserted the text of an antislavery address that he had delivered before the concluding public call at London's Finsbury Chapel on 22 May 1846.

After reflection the editors have decided to avoid pointless repetition in reproducing the end matter of the *Narrative*. Because the first edition of the project's Speeches, Debates, and Interviews Series already published a text of Douglass's Finsbury Chapel speech, found on pages 133–66 of the E1 edition, it is not reproduced in this volume. Likewise, because the D2 edition reprints all sections of the end matter found in the D1 edition, the latter material has not been reproduced. Therefore, all of the end matter that follows the two prefaces printed below originally appeared in the D2 edition.

Douglass, *Narrative* (Dublin, 1845), iii–iv.

PREFACE.

In May last the present Narrative was published in Boston, U.S., and when I sailed for England in September, about 4,500 copies had been sold. This rapid sale may be accounted for by the fact of my being a fugitive slave, and from the circumstance that for the last four years I have been engaged in travelling as a lecturing agent of the American Anti-slavery Society, by which means I became extensively known in our country.

My visit to Great Britain had a threefold object. I wished to be out of the way during the excitement consequent on the publication of my book; lest the information I had there given as to my identity and place of abode, should induce my *owner* to take measures for my restoration to his 'patriarchal care.' For it may not be generally known in Europe, that a slave who escapes from his master is liable, by the Constitution of the United States, to be dragged back into bondage, no matter in what part of the vast extent of the States and their territories he may have taken refuge.

My next inducement was a desire to increase my stock of information, and my opportunities of self-improvement, by a visit to the land of my *paternal* ancestors.

My third and chief object was, by the public exposition of the contaminating and degrading influences of Slavery upon the slaveholder and his abettors, as well as the slave, to excite such an intelligent interest on the subject of American Slavery, as may react upon my own country, and may tend to shame her out of her adhesion to a system so abhorrent to Christianity and to her republican institutions.

I beg to refer my reader to the Preface to the First edition, and the Letter which follows it; to some notices of my Narrative extracted from American newspapers, which will be found at the end of the book; and to the following notice of a meeting held the evening previous to my departure from home, in the town of Lynn, Massachusetts, where I have resided for the last two years;—

"Last Friday evening a meeting was held in Lyceum Hall, for the purpose of exchanging farewells with Frederick Douglass and James N. Buffum, prior to their departure, on the ensuring day, for the Old World. The spacious hall was crowded to its utmost capacity—hundreds of men and women being obliged to stand all the evening. This was a most gratifying fact, and spoke volumes for the onward progress of the anti-slavery movement—since but six or seven years back, the people, instead of meeting with two such anti-slavery men for the interchange of kindly feelings, would have been more likely to meet them for the purpose of inflicting some summary punishment. Hundreds of persons enjoyed on this occasion the first good opportunity they have had to judge of Frederick Douglass's ability as a speaker and a reasoner; and unless I am much mistaken, their judgment was such as not only to increase their respect for him, but for his race, and the great movement now on foot to release it from thraldom. He spoke twice, and both times with great power. His second effort sparkled with wit from beginning to end.

"The following resolutions were adopted, *nem. con.*

RESOLVED—As the sense of this great gathering of the inhabitants of Lynn and vicinity that we extend to our esteemed fellow-citizens Frederick Douglass and James N. Buffum, whose proposed departure for England has brought this multitude together, our heartiest good wishes for a successful issue of their journey.

RESOLVED—That we are especially desirous that Frederick Douglass, who came to this town a fugitive from slavery, should bear with him to the shores of the Old World, our unanimous testimony to the fidelity with which he has sustained the various relations of life, and to the deep respect with which he is now regarded by every friend of liberty throughout our borders.

Douglass, *Narrative* (Dublin, 1846), iii–vi.

PREFACE
TO THE
SECOND DUBLIN EDITION.

In May last, the present Narrative was published in Boston, Massachusetts, and when I sailed for England in September, about 4,500 copies had been sold. I have lately heard that a fifth edition had been called for. This rapid sale may be accounted for by the fact of my being a fugitive slave, and from the circumstance that for the last four years I have been engaged in travelling as a lecturing agent of the American Anti-slavery Society, by which means I became extensively known in the United States.

My visit to Great Britain had a threefold object. I wished to be out of the way during the excitement consequent on the publication of my book; lest the information I had there given as to my identity and place of abode, should induce my *owner* to take measures for my restoration to his 'patriarchal care.' For it may not be generally known in Europe, that a slave who escapes from his master is liable, by the Constitution of the United States, to be dragged back into bondage, no matter in what part of the vast extent of the States and their territories he may have taken refuge.

My next inducement was a desire to increase my stock of information, and my opportunities of self-improvement, by a visit to the land of my *paternal* ancestors.

My third and chief object was, by the public exposition of the contaminating and degrading influences of Slavery upon the slaveholder and his abettors, as well as the slave, to excite such an intelligent interest on the subject of American Slavery, as may react upon my own country, and may tend to shame her out of her adhesion to a system so abhorrent to Christianity and to her republican institutions.

My last object is, I am happy to say, in a fair way of being accomplished. I have held public meetings in Dublin, Wexford, Waterford, Cork, Youghal, Limerick, Belfast, Glasgow, Aberdeen, Perth, and Dundee, within the five months which have elapsed since I landed in England. An edition of 2000 copies of my Narrative has been exhausted, and I am in great hopes that before my visit to Great Britain shall be completed, thousands and tens of thousands of the intelligent and philanthropic will be induced to co-operate with the noble band of American abolitionists, for the overthrow of the meanest, hugest, and most dastardly system of iniquity that ever disgraced any country laying claim to the benefits of religion and civilization.

I beg to refer my reader to the Preface to the First edition, and the Letter which follows it; to some notices of my Narrative from various sources, which will be found at the end of the book; and to the following notice of a public meeting held the evening previous to my departure from home, in the town of Lynn, Massachusetts, where I have resided for the last two years:—

"Last Friday evening a meeting was held in Lyceum Hall, for the purpose of exchanging farewells with Frederick Douglass and James N. Buffum, prior to their departure, on the ensuing day, for the Old World. The spacious hall was crowded to its utmost capacity—hundreds of men and women being obliged to stand all the evening. This was a most gratifying fact, and spoke volumes for the onward progress of the anti-slavery movement—since but six or seven years back, the people, instead of meeting with two such anti-slavery men for the interchange of kindly feelings, would have been more likely to meet them for the purpose of inflicting some summary punishment. Hundreds of persons enjoyed on this occasion the first good opportunity they have had to judge of Frederick Douglass's ability as a speaker and a reasoner; and unless I am much mistaken, their judgment was such as not only to increase their respect for him, but for his race, and the great movement now on foot to release it from thraldom. He spoke twice, and both times with great power. His second effort sparkled with wit from beginning to end.

"The following resolutions were adopted, *nem. con.*

"RESOLVED—As the sense of this great gathering of the inhabitants of Lynn and vicinity, that we extend to our esteemed fellow-citizens Frederick Douglass and James N. Buffum, whose proposed departure for England has brought this multitude together, our heartiest good wishes for a successful issue of their journey.

"RESOLVED—That we are especially desirous that Frederick Douglass, who came to this town a fugitive from slavery, should bear with him to the shores of the Old World, our unanimous testimony to the fidelity with which he has sustained the various relations of life, and to the deep respect with which he is now regarded by every friend of liberty throughout our borders."

It gives me great pleasure to be able to add, in an Appendix to the present edition, an attempted Refutation of my Narrative, lately published in the "Delaware Republican" by Mr. A. C. C. Thompson. My reply will be found along with Mr. Thompson's letter. I have thanked him there; but I cannot refrain from repeating my acknowledgments for the testimony he bears to the substantial truth of my story. We differ in our details, to be sure. But this was to be expected. He is the friend of slave-holders; he resides in a slave state, and is probably a slave-holder himself. He dares not speak the whole truth, if he would. I am an American slave, who have given my tyrant the slip. I am in a land of liberty, with no man to make me afraid. He agrees with me at least in the important fact, that I am what I proclaim myself to be, an ungrateful fugitive from the 'patriarchal institutions' of the Slave States; and he certifies that many of the heroes of my Narrative are still living and doing well, as "honored and worthy members of the Methodist Episcopal Church."

FREDERICK DOUGLASS.

Glasgow, Feb. 6th, 1846.

Douglass, *Narrative* (Dublin, 1846), cxxiii–cxxviii.

APPENDIX.

The following comments on my Narrative appeared very lately in the "Delaware Republican," a newspaper published in the most northern of the Slave States, and not very remote from that part of Maryland where my early days were spent. Although put forth as a refutation of my statements, under the unflattering title of "Falsehood Refuted," I have great pleasure in presenting it to my readers. The writer's admissions are valuable as a confirmation of the main facts of my Narrative, while the denials are only such as might be expected from an apologist of slavery. My reply to Mr. Thompson will be found at the end of his letter.

FALSEHOOD REFUTED.

It is with considerable regret that I find myself measurably compelled to appear before the public; but my attention has lately been arrested by a pamphlet, which has been freely circulated in Wilmington and elsewhere, with the following superscription:—*Extract from a Narrative of Frederick Douglass, an American Slave, written by himself.*

And although I am aware that no sensible, unprejudiced person will credit such a ridiculous publication, which bears the glaring impress of falsehood on every page, yet I deem it expedient that I should give the public some information respecting the validity of this Narrative, because I was for many years a citizen of the section of country where the scenes of the above-mentioned Narrative are laid; and am intimately acquainted with most of the gentlemen whose characters are some shamefully traduced, and I am also aware that the Narrative was not written by the professed author; but from statements of this runaway slave, some evil-designed person or persons have composed this catalogue of lies, to excite the indignation of the public opinion against the slaveholders of the South; and have even attempted to plunge their venomous fangs in the vitals of the Church.

I shall, therefore, briefly notice some of the most glaring falsehoods contained in the aforesaid Narrative, and give a true representation of the character of those gentlemen who have been censured in such an uncharitable manner, as murderers, hypocrites, and everything else that is vile.

I indulge no animosity against the fabricators and circulators of this Narrative, neither do I know them; but I positively declare the whole to be a budget of falsehoods, from beginning to end.

1st. The identity of the author. About eight years ago, I knew this recreant slave by the name of Frederick Baily, (instead of Douglass.) He then lived with Mr. Edward Covey, and was an unlearned, and rather an ordinary negro, and am confident he was not capable of writing the Narrative alluded to; for none but an educated man, and one who had some knowledge of the rules of grammar, could write so correctly; although, to make the imposition at all creditable, the composer has labored to write it in as plain a style as possible; consequently, the detection of this first falsehood proves the whole production to be most notoriously untrue.

Again—"It is a common custom, in the part of Maryland from which I ran away, to separate children from their mothers at a very early age."

This, also, I know to be false. There is no such custom prevalent in that section of the country; but, on the contrary, the children are raised with their mothers, and generally live with them in the same house, except in some few instances where the mother is hired out as a cook or laborer in some other family.

The gentlemen whose names are so prominently set forth in the said Narrative, are Col. Edward Lloyd, Capt. Anthony, Austin Gore, Thomas Lamdin (not Lanman,) Giles Hicks, Thomas Auld, and Edward Covey. Most of these persons I am intimately acquainted with, and shall give a brief sketch of their characters as follows:—

Col. Edward Lloyd was one of the most wealthy and respectable planters in the state of Maryland. He was at one time the Governor of the State, and for several years a member of the legislature. He owned several thousand acres of land, and between four and five hundred slaves. He died before I had much knowledge of him: but I know that he was a kind and charitable man, and in every respect an honorable and worthy citizen.

Most of the same slaves are now owned by his three sons, and they manage their servants in the same manner as did their father; and I know there are no such barbarities committed on their plantations.

Could it be possible that charitable, feeling men could murder human beings, with as little remorse of conscience as the Narrative of this infamous libel wishes to make us believe; and that the laws of Maryland, which operate *alike upon black and white,* bond or free, could permit such foul murders to pass unnoticed? No! it is impossible; and every sensible man knows that these false accusations are the ebullition of an unchristian prejudice.

Captain Anthony and Giles Hicks I know but little of. The accused murderer, Mr. Gore, is a respectable citizen, living near St. Michael's, and I believe a worthy member of the Methodist Episcopal Church; he was formerly an overseer for Col. Lloyd, and at this time all who know him think him anything but a murderer.

Thomas Lamdin, who, it is said in the Narrative, boasted so frequently of his murders, is, at this time, an honest school-teacher in the district where I formerly lived; and all the harm that can be said of him is, that he is too good-natured and harmless to injure any person but himself.

Captain Thomas Auld, whose hypocritical meanness is so strongly depicted in the aforesaid Narrative, was for many years a respectable merchant in the town of St. Michael's, and an honorable and worthy member of the Methodist Episcopal Church; and only notable for his integrity and irreproachable Christian character. He is now retired from the turmoil of a mercantile life, and engaged in the worthy occupation of tilling the soil, little dreaming of the foul accusations that are circulated against him.

Edward Covey, the renowned "negro breaker," is also a plain, honest farmer, and a tried and faithful member of the Methodist Episcopal Church. Mr. Covey lived for several years on a farm adjoining my father's, at which time this runaway negro lived with him, and I am well aware that no such bloody tragedy as is recorded in that lying Narrative, ever occurred on Mr. Covey's farm. All that can be said of Mr. Covey is, that he is a good Christian and a hard working man, and makes every one around him work, and treats them well. By his honest industry, he has purchased a fine farm, and is now reaping the reward of his labor.

Such are the characters of the men whom the imposers of this dirty Narrative have so uncharitably traduced, and by blending these false accusations with the Methodist religion of the South, they wish to lacerate her already bleeding wounds.

I was raised among slaves, and have also owned them, and am well aware that the slaves live better and fare better, in many respects, than the free blacks.

Yet I am positively opposed to slavery, for I know it is a great evil; but *the evil; falls not upon the slave,* but on the owner.

Intrigue and false accusations will never liberate the slave of the South; but, on the contrary, every such attempt will only forge for them new and stronger fetters.

Let the tender-hearted philanthropists of the North speak truth and love towards their Southern brethren, and make a liberal application of their gold for the removing the blacks from the country, and their chance of success will be more flattering.

I have given a true representation of the persons connected with the aforesaid Narrative, and I respectfully submit the facts to the judgment of an impartial public.

A. C. C. THOMPSON.

101, *Market-street, Wilmington, Delaware.*

REPLY TO MR. A. C. C. THOMPSON.

SIR,

For the sake of the abolition cause, I was delighted to see by an extract copied into the "Liberator" of 12 Dec. 1845, from the "Delaware Republican," that a Mr. A. C. C. Thompson, No. 101, Market-street, Wilmington, has undertaken to invalidate my testimony against those slave-holders, whose names I have made prominent in the humble Narrative of my experience in slavery. Slaveholders and slave-traders never betray greater indiscretion than when they venture to defend themselves, or their system of plunder, in any other community than a slave-holding one. Slavery has its own standard of kindness, morality, humanity, justice, and Christianity. Tried by its own standard, it is a system of the greatest kindness to the slave, sanctioned by the purest morality, perfectly agreeable to justice, and of course not inconsistent with Christianity. But tried by any other, it is doomed to condemnation. The naked relation of master and slave is one of those monsters of darkness, to whom the light of truth is death. The wise ones among the slave-holders know this, and they studiously avoid doing anything which will in their judgment tend to elicit truth. They seem to understand that their safety is in their silence. They have probably learned this wisdom from Junius, a distinguished political writer, who counselled his opponent, Sir Wm. Draper, when defending Lord Granby, "never to attract attention to a character, which would only pass without condemnation when it passed without observation."

I am almost too far off to answer your attempted refutation of my Narrative. I fear your article will be forgotten before you get my reply. I however think the whole thing worth reviving, as it is seldom we have so good a case for dissection. In any other country than America, I might hope to get a hearing through the columns of the paper in which I was attacked; but this would be inconsistent with American magnanimity, and it would be folly to expect such a hearing. They might be willing to advertise me as a fugitive slave, but on no other condition. Their motto is, "we don't allow niggers in here." I may, however, in this judge "The Republican" harshly. If so, we shall see. In replying to your epistle, I shall proceeed as I used to do in preaching the Slave-holder's Sermon; dividing the subject under two general heads. Firstly his statement in confirmation of the truth of my Narrative; and secondly, his denials of its truthfulness. Under the first, I entreat you to accept my thanks for your full, free, and unsolicited testimony in regard to my identity. There now need be no doubt on that point, however much there might have been before. You, Mr. Thompson, have for ever settled them. I give you the fullest credit for the deed, saying nothing of the motive. But for you, the proslavery people of the North might have persisted in representing me as an imposter, a free negro, who had never been south of Mason and Dixon's line; whom the abolitionists had educated, and sent forth as a fugitive slave, to attract attention to their faltering cause. I am greatly indebted to you for silencing these truly prejudicial rumours and hurtful slanders. I wish, sir, that I could make you understand the amount of service which you have done me. You have completely tripped up the heels of your proslavery friends, and laid them flat at my feet. You have done a piece of anti-slavery work, which no anti-slavery man could do. Our cautious and truth-loving people in New England would never have believed this testimony in proof of my identity, had it been borne by an abolitonist. Not that they really think such persons disposed intentionally to bear false witness, but they are thought fanatical, and apt to see every thing through a distorted medium. They will believe you; they will believe slave-holders, or their apologists. They have, somehow, strangely imbibed the idea that persons such as yourself are impartial, dispassionate, and disinterested witnesses. Now, under these circumstances, your testimony was and still is of the utmost importance. It will serve to give effect to my exposure of Slavery both at home and abroad. Do not think I wish to administer to your vanity, when I tell you that you seem to have been raised up for the purpose! I came to this land with testimonials of the most satisfactory character from some of the most distinguished abolitionists in America. Yet some here have entertained doubts as to whether I have ever been a slave. You may easily imagine the perplexing and embarrassing nature of those doubts, and the desirableness of having them removed. Thanks to a kind Providence, you have come to my aid; you have removed all doubt, and relieved me of all embarrassment. I now stand before both the American and British public; indorsed by you as being just what I have represented myself to be, an American slave. For you say, "*I know* this recreant slave by the name of Frederick Bailey, instead of Douglass." Now leaving out the term *recreant,* which is rather severe, your testimony is direct and perfect, just what I have long been in want of. But you are not yet satisfied; you seem determined to bear the most ample testimony in my favour. You say you knew me when I lived with Mr. Covey; this is excellent. Then Mr. Covey is no creature of my imagination, but really did exist, and yet lives, and moves, and has a being. And with most of the persons mentioned in my narrative, you say you are intimately acquainted. This also confirms my statements. It shows that I have given the real names of the parties of whom I have spoken. You thus destroy the force of the miserable insinuation of my enemies, that I have used fictitious names and not real names. You go on. *"Colonel Lloyd was a wealthy planter. Mr. Gore was once an overseer for Colonel Lloyd; but is now living near St. Michael's, is respected, and you believe he is a member of the Methodist Church. Thomas Auld (the man who now claims property in my body and soul) is an honourable member of the Methodist Episcopal Church. Mr. Covey too is a member of the Methodist Church."* Once more, allow me to thank you for this triumphant vindication of the truth of my statements; and to show you how highly I value your testimony, I will inform you that as I am now publishing a second edition of my Narrative, (having already disposed of two thousand copies since my arrival on this side of the Atlantic) I will insert your article with my reply, as an appendix to the edition now in progress.

Now then, to the second part, or your denials. You are confident I did not write the book. The reason of your confidence on this point is, that I was, when you knew me, an unlearned and rather ordinary negro. Well, I have to inform you, that you knew me under very unfavourable circumstances; it was when I lived with Mr. Covey, the negro breaker. The degradation to which I was then reduced, and my condition now, contrasted with what it then was, are truly marvellous. I can easily understand that you sincerely doubt my having written the Narrative in question. For if any one had told me seven years ago, that I should ever be able to *dictate* such a Narrative, to say nothing of *writing* it, I should have disbelieved the prophecy. I was then a mere wreck; Covey had beaten and bruised me so much, that my spirit was crushed and broken. Frederick the Freeman is a very different person from Frederick the Slave. To judge me now by what I was then, is to do me great injustice. I feel myself a new man. Freedom has given me new life. The change wrought in me is truly amazing. If you should meet me, now you would scarcely know me. You know when I used to meet you near Covey's wood-gate, I hardly dared to look up at you. If I should meet you where I now am, amid the free hills of Old Scotland, where the ancient "Black Douglass" once met his foes, I presume I might summon sufficient fortitude to look you full in the face. It may be that, wearing the brave name which I have assumed, might lead me to deeds which would render our meeting not the most agreeable. Especially might this be the case, if you should attempt to enslave me. You would see a wonderful change in me. I have really got out of my place; that is, I have got out of slavery, which you know is "the place" for negroes in Christian America. I have now explained away your reason for thinking I did not write the book. You next deny the existence of such cruelty as I reveal in my narrative. You ask: *"Could it be possible that charitable feeling men could murder human beings with as little remorse of conscience as the narrative of this infamous libel wishes to make us believe; and that the laws of Maryland, which operate alike upon black and white, bond and free, could permit such foul murders to pass unnoticed? No!"* You say *"It is impossible."* Now I am not to say here, what charitable feeling men can do, but to show what Maryland slaveholders do. Their charitable feeling is to be determined by their deeds, and not their deeds by their charitable feeling. The cowskin makes as deep a gash in my flesh when wielded by a professed saint as it does when wielded by an open sinner. The musket does as fatal execution when its trigger is pulled by Austin Gore the Christian, as it does when pulled by Beal Bondly the infidel. The best way to determine what these charitable feeling men can do, will be to point you to their laws, which you say operate alike upon the black and white, the bond and the free. By consulting the statute law of Maryland, 8th section, you will find the following law:—"Any slave, for rambling in the night, or riding horses by day without leave, or running away, may be punished by whipping, cropping, or branding in the cheek or otherwise, not rendering him unfit for labour."—p. 237. Then another:—"any slave convicted of petty treason, *murder, or wilful burning of dwelling houses, may be sentenced to have his right hand cut off, to be hanged in the usual manner, the head severed from the body, the body divided into four quarters, and the head and quarters set up in the most public place in the country where such fact was committed."*—p. 190.

Now when you consider with what ease a slave may be convicted of any one or all of these crimes, how bloody do these laws appear! and yet bloody as they are, they are the mere breath of those charitable feeling slave-holders. You say that the laws of Maryland operate alike upon the bond and the free, the white and the black. If you mean by this, that the parties named are all equally protected by law, you assert what is entirely untrue; and unless you are more than ordinarily ignorant, you knew it to be untrue when you made the assertion. It is a notorious fact that no black man can, upon his own oath or the testimony of any number of blacks, bring a white man before any tribunal in the state of Maryland; while the testimony of one white may subject a black to any punishment this side of death. If a slaveholder beat his slave, no matter how cruelly, he has no redress, not even the right of petition; but if a slave beat his master, his right hand may be cut off, and he may be hanged in the usual way, his head severed from his body, and his body divided into quarters, &c. Now you may exclaim, can it be possible, &c.? But there stands the fact, crimsoning the pages of your statute book.

Your positive opposition to slavery is explained by your declaration that the evils of the system do not fall upon the slave, but upon the slave holder.

Believing that you are condemned out of your own mouth, I subscribe myself,

FREDERICK DOUGLASS.

Perth, Scotland, 27th Jan. 1846.

Douglass, *Narrative* (Dublin, 1846), cxxix–cxxiii.

CRITICAL NOTICES.

FROM THE PHILADELPHIA ELEVATOR.

Frederick Douglass.—We observe that this self-emancipated man has lately sent forth from the press a sketch of his life. Every body should read it. It is an exceedingly interesting as well as an ably written work. While lately in a part of Maryland, we were unexpectedly called upon by at least a dozen colored persons, some of them slaves, and others freemen, who had heard that we knew Frederick at the North, and who wished to hear news from their old friend. They knew him by his assumed as well as by his real name, and related to us many interesting incidents about their former companion.

FROM THE BOSTON (U.S.) COURIER.

Narrative of the Life of Frederick Douglass, an American Slave: written by himself. The above work contains many descriptions of scenes at the South, which, if true, bear sufficient witness against the 'peculiar institution,' to make every honest man wish its downfall soon, and by almost any means. And there seems to be no reason for believing that more than the truth is told. Unlimited power to use always tends to power to abuse, and where might is, there is seldom wanting the will to make the right. The story is a simple one, and reveals nothing more than is to be supposed true of those, who have the power to commit crime without the fear of law.

FROM THE BOSTON (U.S.) TRANSCRIPT.

We have been led to these few but earnest remarks, by reading the life of Frederick Douglass—a runaway felon, as he would probably be termed in the South, but, properly speaking, a freeman by choice and adoption. This little book bears throughout the indelible marks of truth and impartiality; and while the mind is shocked by the unnatural scenes there described, it, at the same time, is forced to acknowledge their truth and reality. Harden our hearts as we may to the sufferings of those with whom we are not immediately connected, yet we cannot shut out from our minds those bitter truths which come pouring in upon us from every side—and how great is the sin, when we have eyes and *will* not see, ears and *will* not hear, and hearts and *will* not feel! This book on the whole is a well written history, and, coming from one who only by snatches was able to instruct himself, and that too with the bloody lash ready, on detection, to punish the crime of acquiring knowledge, it may be pronounced an extraordinary performance.

FROM THE NEW YORK TRIBUNE.

FREDERICK DOUGLASS has been for some time a prominent member of the abolition party. He is said to be an excellent speaker—can speak from a thorough personal experience—and has upon the audience, beside, the influence of a strong character and uncommon talents. In the book before us he has put into the story of his life, the thoughts, the feelings, and the adventures that have been so affecting through the living voice; nor are they less so from the printed page. He has had the courage to name the persons, times, and places, thus exposing himself to obvious danger, and setting the seal on his deep convictions as to the religious need of speaking the whole truth. Considered merely as a narrative, we have never read one more simple, true, coherent, and warm with genuine feeling. It is an excellent piece of writing, and on that score to be prized as a specimen of the powers of the black race, which prejudice persists in disputing. We prize highly all evidence of this kind, and it is becoming more abundant. Douglass seems very just and temperate. We feel that his view, even of those who have injured him most, may be relied on. He knows how to allow for motives and influences. Upon the subject of religion he speaks with great force, and not more than our own sympathies can respond to. The inconsistencies of slaveholding professors of religion cry to Heaven. We wish that every one may read his book, and see what a mind might have been stifled in bondage—what a man may be subjected to the insults of spendthrift dandies, or the blows of mercenary brutes, in whom there is no whiteness except in the skin, no humanity except in the outward form, and of whom the Avenger will not fail yet to demand—'Where is thy brother?'

FROM THE PRACTICAL CHRISTIAN (U.S.)

NARRATIVE OF FREDERICK DOUGLASS—this admirable little volume is just out. It will doubtless prove a valuable auxiliary to the cause of abolition. Frederick is a strong man, and will not fail to arouse the sympathies of his readers in behalf of the oppressed. May he long live with his burning eloquence, to pour truth on the naked conscience of this wicked nation.

FROM THE LONDON ATLAS.

This is a very remarkable little volume. It is remarkable as being the production of a slave, and one of that people whom it has always been the cue of slaveholders and slavery advocates to represent as incapable of intellectual vigour and ability. The narrative is written with singular ability, and, as a story of real life, is at once simply related, and one of the most thrilling and absorbing imaginable. If there yet be a man who is inclined to set up a plea for slavery on the ground that slaves are very happy and are well attended to by their masters, *because they are property,* and therefore it is the interest of masters to use them well, let such person read this little book of only 122 pages, and that last and most shallow reason will be torn from him. The autobiography of FREDERICK DOUGLASS demonstrates in most vivid colors, how deadly is the influence of slavery both on master, mistress, and slave, on all that is connected with it. It is a condition fraught with moral death and darkness to all parties, and the savage cruelties and base degradations which are the inevitable portion of the slave, are in themselves, after all, still less revolting, still less awful, than the debasement, the hardening, the pollution and ruin of heart and soul and character in the slave-master and the slave-mistress. The worst evil of slavery in a country is, that it debauches the public mind, destroys the public sensibility, makes a nation a nation of Jesuits and hypocrites. The very religion of CHRIST is made to pander to the sordid evils of slavery. Its sacred sanction is pleaded for its existence, while it is carefully withheld from the knowledge of the slaves; because the very men who plead that Christianity sanctions slavery know that it is a lie, and need no convincing, that if slaves once know the truths of Christianity, they will feel that "it makes them free." There is nothing so shocking to contemplate as the so-called *religious* slaveholder. It is an exhibition so dreadful, that they who are not indignant as it must soon come to believe that Christianity itself is a farce and an instrument of selfish policy. A national system of slavery is a national system for the inculcation of Atheism; for they who can once come to believe in its propriety, must cease to believe that there is a God of justice. The greatest curse that can befall an empire is to have a black mass of slavery in it; because that is perfectly inseparable from the destruction of everything that is noble in the public character, every clear recognition of human and divine right, every sentiment of sound benevolence and of the onward progress of man and his loftier destinies. Slavery rots the heart of a nation; it eats out, like a canker, its sentiment of the great, the noble, and the generous; it sets it on the defence of what it at the same time is conscious is vile and indefensible, and thus stiffens it, as it were, into a doggedness of defiant evil, most mischievous to its fame and most revolting to contemplate. This is the position of things in America at the present moment, and that great republic, the United States,—

> "Did but some power the giftie gie it,
> To see itself as others see it,"—

would rise in a real phrenzy to get rid of the growing curse of slavery; not because it presses on the slave himself; not because men are brutalized by it, and women are more than brutalized by it, not because blood and tears are made to flow, because flesh is torn and the spirit is trodden out of the negro bosom like sparks of fatal fire;—but because the commission of wrong, the perpetration of cruelty and crime on the weak and defenceless; because justice to men and honor to woman, outraged by its maintenance, are acting worse than the possession of seven devils on the national mind;—are confounding all principles of right and wrong, of justice and magnanimity in it, and sinking the national character from that glorious eminence which it assumed at the Revolution, to the moral position in which none but its enemies would wish to see it. America must continue to raise a joyous grin on the face of Satan; must cast a practical sneer on its present fundamental principle that "every man is born free and equal;" must stand as the worst of obstacles in the path of Christianity, and the growth of belief in it; and must disappoint every one who finally looked towards its career as to a great and unexampled developement of national policy and mind, till she gives freedom to black as well as white Americans.

We will now give a few evidences of the working of slavery from the pen this literary slave. But we may be asked before doing this,—"Who is this FREDERICK DOUGLASS? And what guarantee have we that he is what he represents himself to be?" In answer to this, we have only to say that his book is prefaced by two admirable letters from the well-known champions of American freedom, WILLIAM LLOYD GARRISON and WENDELL PHILLIPS, bearing the highest testimonies to his character and to his services in the abolition cause, and that JAMES HAUGHTON, the Chairman, and RICHARD D. WEBB, the Secretary of the Hibernian Anti-Slavery Society, state that—'He has long been known to us by reputation, and is now introduced to us by letters from some of the most distinguished and faithful friends of the Anti-slavery cause in America.' We hear that Mr. DOUGLASS is now in Ireland, and purposes to visit England, and that he is as efficient a speaker in the cause of his oppressed countrymen as he is a writer."—*William Howitt.*

FROM CHAMBERS'S EDINBURGH JOURNAL.

"We have been much interested in the autobiography of FREDERICK DOUGLASS, a person of color, lately a slave in the United States, and now a lecturer in the cause of abolition. The account he gives of his early life, and the condition from which he was able to relieve himself, bears all the appearance of truth, and must, we conceive, help considerably to disseminate correct ideas respecting slavery and its attendant evils. Some of the passages present a dismal picture of what is endured by the negro race in the slaveholding states of the Union. Mr. DOUGLASS is now, we believe, in Great Britain, lecturing on the subject of slavery, and we suppose few could be more capable of depicting the horrors of this great national iniquity.

FROM THE BRISTOL MERCURY.

A more deeply interesting Narrative than Douglass's can hardly be conceived.

FROM THE REV. THOMAS DREW, D.D.

When one reads the autobiography of FREDERICK DOUGLASS for the first time, the grievous details of the writer absorb all attention. On a second reading, interest in the details is accompanied by an enquiry, "did Frederick Douglass himself, *propria penna,* write this book?" It is a matter of truth, that he wrote every line. Then let God have the praise through Christ; for here is a metaphysical illustration of a mind bursting all bonds, and winning light and liberty for his own good and for good of millions! Frederick Douglass thus goes forth to testify to the truth and goodness of God, "that strengtheneth the spoiled against the strong, so that the spoiled shall come against the fortress."—*Amos,* v. 9.

THOMAS DREW, D.D.
of Cambridge and Dublin,
Minister of Christ Church, Belfast,

January 7, 1845.

FROM THE REV. ISAAC NELSON.

I regard the narrative of FREDERICK DOUGLASS as a literary wonder. The incidents of his life are of such a kind as to hold the reader spell-bound, while they are related in a style simple, perspicuous, and eloquent. I looked forward with much interest and some incredulity to a meeting with the author of this unique piece of autobiography, doubting whether any man reared a slave, and so recently escaped from bonds, could, under the circumstances, produce such a work. My meeting with Frederick Douglass dispelled my doubts; he is indeed an extraordinary man—the type of a class—such an intellectual phenomenon as only appears at times in the republic of letters. I have had opportunities of observing his mind in several attitudes, and applied to various subjects during his stay in Belfast, and I take leave to say that not only do I consider him adequate to the task of writing such a book as the one before us, but also of achieving more Herculean feats. His name may yet be quoted both as an abolitionist and a literary man by those very States of America who now deny him a home. I pity the man who can read his Narrative and not sympathise with the poor slave.

ISAAC NELSON,
Presbyterian Minister.

Donegal-street, Belfast, 5th January, 1846.

Douglass, *Narrative* (Dublin, 1846), cxxxiii–cxxxv.

TO THE
FRIENDS OF THE SLAVE.

WHOEVER may have been moved by the perusal of the foregoing pages, to *do* something for the abolition of Slavery in the United States, is informed that a Society called the AMERICAN ANTI-SLAVERY SOCIETY is in active operation for this purpose. Its members have given their lives to the work, in full determination to spare no effort for the attainment of their object. Amongst the means which they employ are the following:—

They publish a weekly newspaper in New York, called the National Anti-Slavery Standard, which is solely devoted to the advocacy of anti-slavery principles, and to the exposure of the religious, political, and social evils of slavery.*

They also circulate pamphlets and tracts, for the elucidation of such of their views as could not be suitably set forth in the ephemeral pages of a news-paper.

They send throughout the Free States, agents devoted to the cause, for the purpose of stirring up the public mind, and awakening the conscience of the people by lectures and public meetings. They rely more upon the promulgation of sound principles and a correct state of public sentiment, than upon any other instrumen-tality, for the overthrow of American slavery. It is clear, from the popular character of the governments of the United States, that every improvement in the institutions of that country must be preceded by a corresponding change in the minds of the people.

These means have been in operation for nearly fourteen years, and, in the face of violent opposition and appalling difficulties, have had a powerful influence in quickening the action of religious bodies and political parties, and in mitigating the shameful prejudice against colour.

The necessary funds have been obtained by extraordinary munificence on the part of a few, and at great personal sacrifice by the poorer friends of the cause.

The BOSTON FEMALE ANTI-SLAVERY SOCIETY (auxiliary to the national soci-ety, and one of its most effective coadjutors) hold an Annual Bazaar in Boston, which has for a few years past received some assistance from ladies in Great Britain and Ireland. It is now respectfully suggested that the extent of this co-

---

*Any person who wishes to be regularly informed of the position of the Anti-Slavery cause in the United States, will receive the "THE STANDARD" regularly, on forwarding his name and address, with ten shillings and six pence, to RICHARD D. WEBB, DUBLIN. This sum includes a small weekly charge for postage paid on mailing the paper in New York. Two-pence postage is charged upon each paper, on delivery in Great Britain and Ireland.

operation should be greatly increased. Contributions from the British Islands have a double value; the hearts of those who labour in the cause of humanity are cheered by these tokens of sympathy from "the Old Country," whilst the proceeds sustain the efforts of the Society.

Contributions to the BOSTON ANTI-SLAVERY BAZAAR of any articles of use or ornament, which will bear to be packed without injury, ladies' fancy work, or the products of manufactories, especially of such works of taste or art as are not manufactured in the United States; in fine, any products of British taste or industry, as well as donations of money, will be appropriated in an effectual manner for the promotion of the cause.

The following ladies have consented to receive donations for the American Anti-Slavery Society, and contributions for the Annual Bazaar auxiliary to it:—

AMBLESIDE—Miss Harriet Martineau.

BIRMINGHAM—Mrs. George Goodrick, Edgbaston.

BRIDGEWATER—Mrs. Thompson.

BRISTOL—Miss Carpenter, Great George-street.

    Mrs. George Thomas, Great George-street.

CHELMSFORD—Miss Ann Knight.

CLIFTON—Mrs. Grinfield, 25, Richmond Terrace.

CORK—The Misses Jennings, Brown-street.

DARLINGTON—Miss Elizabeth Pease.

DUBLIN—Mrs. Allen, 51, High-street.

    The Misses Haughton, 34, Eccles-street.

    Mrs. Webb, 176, Great Brunswick-street.

EDINBURGH—Mrs. Welsh, 7, Montpelier, Bruntsfield Links.

    Mrs. Jane Wigham, 5, South Gray-street.

EVESHAM—The Misses Davis.

EXETER—Mrs. Bishop.

GLASGOW—Mrs. Dr. Reid, Rutland Crescent.

    Mrs. Robert Smith, 15, Woodside Terrace.

    Miss Catherine Paton, 16, Richmond-street.

LIMERICK—Miss S. Fisher, Lifford.

LONDON—Miss Esther Sturge, New Kent Road.

    Mrs. Hannah Bevan, 20, Finsbury Circus.

    Mrs. George Thompson, Waterloo Place.

MANCHESTER—The Misses Peacock, Park-place, L. Broughton

WATERFORD—Miss Maria Waring.

WEXFORD—Miss E. Poole.

WREXHAM—The Misses Hilditch.

Boxes of contributions to the Boston Anti-Slavery Bazaar are forwarded every year, (generally by the Cunard liner which leaves Liverpool on the 4th of

November,) under the superintendence of the ladies in the preceding list who reside in Bristol, Cork, Darlington, Dublin, Edinburgh, Glasgow, and London. These donations are always warmly acknowledged, as substantial evidence of the interest felt by the friends of humanity in Great Britain and Ireland, in the self-denying labours of the American abolitionists.

Reader Responses, 1845–49

Douglass reproduced many of the newspaper and periodical reviews of the *Narrative* in an appendix to later editions of the book, entitled "Critical Notices." Those reviews are found above in a similarly named appendix to this volume and are not reproduced below. What follows are other contemporary reviews located by the editors. Because many of these reviews contain lengthy excerpts from the *Narrative* text, they have been abridged when a quoted passage exceeds one hundred words. Deleted passages are indicated by means of ellipses and a notation of the page and line location of the omitted text in the 1845 Boston edition. Lengthy portions of these reviews assessing or describing books other than the *Narrative* have been deleted by means of ellipses.

NARRATIVE OF THE LIFE OF FREDERICK DOUGLASS. [James Brown] Y[errinton]. *Lib.,* 9 May 1845.

It will give our friends as much pleasure to hear as it does us to announce, that a 'NARRATIVE OF THE LIFE OF FREDERICK DOUGLASS,' written by himself, is in press, and will be published in a few days. The subject and author of the Narrative is too well known, too highly admired, and too deeply beloved by abolitionists to render any commendation of his highly reflective mirror of slavery, necessary at our hands. In addition to the interest contained in the incidents, and the pleasure to be derived from the perusal of the many noble, manly and eloquent passages of the narrator, the value of the work is greatly enhanced by a Preface from the pen of Mr. GARRISON, and a brief though animated and thrilling Letter to the author, in anticipation of his publication, from WENDELL PHILLIPS. Mr. Garrison being in New York, this week, in attendance at the Annual Meeting, we here transfer the former,—for lack of other matter from him,—to the editorial columns of the Liberator:—y.

PREFACE

In the month . . . [iii.2–xii.34] . . . No UNION WITH SLAVEHOLDERS!"

WM. LLOYD GARRISON.

Boston, May 1, 1845.

[Untitled.]. Prospero. (Concord, N.H.) *Herald of Freedom,* 9 May 1845.

I understand FREDERICK DOUGLASS has written out his life, and that it will soon be for sale; the book will give the real name of his master, and the facts connected with his history; and if Frederick can write with anything like the ability with which he can talk, the book will be both entertaining and instructive, to the reader, and I hope profitable to its author.

169

Yesterday, your friend PIERPONT, preached his farewell discourse as minister of Hollis Street Church. For twenty-six years he has been the firm, consistent, and eloquent preacher of 'Righteousness, Temperance, and Judgment to come.' Nobly has he defended the Independence of the Pulpit; and now, having been successful in all the matters he has undertaken, he retires from his elevated position, covered with honor, with a spotless character, and an undying fame.

With what energy, spirit and zeal, he has conducted the twelve years' warfare in which he has been engaged, and how triumphantly he has sustained himself, amidst all its varied scenes,—with what fidelity to principle, and uncompromising integrity he has stood erect when all seemed hopeless; and when at last, his course was endorsed by the tribunals to which appeals were made, and he had the power to force his enemies to terms, but refused to resort to legal quibbles to enforce his rights,—these are now matters of history, and will shed a lustre around his memory, which will increase with the progress of our race, and the adoption of the truths of which he as been so distinguished an advocate.

Yours,

PROSPERO.

NARRATIVE OF FREDERICK DOUGLASS. [Anon.]. *Lib.,* 23 May 1845; reprinted in *NASS,* 5 June 1845; (Chicago) *Western Citizen,* 19 June 1845.

This long-desired Narrative is now presented to the public, in a neat volume occupying 125 pages. It was written entirely by Mr. Douglass, and reveals all the facts in regard to his birth-place,—the names of his mother, master, overseer, &c. &c. It cannot fail to produce a great sensation wherever it may happen to circulate, especially among the slaveocracy. The edition is going off rapidly. The following extracts will enable the reader to appreciate its spririt and power; others we shall give in future numbers of the Liberator.

Mr. Douglass was born in Tuckahoe, about 12 miles from Easton, in Talbot county, Maryland, and is now in his twenty-eighth year. His father was a white man; his mother (whom he never saw more than four or five times) died when he was quite young. He has had two masters—the first one acted as a clerk and supintendent on the home plantation of Col. Lloyd, a very wealthy slaveholder. He describes that plantation in the following thrilling manner:

The home plantation of . . . [12.10–15.15] . . . by the same emotion.

So much for the songs of the enslaved—so much for their happy and contented lot!

Frederick was sent, when between seven and eight years old, to live with a Mr. Auld, in the city of Baltimore. The way in which his youthful mind became inflamed with a desire to learn how to read, is thus stated by him:

Very soon after I . . . [33.3–34.24] . . . the benefit of both.

From this time I . . . [38.1–41.10] . . . moved in every storm.

Great God! how awful is the pressure brought to bear upon the human intellect and heart by slavery! What a lifting of the veil is this, to convince the skeptical that it is impossible to exaggerate the horrors and enormities of that impious system!

We regret that we have not room for more copious extracts; but these, we are sure, will serve to excite a lively desire in all quarters to possess a copy of this extraordinary volume. It is for sale at 25 Cornhill. Price 50 cents. Accompanying it is a finely executed and admirable likeness of the author.

NARRATIVE OF FREDERICK DOUGLASS. [Anon.]. (Hartford, Conn.) *Christian Freeman,* 29 May 1845.

[This eloquent fugitive slave has recently published a faithful narrative of his life, in which he gives the names of his mother, master, overseer, &c., and makes such a revelation of slavery as cannot fail to increase every honest man's abhorrence of the diabolical system. The Liberator says of the work: 'It cannot fail to produce a great sensation wherever it may happen to circulate, especially among the slaveocracy.' We subjoin an extract as we find it in the Liberator. The period of his history related in the following passages, commences when he was eight years old.]

NARRATIVE OF FREDERICK DOUGLASS. [Anon.]. *Lib.,* 30 May 1845.

We continue our extracts from this thrilling Narrative. The following picture of the brutal treatment and forlorn situation of the author's 'poor old grandmother' is so vividly drawn, that he whose eye does not moisten in contemplating it must possess extraordinary command over his feelings.

Very soon after my . . . [47.12–49.22] . . . visit for these things?

The following extract is one of great power. The apostrophe 'to the moving multitude of ships,' seen from the banks of the Chesapeake bay—'Freedom's swift-winged angels, that fly round the world'—partakes largely of the sublime and pathetic:

If at any one time . . . [63.8–65.26] . . . to my wretched lot.

With what graphic power is the description of the sufferings and perils which await the flying fugitive in every quarter of the country, given below!

At the close of . . . [83.14–85.29] . . . we knew not of.'

I have been frequently . . . [107.22–109.13] . . . whip-scarred fugitive slave.

FREDERICK DOUGLASS. [Anon.]. Lynn *Pioneer,* n.d., reprinted in *Lib.,* 30 May 1845.

My readers will be delighted to learn that Frederick Douglass—the fugitive slave—has at last concluded his narrative. All who know the wonderful gifts of friend Douglass know that his narrative must, in the nature of things, be written with great power. It is so indeed. It is the most thrilling work which the American press ever issued—*and the most important.* If it does not open the eyes of this people, they must be petrified into eternal sleep.

The picture it presents of slavery is too horrible to look upon, and yet it is but a faint *picture* of what to millions is a vivid *life*. It is evidently drawn with a nice eye, and the coloring is chaste and subdued, rather than extravagant or overwrought. Thrilling as it is, and full of the most burning eloquence, it is yet simple and unimpassioned. Its eloquence is the eloquence of truth, and so is as simple and touching as the impulses of childhood. There are passages in it which would brighten the reputation of any living author,—while the book, as a whole, judged as a mere work of art would widen the fame of Bunyan or De Foe. A spirit of the loftiest integrity, and a vein of the purest religious sentiment, runs through its pages, and it must leave on every mind a deep conviction of the author's strength of mind and purity of heart. I predict for it a sale of at least twenty thousand in this country, and equally great in Europe. It will leave a mark upon this age which the busy finger of time will deepen at every touch. It will generate a public sentiment in this nation, in the presence of which our pro-slavery laws and constitutions shall be like chaff in the presence of fire. It contains the spark which will kindle up the smoldering embers of freedom in a million souls, and light up our whole continent with the flames of liberty. Great efforts will be made in the name of the Constitution and the Bible, of James Polk and the Apostle Paul, to suppress it: but it will run through this nation from house to house, and from heart to heart, as the wild fire, *finding wings in every wind which blows,* flies across the tall and boundless prairies. Its stirring incidents will fasten themselves on the eager minds of the youth of this country with hooks of steel. The politics of the land will stand abashed before it, while her more corrupt religion will wish to sink back into the hot womb which gave it birth. It will fall in among the churches and state-houses of the land like a bomb-shell, and those who madly undertake to pick it to pieces will share the fate of that poor New-Yorker who attempted something of the kind on a bomb-shell picked up on the shores of Jersey, i.e., they will be blowed to atoms at the first blow.—*Lynn Pioneer.*

NARRATIVE OF DOUGLASS. A. M. *Lib.,* 6 June 1845.

DEAR GARRISON: I received, yesterday, through the kindness of some friend in Boston, the Narrative of Frederick Douglass—his *multum in parto*. His account is brief, though admirable for its comprehensiveness. Whole volumes are therein contained, it being replete with the strong features of that most odious monster Slavery. The scenes through which he passed are exhibited with a clearness, and stamped upon the mind with a strength, which ever accompanies a strong, commanding evidence of truth.

My language is inadequate; therefore I shall not attempt to describe my feelings, as I went with the Narrator through his twenty years' experience in slavery.

I have wept over the pages of Dickens' 'Oliver Twist'—I have moistened with my tears whole chapters of Eugene Sue's Mysteries of Paris—but Douglass's history of the wrongs of the American Slave, brought, not tears—no, tears refused me their comfort—its home truths crowded in such quick succession, and entered so deep into the chambers of my soul, as to entirely close the relief valve. For I am an American woman, and for American women I bleed. I groaned in the agony of my spirit, and said, 'Oh, Lord! how long shall these things be? How long shall the spoiler mark his prey?' I have many times heard the author vividly portray the evils of slavery. I have often heard him recount with deep feeling the endless wrongs they are made to endure—but, oh! never before have I been brought so completely in sympathy with the slave—never before have I felt myself so completely bound with them—never before have I so fully realized the doctrine of our blessed Savior, 'whatsoever ye do unto the least one of these, ye do it unto me.'

May his Narrative incite us to renewed diligence in our labors for the slave! May the author become a mighty instrument to the pulling down of the strong holds of iniquity, and to the establishing of righteousness in our land!

Affectionately thine for the slave,

A. M.

P.S.—I know of no way in which I can better serve the cause of the oppressed, than to enclose $5 to the author of the book, for the extension of its publicity.

Albany, May 24, 1845.

☞ Our correspondent chooses to affix to her letter only the initials of her name; but we know her to be a most faithful friend of the oppressed. Copies of the Narrative, to the extent of her donation, shall be distributed with judgment and care.

In this connexion, we make other extracts from this remarkable work. The following sketch of the effects of the holidays which are granted to the slaves, is highly instructive, as revealing the arts of the slaveholders to make their victims disgusted with the idea of perpetual liberty:

The days between Christmas . . . [74.2–77.2] . . . a very common one.

How startling, yet how true is the description of the religion of the United States, given in the following extract:—

What I have said . . . [118.8–120.12] . . . the semblance of paradise.

Dark and terrible as . . . [121.31–122.26] . . . my duty to testify.

TESTIMONY IN RELATION TO SLAVERY. W. Boston *Courier*, n.d., as quoted in *Lib.*, 6 June 1845.

I was talking yesterday with a defender of slavery, and when I gave a negative reply to his inquiry whether I had ever lived at the South, he exclaimed triumphantly, 'I thought so! That is the reason why you have so many prejudices against slavery, and so many unfounded notions as to the manner in which the slaves are treated. Why don't you go to the South, and see for yourself?'

The cases of Captain Walker and Miss Webster, (not to speak of the case of Mr. Hoar of Concord, who was not an abolitionist,) furnish some strong reasons why an abolitionist, who values his life and liberty on one hand, and his right to free speech and action on the other, should *not* go to the South. And since the opponents of slavery at the North are likely to remain for years under this disability, it is a fortunate and happy circumstance that the South has come here, by her representative, to give us authentic information from the very fountainhead of slavery.

This representative is Frederick Douglass of Easton, Talbot county, Maryland. Let those who have believed the oft-repeated assertion that the slaves are contented and happy, read the autobiography of a slave. The Narrative of the Life of Frederick Douglass, written by himself, and just published, contains abundant and incontrovertible evidence of the misery which the mere condition of slavery, irrespective of what is commonly called bad treatment, (as if privation of liberty were not bad treatment,) entails upon its victims. The author of this book, who has for six years past proved himself a man, by the possession and exercise of the noblest qualities of humanity, was, previously to that time regarded and treated as a chattel, a mere piece of property, whose capabilities were to be worked up and expended in whatever way might appear most profitable to its owner. That property, thank God, is now in the possession of its true proprietor; that body is found to be inhabited by a mind and a soul; and whoever reads the thrillingly interesting narrative above mentioned, will know, on better evidence than that of a walk around the plantation after dinner with its proprietor, the unspeakable wretchedness of the American slave.

W.

NARRATIVE OF THE LIFE OF FREDERICK DOUGLASS, AN AMERICAN SLAVE. Margaret Fuller. New York *Daily Tribune,* 10 June 1845.

NARRATIVE OF THE LIFE OF FREDERICK DOUGLASS, AN AMERICAN SLAVE. Written by himself. Boston: Published at the Anti-Slavery Office. No. 25 Cornhill. 1845.

Frederick Douglass has been for some time a prominent member of the Abolition party. He is said to be an excellent speaker—can speak from a thorough personal experience—and has upon the audience, beside, the influence of a strong character and uncommon talents. In the book before us he has put into the story of his life the thoughts, the feelings and the adventures that have been so affecting through the living voice; nor are they less so from the printed page. He has had the courage to name the persons, times and places, thus exposing himself to obvious danger, and setting the seal on his deep convictions as to the religious need of speaking the whole truth. Considered merely as a narrative, we have never read one more simple, true, coherent, and warm with genuine feeling. It is an excellent piece of writing, and on that score to be prized as a specimen of the powers of the Black Race, which Prejudice persists in disputing. We prize highly all evidence of this kind, and it is becoming more abundant. The Cross of the Legion of Honor has just been conferred in France on Dumas and Soulie, both celebrated in the paths of light literature. Dumas, whose father was a General in the French Army, is a Mulatto: Soulie, a Quadroon. He went from New Orleans, where, though to the eye a white man, yet, as known to have African blood in his veins, he could never have enjoyed the privileges due to a human being. Leaving the Land of Freedom, he found himself free to develope the powers that God had given.

Two wise and candid thinkers,—the Scotchman, Kinment, prematurely lost to this country, of which he was so faithful and generous a student, and the late Dr. Channing,—both thought that the African Race had in them a peculiar element, which, if it could be assimilated with those imported among us from Europe, would give to genius a development, and to the energies of character a balance and harmony beyond what has been seen heretofore in the history of the world. Such an element is indicated in their lowest estate by a talent for melody, a ready skill at imitation and adaptation, an almost indestructible elasticity of nature. It is to be remarked in the writings both of Soulie and Dumas, full of faults but glowing with plastic life and fertile in invention. The same torrid energy and saccharine fulness may be felt in the writings of this Douglass, though his life being one of action or resistance, was less favorable to *such* powers than one of a more joyous flow might have been.

The book is prefaced by two communications,—one from Garrison, and one from Wendell Phillips. That from the former is in his usual over emphatic style. His motives and his course have been noble and generous. We look upon him with high respect, but he has indulged in violent invective and denunciation till he has spoiled the temper of his mind. Like a man who has been in the habit of screaming himself hoarse to make the deaf hear, he can no longer pitch his voice on a key agreeable to common ears. Mr. Phillips's remarks are equally decided, without this exaggeration in the tone Douglass himself seems very just and temperate. We feel that his view, even of those who have injured him most, may be relied upon. He knows how to allow for motives and influences. Upon the subject of Religion, he speaks with great force, and not more than our own sympathies can respond to. The inconsistencies of Slaveholding professors of religion cry to Heaven. We are not disposed to detest, or refuse communion with them. Then blindness is but one form of that prevalent fallacy which substitutes a creed for a faith, a ritual for a life. We have seen too much of this system of atonement not to know that those who adopt it often began with good intentions, and are at any rate, in their mistakes worthy of the deepest pity. But that is no reason why the truth should not be uttered trumpet tongued, about the thing. "Bring no more vain oblations": sermons must daily be preached anew on that text. Kings, five hundred years ago built Churches with the spoils of War; Clergymen to-day command Slaves to obey a Gospel which they will not allow them to read, and call themselves Christians amid the curses of their fellow men.—The world ought to get on a little faster than that, if there be really any principle of improvement in it. The Kingdom of Heaven may not at the beginning have dropped seed larger than a mustard-seed, but even from that we had a right to expect a fuller growth than can be believed to exist, when we read such a book as this of Douglass. Unspeakably affecting is the fact that he never saw his mother at all by day-light.

"I do not recollect of ever seeing my mother by the light of day. She was with me in the night. She would lie down with me; and get me to sleep, but long before I waked she was gone."

The following extract presents a suitable answer to the hacknied argument drawn by the defender of Slavery from the songs of the Slave, and is also a good specimen of the powers of observation and manly heart of the writer. We wish that every one may read his book and see what a mind might have been stifled in bondage,—what a man may be subjected to the insults of spendthrift dandies, or the blows of mercenary brutes, in whom there is no whiteness except of the skin, no humanity except in the outward form, and of whom the Avenger will not fail yet to demand—"Where is thy brother?"

"The home plantation of . . . [12.10–15.15] . . . by the same emotion."

☞Copies of the work may be had of W. H. Graham, Tribune Buildings. Price, 50 cents.

NARRATIVE OF THE LIFE OF FREDERICK DOUGLASS. [Maria Weston] C[hapman]. *NASS*, 12 June 1845.

Narrative of the life of Frederick Douglass, written by himself. Boston. Anti-Slavery Office, 23 Cornhill, pp. 125.

This book ought be read by all before whose mental blindness visions of happy slaves continually dance. It is the story of the life of a man of great intellectual power, in the very circumstances so often alluded to by the advocates for the longer continuance of Slavery;—in the Northernmost of the slave States, and under kind masters. No wonder that those States patronize the Colonization Society for the removal of characters so dangerous to the perpetuity of Slavery. Once, the kind master made a merit of giving *such* a slave his freedom on condition of consenting to go to Liberia. *Nous avons changé tout cela;* the anti-slavery enterprise has drawn to itself the most effectual advocates from the victims of the system it opposes. It has, while shaking that system to its foundation, been unavoidably and incidentally the means of freeing and educating in their own native country, more of these single victims, than the Colonization Society, while doing its best to uphold Slavery, has been able to doom to African exile.

All pro-slavery men, all Abolitionists, and all those who are merely indifferent should buy this book. It will convince the first class, confirm the second, and by the mere interest of its delineation, amply satisfy the third. It is illustrated by a remarkably good engraving of the author. The condition of the infant and of the aged slave, the sorrowful songs of bondage so often quoted by Northern men as an excuse for standing aloof from the Anti-Slavery enterprise, and the swell of heart with which the thought of freedom fills the bosom of the fugitive, are all dwelt upon with that deep impressment which artistical skill strives in vain with melancholy experience, to equal. "I never saw my mother in the day-time. She used to travel in the evening twelve miles to see me, and return before morning." Shall not the simple pathos of this fact, one of a class of facts necessary in Slavery, raise the soul of every mother that reads it?

We have no space for extracts this week, nor do we wish to lessen the value of the narrative to purchasers by forestalling its deeply interesting contents. It is accompanied by a letter from Wendell Phillips, which so truly expresses our own feelings, that we subjoin it.—c.

LETTER OF W. PHILLIPS TO FREDERICK DOUGLASS.

BOSTON, April 22, 1845.

My Dear Friend:—You . . . [13.4–16.23] . . . Yours truly,

WENDELL PHILLIPS.

FREDERICK DOUGLASS.

FREDERICK DOUGLASS—HORRORS OF SLAVERY. [Anon.]. *Religious Spectator,* n.d., reprinted in *NASS,* 7 August 1845.

We had a book put into our hands the other day, purporting to be the autobiography of a slave, who had escaped from bondage, by the name of Frederick Douglass, and we frankly acknowledge, that had it not been for our confidence in the good judgment of the friend from whom the book came, who we knew had little sympathy with the class of technical Abolitionists, we might possibly have laid it aside, without reading it, from perceiving that it was published under the patronage of several individuals, whose course on the subject of Slavery we have never regarded as either politic or right.

On looking into the book, however, we have found it to contain one of the most remarkable and thrilling narratives that have ever fallen under our eye; and though there are some things in it which we regret, particularly the strong expressions against professing Christians at the South, yet we see nothing to cast even a shade of doubt over the authenticity of the narrative, even in respect to its minutest details. We should indeed, have made a single exception to this remark—that is, we should have doubted the practicability of such a book being produced by a poor runaway slave, had it not been that we are assured that his efforts as a public speaker are quite equal to what he has here shown himself to be as a writer; and we have it upon good authority, that his lectures are characterized by as able reasoning, as genuine wit, and as bold and stirring appeals, as we almost ever find in connection with the highest intellectual culture.

Unless we greatly mistake, this small work to which we are referring is destined to exert a mighty influence in favor of the great cause of Emancipation. We acknowledge for ourselves, that we might have heard the system of Slavery reasoned against abstractly, no matter how ably, and no matter how long, and yet we could not have been so deep impressed with it as an outrage against humanity, as we have been by reading this simple story. It is especially fitted to correct a too prevalent error that Slavery *in itself* is not deserving of any severe reprobation—that it is only the abuses of the system with which we have a right to find fault.

And we acknowledge ourselves to be among those who look for its removal at no distant day. It seems to us as clear as the shining of the sun, that there are signs of the times which betoken a speedy and mighty revolution on this subject. The march of public opinion is evidently in favor of emancipation; and opposition can no more arrest it than it can arrest the motion of the planets. There is a spirit awake throughout all the North, that cries out for universal Freedom, and all the agitation and opposition that we witness at the South is but the heaving of the same spirit under different circumstances. It tells of a terrible conflict between selfishness and conscience, which will certainly terminate at last in favor of the better principle.

What particular mode of abolishing Slavery from our land, Providence may ordain—whether it shall be by bringing the South to bow to the high dictates of conscience and of duty, or by suffering the slaves themselves to become ministers of vengeance toward their oppressors, or by some other means, of which we know nothing—we pretend not to say; but the event of ultimate emancipation, in some way, we consider as absolutely certain; and while we would have all labor to bring it about, we would have all take counsel of the spirit of prudence, as well as philanthropy, in respect to the channel in which their labors shall be directed.

[Untitled.]. [Anon.]. (Boston) *Christian Register,* 20 September 1845.

The same publishing establishment have also issued the 'Narrative of Frederick Douglass written by himself.' He was a slave in Maryland, and his account is written with clearness and ability. He is of respectable and rather interesting deportment, and by his personal history and his eloquence as a speaker, is producing an effect equal to that of any of the prominent actors in the anti-slavery movement.

GLEAMS OF LIGHT. A Citizen of Maryland. *Lib.,* 26 September 1845.

A Baltimore correspondent of the Albany Patriot writes to the editor of that paper a letter, which contains the following interesting and encouraging statements:

We can buy anti-slavery documents now in this city at Shurtz & Wilde's Periodical Bookstore. The following are for sale: Review of West India Emancipation, by a Virginian; Bascom's and Peck's Pamphlets; Wayland and Fuller's Letters; and 'Slavery in Maryland,' by John L. Carey of this city, Editor of the Baltimore American. Frederick Douglass's Narrative is now circulating and being read in this city, and five hundred copies are still wanted here. They would be read with avidity, and do much good. And thus Garrison, who is proscribed here in person, would be heard in Baltimore, in the burning language of his Preface to the Narrative.

One word in regard to the truth of the narrative. I have made some inquiry, and have reason to believe his statements are true. Col. Edward Lloyd's relatives are my relatives! Let this suffice for the present. There is one particular slave mentioned in the book that I have often heard spoken of; that is, poor 'Jake,' who was bought by my brother-in-law, a nephew of Col. L. The northern people fight slavery at a distance: I have to fight it every day, and every where, in all the highways and byways of life. I board with a slaveholder, and am waited on by a slave, and see all the laziness and inefficiency on the part of the whites, and the *puttering,* do-nothing, sulky habits of the poor blacks. Every thing about slavery is mean, dirty, lazy, hateful, and *undignified.* There is nothing about it to promote self-respect, or any other noble or virtuous feeling.

Dr. Stewart, a noble-minded philanthropist, the owner of 150 slaves and a plantation, is now writing a pamphlet on slavery and emancipation, and in favor of the freedom of the slaves. Dr. S. is a brother of Gen. Stewart of this city, of whom your correspondent some months since stated, that he sold a colored woman by whom he had children with her offspring, his own flesh and blood, to Hope H. Slatter. No wonder Dr. Stewart is disgusted with slavery, when his own brother is such a monster of iniquity.

We are full of hope in this State. The 'Saturday Visiter' is our leader. Pray for us, till hope is lost in victory.

A CITIZEN OF MARYLAND.

FREDERICK DOUGLASS. [Anon.]. Cork *Examiner,* 22 October 1845.

Our readers will perceive by our advertising columns, that this eloquent Anti-Slavery Advocate, will deliver an address tomorrow, at the Imperial Hotel. He is undoubtedly a man of genius—a man of high mental gifts—whose mental and physical powers are all harmoniously developed. All who would wish to see how the gifts of nature can triumph over the most disheartening circumstances, ought to avail themselves of the opportunity which tomorrow offers. FREDERICK DOUGLASS has published a Narrative of his Life, of which the American press, as will be seen by our advertisement speak in the strongest terms of commmendation. It gives an insight into the slave system in America, which cannot elsewhere be obtained in so concise and interesting a form; and should be in everyone's possession—especially as the profits arising from its sale sustain Mr. DOUGLASS in his career of usefulness in these countries.

NARRATIVE OF FREDERICK DOUGLASS. WRITTEN BY HIMSELF.
[Anon.]. Cork *Southern Reporter,* 21 October 1845, and (London) *League,* n.d.,
reprinted in *Lib.,* 28 November 1845.

We refer our readers to our advertising columns for notices from the American
press, of this work. We are sure that no honest man can arise from its perusal
without deepened convictions of the power which true men everywhere possess of
triumphing over the most formidable obstacles—nor without the belief, that it is
his bounden duty to omit no means, however great or small, which opportunity
affords, of aiding the African people to escape from a worse than Egyptian bondage, and of cheering on their devoted friends, the abolitionists of America. It
appears from the advertisement that Mr. Douglass will deliver an address on
Thursday evening next at the Imperial Hotel. Those who are desirous to see
nature's nobleman, and hear the native eloquence of a self-educated man, ought to
avail themselves of this opportunity to hear Mr. Douglass.—*Cork Southern Reporter, Oct.* 21.

The League, at London, notices the Narrative of Frederick Douglass, as follows:

This book is a curiosity, however we view it. It comes to us certified by highly
respectable persons on this and the other side of the Atlantic as the authentic
production of one who has witnessed and experienced the bitter fruits of slavery.
To understand and appreciate the Narrative, it is necessary to lay aside the office of
critic, and realise the condition of the author, whose whole mind seems to be filled
with the subject of slavery and its victims, whether slaves, overseers, or slaveholders. Only in this way can the writer be forgiven his occasionally elaborate portraits
of individuals having nothing about them worthy of notice, save their almost
incredible brutality. But even as a literary production, this book possesses no
ordinary claims. The author, though uneducated, or rather self-educated, displays
great natural powers; he utters his thoughts always lucidly, and often with a
polished and vigorous eloquence. Indeed the book convinces us, and must convince any impartial reader, that the argument, if it can be so termed, which would
uphold slavery on the ground of the slaves' natural inferiority, has no foundation as
regards such men as the writer, and therefore totally fails in its general application.

Where there is so much to interest the reader and excite the philanthropist—
now with pain at human suffering from inhuman oppression, and now with hope-
fulness that that suffering, and the causes of it, promise soon to be brought to a
termination, we can only afford space for a striking extract, in which the author
exhibits his style and power as a writer, while accounting for and refuting the pro-
slavery assertion of the contentedness of the poor African under his bondage.

THE LIFE OF FREDERICK DOUGLASS. [Anon.]. (London) *Spectator,* 29 November 1845, reprinted in (London) *Littell's Living Age,* 8:64–65 (10 January 1846).

FREDERICK DOUGLASS appears as a Maryland slave, who escaped from his
master in 1838, and, after working as a free labourer in the Northeastern States till

1841, was engaged by an American Anti-Slavery Society as itinerant lecturer. Having a natural force and fluency of language, and dealing with things within his own experience, he appears to have spoken with so much acceptance as to have been stimulated to commit to paper the autobiographical portion of his addresses, which is before us in a Dublin reprint.

In his life there is not much of hairbreadth escape. He is a Mulatto, and supposes that his first owner was his father. Time, to a slave, is not known in its particulars, such as birthdays and exact dates; so that he does not know his own age, but supposes it now to be about seven-and-twenty. According to this reckoning, he was sent in his sixth year from the estate where he was born to wait upon a little boy in Baltimore. Here he was treated kindly; and his mistress began to teach him to read, till his master forbade it: but Frederick, having, as he says, had his mind a little opened, persevered in teaching himself, and succeeded by dint of casual assistance from poor White boys in the street: and to reading, at a subsequent period, he added writing. When about fifteen, his owner in the country took him from his master in town, in consequence of a family quarrel; and Frederick was transformed from a sort of page or footman to a field-labourer. His first two country masters were religious men, but very cruel and exacting; so that he had no time to think of anything but work. His third master was more liberal; and, having time to meditate, he planned an escape, with some fellow-slaves: but it was detected; and Frederick, after being imprisoned and threatened with sale, was sent back to his old quarters in Baltimore, whence he finally managed to escape in reality. Up to this point his narrative is pretty full; but he designedly suppresses the particulars of his escape, lest he should expose others to danger, and prevent some unfortunates from attaining their freedom. In plain English, he was assisted by those secret agents who are scattered through some of the Southern States for the especial purpose of aiding the escape of runaway slaves.

We assume that Frederick Douglass is really what he professes, and not a Coloured free man in masquerade, upon the Jesuit's principle that the end justifies the means. On the one hand, we note the very extraordinary manner in which he taught himself to read; some contentions with different masters, in one case proceeding to a fight,—which seems an improbable insubordination in a slave country, though it may have been heightened to add dignity to Douglass; and a precocious air in the more youthful part of his career, but which also may have been unconsciously coloured by his feelings at the period of composition. On the other hand, the facts and incidents have a strong character of truth. Frederick deals a little in atrocities, though he admits them to be exceptions; but they do not make the greatest impression on the reader as to the horrors of slavery. This appears rather in the brutish degradation to which the mind of the slave is reduced, the destruction of all family ties which is systematically aimed at, and the reaction of the "institution" upon the Whites themselves, lowering their character, and often, according to Douglass, wringing their affections in the case of their Coloured children.

"It is worthy of remark, that such slaves [children of the planter] invariably suffer greater hardships . . . [4.8–4.28] . . . would protect and defend."

There is something natural and touching in this instance of maternal feeling. "My mother and I . . . [2.15–3.12] . . . waked she was gone."

According to Frederick, slaveholders professing religion are a great deal worse than others; more gravely cruel, more exacting, and very mean—not even giving their people enough to eat, which in Maryland is very contrary to public opinion. "Not to give a slave enough to eat, is regarded as the most aggravated development of meanness even among slaveholders. The rule is, no matter how coarse the food, only let there be enough of it." This meanness the professors seem to carry into punishment; assigning Scriptural reasons for it.

Here is a text for stripes.

"I have said my master found religious sanction for his cruelty. As an example, I will state one of many facts going to prove the charge. I have seen him tie up a lame young woman, and whip her with a heavy cowskin upon her naked shoulders, causing the warm red blood to drip; and, in justification of the bloody deed, he would quote this passage of Scripture—'He that knoweth his master's will, and doeth it not, shall be beaten with many stripes.'"

If this narrative is really true in its basis, and untouched by any one save Douglass himself, it is a singular book, and he is a more singular man. Even if it is of the nature of the true stories of De Foe, it is curious as a picture of slavery, and worth reading.

NARRATIVE OF THE LIFE OF FREDERICK DOUGLASS—AN AMERICAN SLAVE:—Dublin: WEBB & CHAPMAN, pp. 128. 1845. [Anon.]. *British Friend,* 3:174 (November 1845), reprinted in *Lib.,* 26 December 1845.

WE would especially call the attention of our readers to this deeply interesting little volume. It is impossible to read it and not have every sympathy awakened in behalf of our fellow beings, held as "chattels," in that land of professed Republicans and Christians—the United States of America. The reader is impressed with a feeling that the *slave-holding* portions of that country are yet in ignorance of the first principles of liberty, of justice, and Christianity. Truth seems stamped on every page of this narrative. If it be true, as no reader can doubt that it is, how fearful the responsibility of the General Assembly of the Free Church of Scotland, of the American Board of Commissioners for Foreign Missions, and of all professedly religious bodies that stand sponsor for the Christianity of American Slaveholders! We earnestly entreat all our readers, and every abolitionist, and friend of justice, and humanity, in this kingdom, to obtain and read this little work. It will do more to give them correct views of American Republicanism, and American Religion, as these are developed in the Slave-States, and do more to give them just views of duty in reference to the Slave-holding churches, and minsters of America—than a thousand lecturers could do.

This is a plain, but eloquent narrative of the experience of a man who was born and trained to regard himself, and to be regarded by all around him, as a "chattel." In reading it, one sees before him the fearful tossings and heavings of an immortal soul, herded with beasts, and compelled to grope about, feeling after God among reptiles. The reader feels himself in communion with immortality—sunk to a thing—with the image of God turned into a brute. One feels that the distinction between Christianity and the Slave-holding Religion of America, is justly and forcibly drawn. It is impossible for the American Slaves not to be infidels to the religion of their masters. Every reader of this narrative must feel, that a religion which can receive a Slave-holder to its loving and honoured embrace, cannot be true Christianity—cannot be of God. This book clearly indicates that the only way peacefully to abolish American Slavery is, to exclude all Slave-holders from all respectable and Christian society.

FREDERICK DOUGLASS, THE FUGITIVE SLAVE. [Anon.]. Bristol *Mercury,* 6 January 1846, reprinted in *NASS,* 5 March 1846.

But little is yet known in England respecting this remarkable man. A few years ago he was suffering under the horrors of hopeless slavery, in Maryland, United States. Happily for him, and probably for his suffering fellow-slaves, he escaped from his cruel bondage to the free States of America, where he remained in obscurity for a year or two, working at any employment he could procure, exposed only to the contempt and indignity with which *independent* and republican America, even its *free* States, treats that portion of its population, however well educated and refined they may be, whose misfortune it is to have any color in their skin. After a time, on a casual attendance upon an anti-slavery meeting, Douglass ventured to make himself known to some members of an abolition society. The Abolitionists found him to be a young man of unusual ability, of sound judgment, serious, of excellent character, and with a degree of cultivation of mind quite extraordinary for the opportunities he had while in the slave States, where teaching slaves to read, and even giving them Bibles, subject the offenders to severe penalties! The American Anti-Slavery Society having ascertained that, in addition to the dependence that could be placed upon all of Frederick Douglass's statements, he had a peculiar facility of expressing himself with fluency and correctness, employed him as a lecturer upon Slavery, the evils of which he was able to expose from personal experience. His lectures occasioned much excitement in the free States, and much indignation, when his statements had gone southward, in the slave States from whence he had escaped. Doubts having been circulated as to the truth of the appalling revelations he made, he resolved to publish a narrative of his life, giving the names of the masters under whom he had lived, and dates and events which would at once prove the correctness of his account, and suppressing only some names and circumstances connected with his escape, which, if known, would have involved some of his benefactors in difficulties, and have diminished the facility of escape of other slaves by similar means. Wendell Phillips, Esq. an eminent barrister of Massachusetts, and an active Abolitionist, to whom Douglass showed his narrative in MS., advised him not to publish it, as it would probably lead to successful efforts for his being re-taken, and returned to Slavery, a fugitive slave not being safe even in the free States, their laws compelling them to give up such runaways if claimed by their owners. Douglass, however, with that courage which has distinguished him throughout his career, printed the narrative, and most rapid was its sale in America. Prudence, however, as well as other powerful motives, decided him upon taking the occasion of the excitement produced by the wide dissemination of his narrative, to leave America for awhile, and visit Great Britain. In accordance with this intention he sailed in the *Cambria,* Government steamer, from Boston, last August, in company with Mr. Buffum, a highly respectable man, an Abolitionist, and with the Hutchinsons, a remarkable family of singers, consisting of four brothers and one sister, who have been performing in Liverpool, and occasioning much interest by the originality of their music and their anti-slavery songs. The party arrived in Liverpool, August 28th, and Douglass immediately repaired to Dublin, where, as well as in Cork and at Belfast, (where he at present is,) he has been lecturing to thronged assemblies.

The papers contained an account of a fracas on board the *Cambria* when Douglass came to England. The passengers having ascertained what an interesting man they had with them, expressed a desire to hear him give some history of himself and of Slavery, and the captain saw no reason for objecting to their wishes. Notice having been given of what was to take place, that the passengers might attend or absent themselves as they wished, Douglass began to speak, but he had not proceeded far, before he was interrupted by two American gentlemen accusing him of falsehood. Douglass, to prove his statements, began to read the laws of the slave States; the Americans, however, would not allow him to proceed, and threatened to throw him overboard. An Irish gentleman assured them that any attempt at violence would be a dangerous expedient for their own safety. The disturbance rose so high, that Captain Judkins was at length compelled to declare he would put in irons any one who ventured upon an act of aggression. The Abolitionists in Massachusetts have been voting resolutions of thanks to Captain Judkins for his manliness on the occasion, and the papers in the interest of the slaveholders abuse him, and threaten him with no more American passengers for allowing their nation to be insulted.

Douglass's lectures are said to be very eloquent. He is now finishing some at Belfast, where the chapels of the Wesleyan Methodists, Independents, and Presbyterians have been thrown open to him. His next visit will be to Glasgow, and he will probably come to Bristol (an invitation from which place he has accepted) in the spring.

A more deeply interesting "Narrative" than Douglass's can hardly ben conceived. An edition of it has been reprinted by a warm friend of his in Dublin, and is being sold chiefly among private friends, without any advertisements or commission charges, for Douglass's benefit. A few copies have come to Bristol. Douglass, whose feelings are very independent, hopes to support himself while in England solely by the sale of the "Narrative."

He states in his preface to the Irish edition that his inducements to come to Great Britain were—First, to be absent from America during the sale of his book, on account of his personal safety, "lest his *owner* should adopt measures to restore him to his *'patriarchal care.'*" Second, that he might improve his stock of knowledge by visiting this kingdom. Third, chiefly to extend in England an enlightened knowledge of the contaminating and degrading influences of American Slavery upon both slaveholders and slaves, and thus excite such an intelligent interest in behalf of his suffering countrymen as may react upon America, and aid in the eventual extinction of this sinful institution.

Mr. Douglass speaks with much feeling of the gratification it has been to him, during his limited experience of travelling in this country, to move about from place to place in public conveyances without being despised and insulted in consequence of his color, and of his meeting everywhere with that respect which is due from man to man; and he has drawn a strong contrast on this point, between the freedom of monarchical England, and the thraldom of republican America.

NARRATIVE OF FREDERICK DOUGLASS. [Anon.]. Albany *Patriot,* reprinted in *Lib.,* 20 February 1846.

In the Patriot of Dec. 31, we published an article from the Delaware Republican, signed 'A. C. C. Thompson,' in which the truthfulness of Douglass's narrative is denied—to which we subjoined a remark or two of our own, and also some extracts of letters recently received in this country from Ireland, showing the opinion formed there in relation to the character of Douglass, and his abilities as a man—the latter having been impugned and denied by Mr. Thompson, no less than his veracity.

We have received from Mr. Thompson the following letter, enclosing a slip cut from some newspaper, containing the four certificates which we insert at his request. The certificates are evidently cut out of the body of some article, the whole of which he seems unwilling we should see. Why did he not send us the paper?

WILMINGTON, (Del.) Jan. 12, 1846.

To the Proprietor of the Albany Patriot:

DEAR SIR:—In your paper of Dec. 31, I notice that you have copied my communication to the Delaware Republican, upon which you make some very worthy comments. You say:

'Mr. Thompson will have to produce some better testimony than his own opinion of the general religious character of slaveholders, before he can disturb the stern facts recorded by Frederick Douglass.'

Herein you grossly misrepresent me, as you do every thing connected with slavery. It would not answer your purposes to publish plain truth upon all occasions, as it would not coincide with your perverted opinions.

What I intended by my communication in the Delaware Republican, was only to prove the assertions in the narrative of Frederick Douglass to be false, which I knew to be so. But as you do not consider the evidence of one respectable white man as creditable as the assertions of a ranting negro, I will produce other testimony than my own, from gentlemen of respectable standing, to show you that the assertions of this negro Douglass are nothing more than gross misrepresentations. Now for the testimony.

Extracts from the letter of Mr. Auld, the master of Frederick Douglass.

'He states that I used to flog and starve him; but I can put my hand upon my Bible, and with a clear conscience swear that I never struck him in my life, nor caused any person else to do it. I never allowanced one of my slaves: but the tale would not have answered their (the Abolitionists,) purposes, unless the slave had been starved, or nearly whipped to death.

Can it be believed that Mr. Gore should deliberately shoot one of Col. Lloyd's slaves, and still be retained in his employ? Col. Lloyd was not the man to suffer such an imposition, and I know the whole story to be false.

I placed him in Baltimore to learn a trade, and told him that if he would behave himself and learn his trade well, when he was 25 years old I would emancipate him; and he promised me faithfully that he would do it. He does not say one word about this in his Narrative, as it would not have answered to have mentioned so much truth.'

Extract from the letter of Dr. A. C. Thompson.

CAMBRIDGE, Dorchester Co., Md.

'I always knew Thomas Auld to be a worthy and pious man, but he was never a class leader nor an exhorter.'

Letter from Dr. James Dawson.

ST. MICHAELS, Talbot Co., Md.

DEAR SIR:—I have seen and read a Narrative of the life of negro Frederick Douglass, purporting to have been written by himself; (doubtful) in which the character of Mr. Thomas Auld is most foully aspersed. I lived in the family of Mr. Auld at the time when this cruel and inhuman conduct is said to have taken place; and so far as my knowledge of himself and an acquaintance with his domestic affairs goes, (which was thorough) I can unhesitatingly pronounce it a base and villanous fabrication. I could say much more in confirmation of the falsity of the charges, but deem it unnecessary.

Yours, &c.

JAMES DAWSON.

A. C. C. THOMPSON, Wilmington.

Letter from Mr. Thomas Graham.

St. Michaels, Talbot Co., Md.

Mr. A. C. C. Thompson:

Dear Sir:—During Mr. Auld's entire residence in St. Michaels, he was my immediate neighbor, and the intercourse between our families gave me an opportunity of knowing the situation and condition of his servants. The statements of Frederick Douglass respecting Mr. Auld's treatment to them, is, in every word, most basely false. They were well fed and well clothed; never allowanced in food, but had as much as they could eat.

Mr. Auld's indulgence to his servants is well known throughout this neighborhood; and I have no hesitancy in saying that I know beyond the possibility of a doubt that the whole statement relating to this gentleman is most ungrateful and false. And from my acquaintance with other individuals accused, and from their unimpeachable Christian character, I believe the entire narrative of accusations to be a manufactured compound of falsehoods.

I lived within 30 feet of Mr. Auld's residence for several years, and during that time his conduct to his servants was more like an indulgent father than a master. He has invariably emancipated his slaves when they arrived at the age of 25 years, and their services to him were almost voluntary.

THOMAS GRAHAM.

Letter from L. Dodson.

St. Michaels, Talbot Co., Md.

Mr. Thompson:

Dear Sir:—If it will be of any service to you, in your attempt to expose the base falsehoods contained in the 'Narrative of Frederick Douglass,' I will say, that so far as his narrations refer to Mr. Auld's treatment toward his servants, they are most palpably untrue. For nine years I was connected with Mr. Auld's family; the greater part of the time boarding with him; and I speak from personal knowledge, when I say that Fred. and all his servants were treated well. Indeed, I never knew him to strike, much less abuse them.

I knew Fred. well; we were boys together, in the same family, and his narrations are little less than gross misrepresentations.

The cruelties which are charged upon Mr. Covy, Gore, and others, are equally false; for every man acquainted with these gentlemen will say that they are incapable of such offences against humanity.

You may confidently hold up this 'Narrative' as the latest and perhaps the most unpardonable effort of Abolitionism. If 'truth is mighty and must prevail,' I have no doubt that this attempt like many others will prove ineffectual.

Yours truly,

L. DODSON.

If you are not carried away by prejudice, I think the evidence I have adduced from these gentlemen's letters should be sufficient to convince you that 'the stern facts recorded by Mr. Douglass' are very stern falsehoods. I care not how great a man you make of him—if he is 'one of God's best gifts to the world'—yet with all his greatness, he is a liar. And surely you will never again attempt to palm his narrative upon the public for truth.

I do not wish to be understood as advocating slavery, for I am convinced that it is a great evil—but not sinful under ordinary circumstances. Neither do I attempt to vindicate the religious character of the slaveholders of the South; for it is evident that there are bad men among them, as well as in every other community. But tell me, is the Southerner to be deprecated because he owns a slave, more than the Northern Abolitionist, who, in defiance of all law and honor, steals a slave from his lawful owner, and will then manufacture an incredible story without the least shadow of truth, to defame the character of slaveholders? If such is your opinion, you have studied some code of morality that I have never seen.

If you wish to persuade the Southerners to abolish slavery, you must talk to them in a more sensible manner; you must not fabricate such horrid tales of murder, man-stealing, &c., as you have done heretofore. And perhaps when you shall be cured of this evil spirit, then the slaveholders will have some confidence in your abilities to advise. But be assured that all the venom that you can disgorge will never add one laurel to your brow, but on the contrary, will engender jealousy and hatred, and make the condition of the slave much worse.

Yours, very respectfully,

A. C. C. THOMPSON.

We publish with the utmost willingness the above letter and certificates, not only because it is fair play to let the slaveholders, as well as other evil doers, be heard in their own defence, but also because we want no better confirmation of the general credibility and truth of Douglass's narrative than such certificates afford.

If any of our readers have never read the Narrative, we wish they would do so. It purports to be a plain statement of facts and circumstances which occurred to the writer, or within his immediate knowledge—giving names and incidents, and a part of the time, dates, with minute particularity. Scenes of common and ordinary interest exemplifying many of the peculiar characteristics of the slave system as it prevails in Maryland, are detailed, and others of great cruelty, and inhumanity are narrated. Of a great part of this cruelty, Douglass was the victim, and of many other instances he was the witness. There is a peculiarity of detail, and other internal evidence of veracity, which, we repeat, will require something more than Mr. Thompson's opinion that the story is false, or the certificates of the good character of Mr. Auld which he has published, to overthrow. In all the above certificates, formidable as they may seem, there is but one distinct fact stated by Douglass contradicted. Douglass says, page 57:

'I had lived with him (Auld) nine months, during which time he had given me a number of severe whippings, all to no good purpose.

This Mr. Auld in his certificate denies. He says he never struck him in his life, 'nor caused any person else to do it.' It must be borne in mind, that Mr. Auld is the accused person, and is testifying in his own behalf—so it is a question of credibility. Douglass says he was whipped and ill-fed by Auld. Auld denies it—pleads not guilty, as accused people generally do. All the other certificates, and the things stated in them, amount to this, and this only—that the certifiers have too good an opinion of Mr. Auld, Mr. Gore, and Mr. Covy, to believe they would do the inhuman and abominable things Douglass says they did.

Mr. Thompson must be very green, or else he must suppose others very green, if he thinks that such wordy opinions of accomplices in wickedness will satisfy the candid public mind of this nation, which has commenced a searching scrutiny into the secret and hidden, as well as manifest abominations of the infernal system of slavery, that Mr. Douglass's statements are 'stern falsehoods.'

We hope Mr. Thompson will not rest here, but will proceed with his investigations into the truth or falsity of Douglass's statements, and give the public the *evidences* of lying which he shall discover—not the opinions of one man as to what another would do, who should be as deep in the mud as the witness himself might be in the mire, but good legal testimony, such as courts would receive in a *civilized* country—as to *facts,* some of the specific occurrences with which the narrative abounds. Come, Mr. Thompson, an honest, manly effort to overthrow by disproving the *events* which he states took place, would do you good. And when you have done that, we will give you another batch of facts to work at. We will furnish you with a book entitled 'American Slavery as it is, or the Testimony of 1000 Witnesses,' published in 1839. Perhaps our friends C. D. Cleveland or Thomas Earle, of Philadelphia, can furnish you with the book now, if you choose. Come, go at that book, and not spend your time upon such small game as poor Frederick Douglass, the 'recreant slave.' These 1000 witnesses are not abolitionists generally, but Southern men and women, statesmen, governors, congressmen, bad men and good men, from high places and low places and sacred places, ministers, deacons, and bishops—and their testimony challenges scrutiny. The vouchers are mostly on file. The work has been extensively circulated for the last six years, as well at the South as the North, and no man has yet undertaken to invalidate the horrid charges it prefers against the system. If Mr. Thompson will once peruse that work with candor and attention, he will find a larger business than defending the religion of the South against the slanders of a 'ranting negro.' He will find also that we have some reasons to know, that high professions of religion, and exalted piety towards God, are, in the ethics of the slave code, deemed consistent with monstrous inhumanity to man.

THE HEART OF A SLAVE. [Anon.]. *Oberlin Evangelist,* 29 April 1846.
[From the Autobiography of Frederick Douglass.]
"Very soon after my . . . [47.12–49.22]] . . . visit for these things?"

[What a portraiture, this, of some of the noblest sentiments of the human heart! Who shall any longer doubt that slaves may have their full share of human sympathies, and of the most exalted kind? We should like to see some apologist for slavery set himself to search the records of history for a better or a like specimen of noble-hearted humanity in bosoms where the genuine slave-spirit has had sway from youth up. Nay, those finer and nobler sensibilities of human hearts are not begotten by the exercise of oppression.

Let it not be said in the oppressor's vindication that every slave is not a Frederick Douglass. We know that but too well. It is Slavery's worst fault that with iron heel it crushes down, not the body only, but the *soul*—as much as it possibly can. Thousands among the colored race might and would have had all the noble sentiments and sensibilities of a Douglass if Slavery had not crushed their spirits. The few whose souls no earthly tyranny can crush, show what the colored race, redeemed from Slavery's curse, might be.

Let Frederick Douglass go on and lift up his voice for humanity, and for his down-trodden brethren. Our full hearts bid him God speed. O, rise a thousand other such! Then the pillars of Oppression would shake to their deep foundation. Such men as Douglass will find a refuge for themselves and for their brethren in the sanctuary of the great hearts of our race, and their bondage shall be to us as the bondage of our own children. Then the days of Oppression are numbered. Ed.]

FREDERICK DOUGLASS. [Anon.] (Chicago) *Western Citizen,* n.d., reprinted in *Lib.,* 15 May 1846.

'*As sure as his feet shall touch American soil, he shall be taken back again to Slavery.*'

Such, as I have been informed from an authentic source, is the declaration of the former owner of Frederic Douglass, and such I doubt not will be the attempt, if he return to his native land. It is only recently that I have had an opportunity of reading the life of this extraordinary man, and from my knowledge of slavery as it really exists—the pernicious effects of the system upon the minds and characters of those so unfortunate as to have been born and brought up beneath its soul-destroying influence—I am fully prepared to bear a decided testimony to the truth of all his assertions, with regard to the discipline upon the plantations of Maryland, as well as his descriptions of cruelty and murder. Of Col. Lloyd, or his family, I have personally but little knowledge, although during years of my childhood and youth, I have occasionally met them in Annapolis, where they frequently visited, and where also a number of their relatives reside. Aristocratic in the extreme, they moved and lived in the style of the nobility of foreign lands; and however amiable the Col. or his family might appear, I'll venture to say he was willing to wink at, and permit any cruelty or oppression which an unprincipled overseer might say was necessary. Well I know that the doctrine of the slaveholder is—'Tis better that a nigger should be killed than the authority of the overseer should in the least be opposed or resisted.' I have heard masters and mistresses too, say to their over-seers, 'Knock them down or shoot them, or anything else, sooner than not enforce and secure implicit obedience.'

NARRATIVE OF THE LIFE OF FREDERICK DOUGLASS, AN AMERICAN SLAVE. [Anon.]. (Edinburgh) *Scotsman,* 27 June 1846.

Written by Himself. Dublin: Webb & Chapman, &c.

THIS little volume has been for some time before the public, but we have not hitherto had an opportunity of recommending it to the notice of our readers. We now do so, as containing a most interesting and instructive narrative, illustrative in a very striking manner of the monstrous evils of slavery.

Without at all touching upon the recent controversy with which Mr. Doug-lass was connected, we may be permitted to remark, that no one who had an opportunity of hearing him at any of the late meetings in the Music-hall, could avoid being impressed with a sincere conviction of the truth of his statements, or fail to admire the good taste and natural eloquence which marked his style of composition and delivery. The same characteristics prevail in his written narra-tive. It has all the simplicity of truth, while at the same time it exhibits a degree of strength and elegance of expression, which would scarcely have been ex-pected in the writings of a man born and brought up in the darkness of slavery, and whose education was not only self-acquired, but obtained in hasty and stealthy snatches.

The very first page of Mr. Douglass's Narrative lifts up a curious corner of the black veil with which slavery, in shame and fear, envelopes itself. A slave does not know his own age:—

"I have no accurate . . . [1.4–2.1] . . . a restless spirit."

The cruelties witnessed and suffered by the narrator are very powerfully described; nor does he shrink from noticing the gross immortalities of which the iniquitous system of slavery is at once the parent and the protector. But for the most of these disclosures we must refer to the work itself, and only spare room for the following pathetic passage:—

"If any one thing . . . [47.20–48.20] . . . the loss of great-grandchildren."

Much of the information which may be found in this little work is such as could only have been furnished by one who had been himself a slave, and who, having become free, and escaped from all fear of his former masters, can speak out with perfect freedom. Slaves, as long as they continue under bondage, are afraid to tell their miseries to any one. The result of speaking freely to any passing inquirer is well exemplified in the following anecdote, and the commentary which accom-panies it is also interesting:—

"Colonel Lloyd was said . . . [18.12–20.4] . . . masters when viewed separately."

Not the least important or suggestive part of Mr. Douglass's book, is his testimony against the so-called religion of the slaveholders, recorded here without reference to recent occurrences, and indeed before anything had been said regarding the transactions of the Free Church in the mission to America:—

"I assert most unhesitatingly, . . . [77.26–79.31] . . . reverend slave-driver, Rigby Hopkins."

And lest any one should receive the false impression that in so speaking of *the appearance of religion* assumed by slaveholders as a cloak for their crimes, he speaks against religion itself, Mr. Douglass distinctly explains the difference in an eloquent "postscript," with a quotation from which we shall conclude our extracts from this interesting and eloquent little book:—

"What I have said . . . [118.9–120.9] . . . the garb of Christianity. There we behold religion and robbery the allies of each other; slavery and piety linked and interlinked; preachers of the gospel united with slaveholders."

MEMOIR OF FREDERICK DOUGLASS. Mary Howitt. (London) *People's Journal,* 2:302–05 (1847).

IF we were to write ten volumes on the atrocities and miseries of slavery in the abstract, we could say nothing half so impressive and conclusive as is the simple, honest narrative of a real slave, written by himself. Listen, then, to a brief outline of such a history, ye good, warm-hearted, working men and women of England. The man whose history it is, is now among you: welcome him kindly, wherever you meet with him, for he is a noble human being; and beyond this—and this is what he will ask from you—waft across the Atlantic the sighs of your deepest sympathy for the millions who suffer daily as he has done—claim the whole coloured race as your brethren, and demand that they shall be free!

Frederick Douglass is a slave. There is one man in America to whom he belongs, as a chattel: were he in Maryland, where that master lives, he might be chained, and scourged with a cowskin whip till blood flowed to his feet. He can read and write, and has very much knowledge. Some minds gather knowledge by intuition; his is of that kind—but for this very cause would his master treat him more savagely. If he escaped, he might be hunted with bloodhounds, and when retaken might be tortured as if he had fallen into the hands of fiends. The *Book of Martyrs* contains nothing more horrible than that master might legally inflict on Frederick Douglass, were he again to fall into his hands.

There are, in the slave States of America, about three millions of slaves: some of these are used better, many of these are used much worse, than Frederick Douglass has been. But now, to his history. Slaves very rarely know their ages, any more than domestic animals do—for there is no parish register for them—no birthday anniversaries: Frederick Douglass, therefore, can only conjecture how old he is. His mother was a slave; his father was a white man and her master. Slave-holders generally have large families by their female slaves; but these children have no claim on the father's affection—he sells them, or makes them his own slaves, just as may suit his convenience. This is one way of increasing his property. Our little new-born slave, Frederick—for the slave has no surname; that is his master's privilege—was, as is customary, separated from his mother soon after he was born; for the slave must have no affections, any more than the horse or cow. He never, he tells us, saw his mother more than four or five times in his life, and then but for a very short period, and in the night. She was hired out to a Mr. Stuart, who lived twelve miles off: and she used to go in the night to see her child, travelling all the way on foot, after her day's work was done; and if she were not back at her work by sunrise, she was severely whipped. He never saw her by daylight; she came to him in the dead of night, lay down beside him, folded him in her arms to sleep—but when he woke next morning, she was gone. Thus, for a few times, met the mother and child; and then Death, the kindest friend to the slave, put an end to these meetings, and to her hardships and sorrows at the same time. He might then have been about seven years old.

The father of the little slave was one Captain Anthony, who lived on a small farm belonging to a large plantation. He was the overseer of the overseers, and possessed about thirty slaves. To give an idea of an overseer, we will give a sketch of the one who had the oversight of this unfortunate thirty. He always went about armed with a cowskin whip and a heavy cudgel. He used to cut and slash the women's heads so horribly, that even Captain Anthony was angry with him; and yet Captain Anthony himself was not merciful—he had considerable pleasure in whipping a slave. One day he tied up a poor female slave to a joist, and whipped her upon the naked back till she was literally covered with blood. No words, no tears, no prayers from his gory victim could move his iron heart. Little Frederick stood not far off, trembling, and saw it. He says "he never shall forget it. It struck him with awful force. It was the blood-stained gate, the entrance to the hall of slavery, through which he was about to pass." These are his own forcible words.

This inhuman wretch thought, nevertheless, that some religious instruction was necessary for the slave. The preacher and religious teacher always enforced obedience to their masters; that was the true pith of the lesson, and therefore they must learn religion betime. During the summer, therefore, little Frederick and about thirty other little lads were sent every evening to the prayer-school, the only school they went to. This was kept by a very old slave, who was fit for nothing else. He had been beaten all his working days, and now that he had a little power himself, he sate with a large whip in his hand, and taught the children the Lord's Prayer; and for every inattention, mistake, or forgetfulness, he gave them a cut with the lash. The Lord's Prayer and the stinging lash became early associated. Thus were they taught.

Captain Anthony had two sons, and one daughter married to one Thomas

Auld, or Captain, as he was called, because he was master of the trading vessel in which the product of the whole plantation was sent to Baltimore. The plantation belonged to Colonel Lloyd, and consisted of about twenty smaller farms. The Colonel's residence was called the Great House Farm, and this was the central place of business. All disputes were settled here, runaway slaves were publicly whipped here, and here, too, each month, the slaves came, or rather a few out of the whole number came, to receive their stipulated allowance of food and clothes. Each slave received for the month eight pounds of pork or fish, and one bushel of corn-meal. This was all they had to live on. Their yearly clothing consisted of two coarse linen shirts, one jacket, one pair of trowsers, one pair of stockings, one pair of shoes, all of the coarsest kind. Two coarse linen shirts a year constituted the sole clothing of the children, until they were fit for work. Beds, the slaves had none, unless one coarse blanket be considered such. But the slaves suffer less from the want of beds, than the want of time to sleep. When their day's work is done, they have to work for themselves—to wash, to mend, to cook: they have nobody to do these things for them, and thus they are done at night; and when they are ended, they lie down in their miserable blankets, and sleep till the driver's horn calls them to the field, and the driver's whip hurries them into it.

A great deal has been said of the irrepressible gaiety of the slave; we have been told that his songs are incessant, and this has been made an argument in favour of his condition. Let us hear, then, why the slaves appointed to fetch from the Great House Farm the monthly allowances of food made the dreary old woods for miles round reverberate with their wild songs, for there is a deep argument in the fact. "Their songs," says Frederick Douglass, "revealed at once the highest joy and the deepest sadness. They composed and sang as they went along . . . [13.14–15.6] . . . relieved by tears."

To return to our little Frederick, yet wearing nothing but his juvenile garment of a shirt. Beside going to the prayer school, his business was to look after Captain Anthony's cows and poultry, and to run errands for Mrs. Auld. They did not very often whip him, but he suffered bitterly from hunger and cold. At length he was seven, and old enough to have a pair of trowsers and to work. He was sent, therefore, to Baltimore, to Mr. Hugh Auld, Captain Auld's brother, to wait on Master Thomas, his little son. Hugh Auld had married a wife from one of the Northern States, a young woman who had worked for her own bread, and never till now had owned a slave: her heart, therefore, was full of human kindness. She received the little slave with a face beaming with good nature, and it caused the most inconceivable happiness to fill his soul. Presently, this kind woman began to teach him to read, and allowed him strange liberties. One Sunday evening, when his master was gone to chapel, he lay down under the table and fell asleep. In awhile he was woke by a sound of reading in his ears—it was his mistress reading the bible aloud to herself. She read the first chapters of Job: the little slave had never heard anything like that before—he raised himself up silently on his elbow and listened. She read with great earnestness, apparently deeply impressed with the sense of the chapter; and as she read, he determined never to rest till he too could read and gather up for himself wonderful histories like that. When, however, he had got so far in reading as to spell words of three or four letters, his master made the discovery of what his wife was doing, and instantly put a stop to it; for it was unlawful, he told her, as well as unsafe, to teach a slave to read. In the hearing of the boy he said, that "learning would spoil the best nigger in the world; it would unfit him for a slave; it would make him discontented and unhappy."

These were not wise words of Mr. Hugh Auld, for they gave rise to a train of reasoning which was never silenced again. "It was a new and special revelation, explaining dark and mysterious things with which his youthful understanding had struggled in vain. He now understood the white man's power to enslave the black man. From that moment he understood the pathway from slavery to freedom."

Seven years went on, and changes took place. The mild, gentle mistress had profited by her husband's words, as well as the slave. Irresponsible power had converted even her into a cruel tyrant; and now, the highest crime which, in her eyes, a slave could commit, was to read. Frederick, however, learned to read, spite of all her efforts to prevent it. He had also a little library of his own, curiously enough collected, and not consisting of volumes, but of minute portions of them; for, whenever he saw printed paper of any kind lying in the kennels, or trodden under foot in the streets, he picked it up, carefully cleaned it from the mud, washed and dried it, and possessed himself of its contents. In this way he became the proprietor of several stray leaves of the bible. But, in the meantime, this reading and thinking had produced that very discontent which his master had foretold. He now understood the difference between a free man and slave, and this knowledge embittered his existence to such a degree, that he often wished for death. All his faculties were alive, and from everything which surrounded him he derived exciting knowledge. He heard people talking a great deal about abolitionists, and one day his master said in his hearing, that "all the wickedness of the slaves was owing to these abolitionists." What in the world could an abolitionist be? By good fortune, he presently fell in with a dictionary, and eagerly looked for the word— but no light was thrown on the subject there, though light came in process of time; and then that knowledge, like all the rest, as Mr. Hugh Auld had said, only made him more discontented and unhappy.

He learned to write, too, by challenging boys in the streets to writing-matches with chalk on the pavement and board-fences, when he himself knew the form only of two or three letters; and later, by practising in Master Thomas's old copy-books when the family were at chapel.

After awhile, Mr. Hugh Auld and his brother Thomas, whose property Frederick was, quarrelled, and he took back his slave. Thus he came back to the place of his birth. Old Captain Anthony was now dead, and Captain Auld was master in his place. This man was mean, cruel, and cowardly; his very slaves despised him. He believed himself, nevertheless, a very religious man; he prayed morning, noon, and night, and seemed to think that this show of religion would cancel the most atrocious cruelties. Of all his slaves he hated most the slave whom he had lent to his brother; he said that a city life had spoiled him, and that he would corrupt the rest of the slaves. A dreadful charge this, and therefore it must be met by severe means. Not far off lived one Edward Covey, a famous negro-breaker—not a *horse*-breaker, good reader, but a *man*-breaker—rather a new occupation to your ears. This man had a little farm, and the slaveholders used to send their reading and writing and thinking slaves—those who had any spark of manhood about them—to be broken-in by him. Covey had immense reputation in this line. What a tophet of misery must his little farm have been!

Let us hear what our poor reading and thinking slave says of it. "If at any one . . . [63.8–63.23] . . . closed in upon me." The house where all this intense misery was endured stood on the shore of Chesapeake Bay. The poor heart-broken slave would often stand for hours in the stillness of the Sabbath, watching with agonised heart and tearful eye the countless number of shipping going forth over the free ocean. The sight affected him powerfully, and from this sight again were rekindled aspirations after freedom.

Covey's savage cruelties increased day by day; they were beyond the endurance of the most spirit-crushed slave. Frederick was hiding one day in a wood, and his master was in chase of him, when he fell in with another slave with whom he was acquainted. This slave, whose name was Sandy, on hearing his troubles promised to get him a certain root out of the woods which, if he always wore on his right side, would entirely disable Covey or any other white man from flogging him. Sandy himself had worn it, he said, for years, and never since so doing had received a blow. The magic root was found and immediately placed in its proper position, and in the strength of this talisman the poor runaway returned back to Covey's house. Strange to say for two days the savage man was mild, but on the third the virtues of the root were put to a severe test.

Covey, who seemed to have waited only for an opportunity for revenge, found it, and fell upon his victim with tenfold fury; at that moment, however, whence came the spirit let the wise say, the soul of the man rose up within the slave, and the end of it was that he was the victor. This, he tells us, was the turning-point in his career as a slave. It rekindled the few expiring embers of freedom, and revived within him a sense of his own manhood. It recalled the departed self-reliance, and inspired him again with the determination to be free. Strange to say, Covey never spoke of the triumph his slave had had over him; no doubt he feared that if this were noised abroad his reputation as a negro-breaker would be gone for ever.

A year or two afterwards Frederick lived with a Mr. Freeland, and here began secretly to teach his fellow slaves to read. He had a Sunday-school, and devoted also three evenings a week to this laudable purpose; and yet, had it been known, he would have been liable to severe whipping, all instruction of the slave being unlawful. Many slaves by this means learnt to read. The utmost affection and unanimity existed among these poor fellows. "They were noble souls," says he; "they not only possessed loving hearts but brave ones also."

In the year 1835 he resolved to make a great attempt to secure his liberty. He communicated his resolve to some of his beloved companions in affliction. Five of them entered into this league. On the Saturday night previous to the Easter holidays they determined to take a boat up the Chesapeake Bay, and then turning their canoe adrift, follow the guidance of the North Star till they got beyond the limits of Maryland. Frederick wrote a pass for each of them, for without such pass no slave could leave his master's plantation.

Nothing could equal their intense anxiety as the time drew near. Each was pledged to each other in the most solemn manner. At length the day came, the coming of which was fixed upon for their enterprise. Early in the morning they went as usual to the field; they were at work, "and all at once," says he in his narrative, "I was overwhelmed with an indescribable feeling, in the fulness of which I turned to Sandy (he who had given him the root), and said, 'We are betrayed!' 'Well,' said he, 'that thought has this moment struck me!'" They said no more.

And they *had* been betrayed. One of their little band was too weak for the trial, and they were all taken at breakfast-time; beaten, bound, and sent off to jail. Upon the whole they managed well; by one way or another they destroyed their passes, and agreed among themselves to own nothing. Contrary to all expectations the others were taken back by their masters, and Frederick alone left to be sold. But he was not sold; he was once more sent to live at Baltimore with Mr. Hugh Auld, and here he again busied his mind with plans for gaining his liberty, and from this place he actually effected his escape.

The means by which this was done he does not tell for a humane and wise reason. Were they known, he says, it would involve others in the most embarassing difficulties, and would also cause still greater vigilance on the part of the slave-holders; and thus, as he says, "perhaps be the means of guarding a door whereby some dear brother bondsman might escape his galling chains." He had for a long time fixed upon the 3d of September, in the year 1838, for the day on which he would make his great attempt; and accordingly, so well were his plans laid, that on that same day he left his bondage and succeeded in reaching New York without the slightest interruption whatever. Of the means he used or the route he took we know nothing. One little characteristic circumstance we must not omit here, which we have heard him relate, and which exhibits the excited state of his feelings whilst this great scheme was agitating his mind. The thought of it was never absent from him; but it could not be spoken aloud. He was known however to his master as a Methodist, and thus he poured out the full current of his thoughts in hymns which, applicable to the captive spirit looking for emancipation in death, were applicable likewise to the living bondsman about to escape from his outward fetters. Thus he would sing words to which the following would be the refrain:—

Run to Jesus, shun the danger;
   I don't expect to stay much longer here!
I thought I heard them say
There were lions in the way:—
   I don't expect to stay much longer here!

It is impossible to give the full effect of these simple, but expressive words; those who have heard this extraordinary man speak of his former life, or have heard him sing, can imagine the deep pathos, the intense significance given to them in this way.

Within a fortnight after his escape he was married in New York to Anna Murray, a free woman, his long intended wife, and one who probably had a hand in his deliverance. Five minutes after his marriage, his bride shouldered one part of their luggage and he the other, and off they went on their way to New Bedford, as happy as if life had all been one pathway of flowers. Wherever they went they found the friends of the poor and the oppressed; he began to feel that he was a free man among the free. At New Bedford he received his permanent sirname of Douglass, hitherto he had changed it many times. A friend of his had just been reading the Lady of the Lake, and suggested her patronymic name as his. He adopted it; and long may he and his descendants bear it!

"I found employment," says he, "the third day after my arrival at New Bedford, in stowing a sloop with a load of oil. It was new, dirty, and hard work, but I went at it with a glad heart and a willing hand. I was now my own master. It was a happy moment, the rapture of which can be understood only by those who have been slaves. It was the first work the reward of which was entirely my own. I worked that day with a pleasure I had never before experienced. I was at work for myself and my newly-married wife. It was to me the starting point of a new existence."

Soon after this he became acquainted with the writings of the Abolitionists, and a new life then, indeed, began in his soul. He now fully understood the meaning of the word. He attended Anti-Slavery meetings, and now and then said a few words in them; the power to speak grew stronger and stronger, and at length he came out as one of the most able advocates of the cause of emancipation. The secrets and horrors of the prison-house were known to him; he was naturally eloquent, endowed with great powers of mind, and one every way calculated to assert the claim of the coloured man to the rights of common humanity. For four years he was employed by the Anti-Slavery Society of America as a lecturing agent, producing by his burning eloquence as he went along a thrill through the heart of the people, and putting forth in his own person the most incontestible argument on behalf of his brethren in bonds, who, though slaves, are yet men. This was not done, however, without considerable risk to himself. In many places the greatest excitement was produced by his exposures of the horrors of slavery. The pro-slavery party followed him with the most inveterate hatred. Great mobs, in many instances, collected to assail him. And in one instance, at Pendleton, Indiana, in 1843, he had his right hand broken by the violence of the people, who assailed him and his companion with sticks and stones. According to his principles as a non-resistant, he could make no reprisals; but endeavoured by mild words and a peaceable demeanour to disarm their fury. A little boy, however, ran up to him and said that the people were killing his companion; whereupon, at once forgetting non-resistance, he rushed in among them, rescued his friend, and came off with an injury the traces of which he will carry to his grave. In 1844 he wrote the narrative of his life—the boldest step which he had yet taken in his career as a free man. This little book sold immensely, but such was the excitement produced by it that it was thought advisable he should for a time leave the United States, more especially as he had in it published his identity and place of abode, by which means his *owner* might take measures for regaining possession of him, it being legal by the constitution of the United States for any master to seize upon his escaped slave in any part of their territories where he might have taken refuge.

This was one reason for his coming to this country, but there were yet others; he wished to acquaint himself with the land of his *paternal* ancestors, and to improve and enrich his mind from the stores of knowledge which would here open to him; but, above all, to advocate with us the cause of his degraded and oppressed people, to excite, as he himself says, "such an intelligent interest on the subject of American slavery as shall re-act upon his own country, and tend to shame her out of her adhesion to a system so abhorrent to Christianity and her republican institutions."

Such is Frederick Douglass, the *chattel* that was, the *man* that is. We have seen something of him, we have heard more, and all tends to place him higher in our esteem. We acknowledge him as a brother man, give him the warm, right-hand of fellowship, and heartily wish him God speed!

ANTI-SLAVERY BOOKS. Giles B. Stebbins. *NS,* 21 April 1848.

Almost every person of even the most ordinary mental culture reads a book now and then. Scarce a family but what has its little library. Books of voyages and travels, strange sights in distant lands, read with eager eyes by old and young; lives of great men of our own and other lands; stories of wars and struggles against tyranny, especially the bloody strife of our revolution; poems, wakening the love for the beautiful; theological works, to confirm long-cherished attachments to a sect: political works proving as clear as day-light that the policy of this, that, of the other party is the only one to save the country. But few, very few books will be found to stir up sympathy or righteous indignation against chattel slavery—few works that speak out with free, bold words of its exceeding sinfulness, its ruinous influence on national morals or national welfare. Yet this is the *great question* of the age, the great sin of this land.

The Narrative of Frederick Douglass, a voice coming up from the prison-house, speaking, like a thousand-voiced psalm, the feelings of a gifted mind, while "cabined, cribbed, confined," and its deep yearnings for liberty; the simple story of Wm. W. Brown, full of incidents that tell volumes of what slavery is: that parting scene when his mother bade him a heart-broken farewell on the deck of the steamboat, broken off by the brutal violence of the soul-driver, has a word of sad pathos in it;—the brief but moving tale of the sufferings of Henry Weston, telling of the fiend-like cruelties of the deepest dungeons, of the prison, the cane-fields of the far south-western these books should be read by all. None can read them without loathing slavery.

"Theodore Parker's Letter to the People, Touching Slavery," a book with a simple title, yet one containing a fund of information as to the ways in which the nation supports the institution, and as a fit reform, the institution robs the nation of freedom, honor and money.

"Facts for the People," a clear history of the Mexican War—the last crusade not to the holy sepulchre, but to the Halls of the Montezumas; not for the safety of the sacred temple; but for the desecration of freedom's holy shrines—facts, like Pelion upon Ossa that must satisfy every reasonable mind.

"Despotism in America," that able philosophical *ex pose* of the influence of the system on the very foundations of American society, manners and morals, written with an eloquence and power worthy the greatest minds of the age. "Slavery, illustrated by its effects on women," a work written in a pure, faultless style, yet giving startling proofs of the poisoning, corrupting effects of striking down the holiest tie that binds heart to heart—these should all have a conspicuous place in every household library. "The Church as it is, or the Forlorn Hope of Slavery," a little book full of proofs of the sad fact that the church is the bulwark of oppression.—Spooner and Wendell Phillips' works on the United States Constitution, efforts of two able men—one to prove the Constitution to be anti-slavery, the other pro-slavery, both able, though, in my poor judgment, the pro-slavery argument has the best, the true side of the question. Jonathan Walker's story, telling how slavery brands and imprisons the Anglo-Saxon, as well as the African, and makes United States officers do the deed in defence of constitutional right. Many other valuable works might be named which ought to be read, which would spread a flood of light over minds now darkened by ignorance and prejudice; and with light must come action, ceasing to do evil, learning to do well—ceasing to support slavery, learning to support liberty. "Let there be light," and with light will come liberty for the captive, free freedom for the nation such as it never yet knew—never can know, so long as slavery exists. All these books, and many others as valuable, can be found at the Anti-Slavery Office in this city.

Will the people read, or will they be ignorant, listless, negligent of duty and right!

FREDERICK DOUGLASS. Wilson Armistead. *A Tribute For The Negro*. (Manchester, Eng., 1848), 454–56.

Was born a Slave, on a plantation in Maryland, about the year 1817, and remained in that servile condition till about twenty-one years of age, when he effected his escape from fetters and chains. The history of his life of Slavery, which has been widely circulated,* presents a dismal picture of what is endured by the Negro race in the Slave-holding states of the Union.

The narrative of Douglass, written by himself, considering how long and dark was the career he had to run as a Slave, in the poorest school for the human heart and intellect, and how few have been his opportunities for subsequently improving his mind, is highly creditable to his head and heart. He who can peruse it without a tearful eye, a heaving breast, an afflicted spirit,—without being filled with an abhorrence of Slavery and all its abettors, and animated with a determination to seek the immediate overthrow of that execrable system,—must have a flinty heart indeed. It presents no exaggerated picture of Slavery. Many have suffered incomparably more, while few on the plantations have suffered less, than himself. Yet how deplorable was his situation! what terrible chastisements were inflicted upon his person! what still more shocking outrages were perpetrated upon his mind! with all his noble powers and sublime aspirations, how like a brute was he treated, even by those professing to have the same mind in them that was in Christ Jesus! to what dreadful liabilities he was continually subjected! how destitute of friendly counsel and aid, even in his greatest extremities! How heavy was the midnight of woe which shrouded in blackness the last ray of hope, and filled the future with terror and gloom! What longings after freedom took possession of his breast, and how his misery augmented, in proportion as he grew reflective and intelligent,—thus demonstrating that a happy Slave is an extinct man! How he thought, reasoned, felt, under the lash of the driver, with the chains upon his limbs! what perils he encountered in his endeavours to escape from his horrible doom! and how signal have been his deliverance and preservation in the midst of a nation of pitiless enemies!

The narrative of Douglass contains many affecting incidents, many passages of great eloquence and power; perhaps the most thrilling one of all is the description he gives of his feelings, as he stood soliloquizing respecting his fate, and the chances of his one day being a free man, on the banks of the Chesapeake Bay—viewing the receding vessels as they flew with their white wings before the breeze, and apostrophizing them as animated by the living spirit of freedom. Who can read that passage, and be insensible to its pathos and sublimity? "Compressed into it is a whole Alexandrian library of thought, feeling, and sentiment—all that can, all that need be urged, in the form of expostulation, entreaty, rebuke, against the crime of crimes,— making man the property of his fellow-man! O, how accursed is that system, which

---

* Narrative of the Life of Frederick Douglass, an American Slave, written by himself. Dublin: Webb and Chapman. 1845.

entombs the god-like mind of man, defaces the divine image, reduces those who by creation were crowned with glory and honour, to a level with four-footed beasts, and exalts the dealer in human flesh above all that is called God! Why should its existence be prolonged one hour? Is it not evil, only evil, and that continually? What does its presence imply but the absence of all fear of God, all regard for man, on the part of the people of the United States? Heaven speed its eternal overthrow!"

What a disgrace on *Free and Enlightened* America! Here we have a man in physical proportions and stature commanding and erect, in intellect richly endowed, in natural eloquence a prodigy, in soul manifestly "created but a little lower than the angels;" yet a Slave, aye, a fugitive Slave, trembling for his safety on American soil. Capable of high attainments as an intellectual and moral being, almost without an education, an ornament to society, and yet, by the law of his country, by the voice of its people, by the terms of the Slave Code, only a piece of property, a beast of burden, a chattel personal, nevertheless!

It would be superfluous to say much here respecting the talents of Douglass, which are so self-evident. Few have not had an opportunity of judging of his abilities for themselves, and thus increasing their respect for him and for his race. As a public speaker, he excels in pathos, wit, comparison, imitation, strength of reasoning, and fluency of language, frequently giving utterance to many noble thoughts and thrilling reflections, and his eloquent appeals have extorted the highest applause of multitudes on both sides of the Atlantic. "There is in him," says W. L. Garrison, "that union of head and heart, which is indispensable to an enlightenment of the heads, and a winning of the hearts of others. May his strength continue to be equal to his day! May he continue to grow in grace, and in the knowledge of God,' that he may be increasingly serviceable in the cause of bleeding humanity;" and let the calumniators of the Coloured race despise themselves for their baseness and illiberality of spirit, and henceforth cease to talk of the natural inferiority of those who require nothing but time and opportunity to attain to the highest point of human excellence.

ART. IV—NARRATIVES OF FUGITIVE SLAVES*. [Anon.]. (Boston) *Christian Examiner,* 47:61–93 (July 1849).

AMERICA has the mournful honor of adding a new department to the literature of civilization,—the autobiographies of escaped slaves. We have placed below the

*1. *Narrative of Henry Watson, a Fugitive Slave.* Written by Himself. Boston: Published by Bela Marsh. 1848. 12mo. pp. 48.

2. *Narrative of the Sufferings of Lewis and Milton Clarke among the Slaveholders of Kentucky.* Boston: Published by Bela Marsh. 1848. 12mo. pp. 144.

3. *Narrative of William W. Brown, a Fugitive Slave.* Written by Himself. Boston: Published at the Antislavery Office. 1847. 12mo. pp. 110.

4. *Narrative of the Life of Frederick Douglass, an American Slave.* Written by Himself. Boston: Published at the Antislavery Office. 1845. 12mo. pp. 125.

5. *The Life of Josiah Henson, formerly a Slave, now an Inhabitant of Canada, as narrated by Himself.* Boston: Arthur D. Phelps. 1849. 16mo. pp. 76.

titles of five narratives of this description. The subjects of two of these narratives, Douglass and Henson, we have known personally, and, apart from the internal evidence of truth which their stories afford, we have every reason to put confidence in them as men of veracity. The authors of the remaining accounts are, for anything we know to the contrary, equally trustworthy. We place these volumes without hesitation among the most remarkable productions of the age,—remarkable as being pictures of slavery by the slave, remarkable as disclosing under a new light the mixed elements of American civilization, and not less remarkable as a vivid exhibition of the force and working of the native love of freedom in the individual mind. . . .

The narrative of Douglass contains the life of a superior man. Since his escape from slavery, he has been employed as an antislavery lecturer, and is now the editor of a newspaper in Rochester, N.Y. He does not belong to the class, always small, of those who bring to light great principles, or who originate new methods of carrying them out. He has, however, the vividness of sensibility and of thought which we are accustomed to associate with a Southern climate. He has a natural and ready eloquence, a delicacy of taste, a quick perception of proprieties, a quick apprehension of ideas, and a felicity of expression, which are possessed by few among the more cultivated, and which are surprising when we consider that it is but a few years since he was a slave. In any popular assembly met for the discussion of subjects with which he has had the opportunity to become familiar, he is a man to command and hold attention. He is a natural orator, and his original endowments and the peculiarity of his position have given him a high place among antislavery speakers.

But while our sympathies go strongly with him, and because they go with him, we are disposed to make a criticism on a mode of address in which he sometimes indulges himself, which we believe is likely to diminish, not only his usefulness, but his real influence. We would not detract from his merits, and we can easily excuse in him a severity of judgment and a one-sidedness of view which might be inexcusable in another. We can hardly condemn one who has been a slave for seeing only the evils of slavery, and for thinking lightly of the difficulty of remedying them; but we have wished, when we have heard him speak, or read what he was written, that he might wholly avoid a fault from which a natural magnanimity does something towards saving him, but to which he is nevertheless exposed. His associates at the North have been among those who are apt to mistake violence and extravagance of expression and denunciation for eloquence;—men who, whatever their virtues otherwise, are not in the habit of using discrimination in their judgments of men or of measures which they do not approve. To him they have doubtless been true and faithful friends, and he naturally adopts their style of speech. But it is a mistaken one, if the speaker wishes to sway the judgment of his hearers and to accomplish any practical end. No matter what the vehemence of tone or expression, whenever a public speaker indulges himself in violent and unqualified statements and in sweeping denunciations, he not only makes it apparent that he is deficient in a sound and fair judgment, but what is worse, he creates in his hearers a secret distrust of his real earnestness,—a vague feeling that after all he is thinking more of his speech than of the end for which he professes to make it. When men are profoundly in earnest, they are not apt to be extravagant. The more earnest, the more rigidly true. A merchant, in discussing the politics of the day, about which he knows or cares little, freely indulges in loose, extravagant, and violent declarations. But follow him to his counting-room; let him be making inquiries or giving directions about some enterprise which he really has deeply at heart, and the extravagance is gone. Nothing will answer here but truth, and the exact truth. His earnestness makes him calm. It is seen in the moderated accuracy, as well as in the decision and strength, of his statements. Extravagance and passion and rhetorical flourishes might do when nothing which he greatly valued was at stake; but here is something too serious for trifling. Just so it is in other cases. A flippant, extravagant speaker, especially if he be gifted with the power of sarcasm, will probably be listened to and applauded, but nothing comes of it. They who applaud the most understand very well that this is not the kind of person whose judgment is to be relied on as a guide in action. His words are listened to with much the same sort of interest that is given to the personated passion of the theatre. A few sober words from a calm, wise, discriminating mind are, after all, the ones which are followed. Nothing is less effective, for any practical end, than the "withering and scorching" eloquence with which American speeches seem so to abound. It conciliates no opponent, and though it may light up the momentary passions, it gives no new strength of conviction to the friends of a cause. It is the last kind of eloquence to be cultivated by those who are heartily in earnest in their desire to promote any great reform.

We by no means think that these remarks apply peculiarly to Douglass. We make them, however, because we think that, more often than he is probably aware, he suffers himself to fall into this mode of speech. He has such ability to appeal to the higher and more generous sentiments, and such appeals do so much to win over enemies and to strengthen friends, he has such personal knowledge of slavery, and is so competent to make all he says effective, through candor and a just appreciation of the difficulties that beset the subject of emancipation, and is withal so much of a man, that we regret any mistake of judgment which tends to diminish his power as an advocate of the antislavery cause.*

* We have hesitated about making these remarks; and now, on reading them over, the sympathy which his narrative excites, and our respect for the force of character he has shown in rising from the depths of bondage to be the equal associate of those who have possessed every opportunity of cultivation and refinement, almost make us erase what we have written. We would avoid giving pain to one who has suffered all that we should most dread for ourselves, and who has risen above obstacles by which we should probably have been crushed. But still, whatever the past has been, he is now free. By his indisputable deserts, he has secured for himself an influential position. The course which he takes is important to others beside himself. Should he read this criticism, we hope that the internal evidence will be sufficient to show that it is written by one who rejoices in his usefulness. And in the faith that he may so read it, and that its suggestions may not be without value, we allow it to stand.

Bibliography of Textual Appendixes

Gerald Fulkerson

I. TEXTS OF THE *NARRATIVE* AND OTHER PUBLISHED PRIMARY MATERIALS

Douglass, Frederick. *Narrative of the Life of Frederick Douglass, an American Slave*. Boston: Anti-Slavery Office, 1845.

———. *Narrative of the Life of Frederick Douglass, an American Slave*. Dublin: Webb and Chapman, 1845.

———. *Narrative of the Life of Frederick Douglass, an American Slave*. 2nd Dublin edition. Dublin: Webb and Chapman, 1846.

———. *Narrative of the Life of Frederick Douglass, an American Slave*. Third English edition. Wortley: Joseph Barker, 1846.

———. *Narrative of the Life of Frederick Douglass, an American Slave*. Third English edition. London: R. Yorke Clarke, 1847.

———. *Narrative of the Life of Frederick Douglass, an American Slave*. Sixth edition. London: Somers & Isaac, 1847.

———. *My Bondage and My Freedom*. New York: Miller, Orton, & Mulligan, 1855.

———. *Life and Times of Frederick Douglass*. Rev. ed. Boston: De Wolfe and Fiske, 1892.

Merrill, Walter M., ed. *The Letters of William Lloyd Garrison*, Vol. III: *No Union with Slaveholders, 1841–1849*. Cambridge: The Belknap Press of Harvard University Press, 1973.

Taylor, Clare. *British and American Abolitionists: An Episode in Transatlantic Understanding*. Edinburgh: Edinburgh University Press, 1974.

Whittier, John Greenleaf. *The Works of John Greenleaf Whittier*. 7 vols. Boston: Houghton, Mifflin, 1892.

II. JOURNALS AND NEWSPAPERS
(DATES INDICATE THE YEARS CONSULTED.)

The British and Foreign Anti-Slavery Reporter (London). 1845–1848.
Frederick Douglass' Paper (Rochester). 1851–1852.
The Liberator (Boston). 1845–1852.
National Anti-Slavery Standard (New York). 1845–1852.
The North Star (Rochester). 1847–1851.
Pennsylvania Freeman (Philadelphia). 1845–1848.
Rochester Daily American. 1848–1852.
Rochester Daily Democrat. 1848–1852.

III. MANUSCRIPT COLLECTIONS

Anti-Slavery Collection. Boston Public Library.
Chapman Family Papers. Boston Public Library.
Frederick Douglass Papers. Microfilm. Library of Congress.
Frederick Douglass Papers. University of Rochester Library.
Estlin Family Papers. Microfilm. Cornell University Library.
William Lloyd Garrison Papers. Boston Public Library.
Weston Family Papers. Boston Public Library.

Index